THE BOOK ON NEGOTIATING REAL ESTATE

PRAISE FOR
THE BOOK ON NEGOTIATING REAL ESTATE

"This is the only book you'll need to learn the strategies and tactics necessary to ensure you get the BEST deals—and the MOST deals—on your investment property, every time!"

—Joe Fairless, Author of *Best Ever Apartment Syndication Book*

"J Scott, Carol Scott, and Mark Ferguson are three of the premier real estate investors in our industry. Their tips and tricks for negotiating great deals are priceless. Read this book and learn from the best."

—Michael Blank, Multifamily Investor, Educator, and Author

"Mark Ferguson and the Scotts offer tales from the trenches like no one else in the business, showing investors tips and tricks you could only pick up from years of success. If I had this book starting out, I'd be light-years ahead of where I'm at now. The Book on Negotiating Real Estate is the real deal, and will put you ahead of your, competition saving you money and time in the process."

—Dave Van Horn, Author of *Real Estate Note Investing*

THE BOOK ON
NEGOTIATING REAL ESTATE

Expert Strategies for Getting the Best Deals When Buying & Selling Investment Property

REVISED EDITION

J SCOTT, MARK FERGUSON, CAROL SCOTT

The Book on Negotiating Real Estate
J Scott, Mark Ferguson, Carol Scott

Published by BiggerPockets Publishing LLC, Denver, CO
Copyright © 2019 by J Scott
All Rights Reserved.

Publisher's Cataloging-in-Publication data
Names: Scott, J, 1971-, author. | Ferguson, Mark, 1979-, author. | Scott, Carol, 1971-, author.

Title: The Book on negotiating real estate : expert strategies for getting the best deals when buying investment properties / J. Scott , Mark Ferguson, and Carol Scott.

Description: Denver, CO: BiggerPockets Publishing, 2019.

Identifiers: ISBN 978-1-947200-06-7 (pbk.) | 978-1-947200-07-4 (ebook) | LCCN 2018942992

Subjects: LCSH Real estate investment--United States. | Personal finance. | BISAC BUSINESS & ECONOMICS / Real Estate / General | BUSINESS & ECONOMICS / Real Estate / Buying Selling Homes | BUSINESS & ECONOMICS / Negotiating

Classification: LCC HD1382.5 .S39 2018 | DDC 332.63/24--dc23

Second Edition

Published in the United States of America
10 9 8 7 6 5 4 3 2 1

This book is dedicated to the investors and real estate professionals everywhere who spend their days working tirelessly to help solve other people's problems.

TABLE OF CONTENTS

Preface 10

Introduction 12

CHAPTER 1 | Introduction to Negotiation 16

CHAPTER 2 | Principles of Negotiation 27

CHAPTER 3 | The Power of Information 42

CHAPTER 4 | Psychology of Rapport 59

CHAPTER 5 | Seller Motivation & Leverage 76

CHAPTER 6 | Opening Bid Considerations 92

CHAPTER 7 | Your Opening Bid Price 110

CHAPTER 8 | Terms & Contingencies 128

CHAPTER 9 | Delivering Your Offer...........................145

CHAPTER 10 | Negotiating Tactics...........................163

CHAPTER 11 | Concessions Strategies.......................182

CHAPTER 12 | Defense & Counter Tactics...................198

CHAPTER 13 | Renegotiation Principles.....................211

CHAPTER 14 | Renegotiation Scenarios.....................221

CHAPTER 15 | Negotiating the Sale.........................236

CHAPTER 16 | Buying from Institutions......................248

Final Thoughts...263

PREFACE

In the summer of 2015, I was asked to give a presentation at a large real estate meetup in New York City, run by my good friend, Darren Sager. I happily accepted—my kids had never been to NYC, my wife loves the city, and we figured we'd make a vacation out of it.

A few days before the presentation, I still hadn't decided what I'd talk about. To help generate some ideas, I asked Darren to send an email to his group, asking if there were any topics in particular they'd be interested in hearing about.

The first response I received was, "I'd love to learn how to be a better negotiator."

Why hadn't I thought of that? I had spent more than a dozen years working for some of the biggest companies in the world doing large scale negotiations and this was a topic I knew a good bit about; it was also a topic that was highly relevant to real estate investing. But, other than an article here or there, I had spent a tremendously small amount of time writing about and discussing negotiation.

So, I put together a presentation I called, "Ten Things You Can Do Today to Become a Better Real Estate Negotiator."

The goal of that presentation was to provide a short list of basic negotiating strategies that, in about two hours, could turn a novice negotiator into someone who was better than 95 percent of the general public. Given how little the average person knows about negotiating and how little time they spend practicing their negotiating skills, I knew that by implementing some very basic tips, almost anyone could considerably improve their ability to negotiate.

I created my presentation on the train ride up to the city—I have a bad habit of waiting until the last minute for these things—and just sort of "winged it" to the group of over 200 investors who had packed the WeWork coworking space where the meeting was being held.

The response was completely unexpected. For several days after the presentation, I received email after email thanking me for delving into a topic that in our business is so important, but is often overlooked or minimized. Even my last-minute PowerPoint slides and unrehearsed talking points apparently didn't detract from the value of the presentation.

In fact, among the responses were several investors who suggested that I write a book on how to negotiate real estate. So I decided to do just that. But this was a topic that was so broad that I didn't feel I could tackle it myself. After following the writing and experiences of my investing colleague, Mark Ferguson, for several years, I knew that I wanted him to help me with the book. I also enlisted the help of my wife, Carol Scott—the one person I know who can consistently out-negotiate me.

Between Mark, Carol, and myself, we have completed nearly 1,000 real estate transactions. Mark is both an investor and licensed real estate agent who has flipped over 100 properties, owns more than a dozen rental units, and manages a team of real estate agents who help their clients buy and sell hundreds of properties per year.

Carol and I spent many years in management positions at Silicon Valley tech companies, where negotiating was a staple of the job. In the real estate space, we've completed over 250 deals, including buying, selling, building, partnering, and lending on projects across the country.

The three of us credit much of our success in the business world and in real estate to the negotiating skills we've acquired over the years, and our goal with this book is to transfer some of that foundational knowledge to the rest of the real estate investor community. If you have any more questions, please find us hanging out in the BiggerPockets.com forums or read any of our blog posts on the site. We hope that all who read this book will achieve greater business success from it!

J Scott

INTRODUCTION

Ask most people to define "negotiation," and the typical response you'll receive is that negotiation is a haggling between parties—each making their case, listening to the other side present theirs, and both sides trying to eventually reach an agreement.

While that back-and-forth part of the negotiation process is most certainly important, good negotiators realize that it's actually the culmination of a lot of upfront work and preparation. And not only upfront work—real estate deals can be unusual in the sense that negotiations often get revisited *after* an agreement is reached, when something goes wrong, like a bad inspection or appraisal.

It's when you can successfully navigate each piece of a negotiation—the upfront preparation, the haggling between parties, and then keeping the deal together when it hits a last-minute snag—that you can call yourself an expert real estate negotiator.

The goal of this book is to get you there.

To give you an idea of how we've organized this book, let's take a look at how a real estate negotiation typically flows:

Because each of these parts of the process is so important to the overall success of a negotiation, we've attempted to present our information in an order that replicates the flow you see above.

Planning, Preparation, & Research

The real estate negotiation process typically begins long before an offer is made or the haggling starts. In fact, it often begins before you even meet or talk to the other party in the transaction. This is the time when you'll be gathering all of the external information you'll need to achieve a successful negotiating outcome.

Diligent negotiators will use this time to try to get as much information about the property, the neighborhood, the local market, the other party, any agents/appraisers/lenders involved in the transaction, etc. It's often said that whichever party comes into the negotiation most prepared is the party likely to get the best result.

This can't be overstated. While knowing lots of strategies and tactics to persuade and influence the other party may give you an advantage in a negotiation, even a novice negotiator should be able to outmaneuver their "opponent" if they are better prepared and have more information about the transaction being negotiated.

We'll talk a lot more about planning, preparation, and research in Chapter 3.

Building Rapport & Determining Motivation

When it comes to preparation for your negotiation, there is one source of information that is more valuable than all the others combined—the other party himself. (For the sake of expediency, in this book we'll randomly assign gender.) At this stage, your goal is to build trust and rapport with the person you'll be negotiating with, and to use that budding relationship to gather information about his motivations and needs. This information will form the foundation of your negotiating path.

There is a deep psychology behind bonding with other people to build trust and rapport, and anyone can do it if they learn the basic skills and techniques. Once you learn these skills and put them to use early and often in your negotiating communication, you'll find that you can gain the information you'll need to ensure a successful negotiation outcome for both sides.

We'll spend Chapter 4 discussing the techniques behind building rapport and how to do it most effectively, and then in Chapter 5 we'll reveal how to put those techniques into practice to start getting important information from the other party.

Making an Initial Offer

Once you have all the data you need to make and support your side of the negotiation, it's time to put together an offer. This is where you will organize the information you've gathered, solidify your goals, and assemble a first proposal that will lay the groundwork for the bargaining period.

At the same time, the other party will likely be defining their goals for the transaction—though they may not be doing it in the same organized and systematic fashion you are. Part of your challenge is to determine what they are thinking (assuming they *are* thinking) and how they might react to your first offer.

We'll spend Chapters 6 through 9 exploring the strategic aspects behind creating your initial offer and the best practices for making and communicating that offer to the other party.

Bargaining

Once an offer is made, the actual haggling begins. This is the back-and-forth discussion that—hopefully—allows both sides to move toward a successful compromise. During this time, the parties will be making offers and counteroffers, trading *concessions* (we'll talk about those soon), revising their strategy based on what they are learning from the other party, dealing with hiccups ("stalls") in the discussion, and trying to keep momentum toward the goal of a mutually agreeable deal.

Depending on the circumstances, this process may take place face-to-face or by using real estate agents as intermediaries. The whole discussion may take just a few minutes, start to finish, or, it may take several days, weeks, or even months. The process may even start and stop several times should either or both parties not feel that a reasonable outcome is possible.

In Chapters 10 and 11, we'll discuss the strategies and tactics you—as the buyer—should be using to get the bargaining started and how to keep it moving forward. We'll discuss the techniques you can, and should, be using to control the negotiations and ensure your interests are best served, while also maintaining a balance of power that will allow the other party to walk away satisfied as well. And, in Chapter 12, we'll review how to defend against tactics that might be used against you.

In Chapter 15, we'll explore strategies and tactics you should be using when you're the seller in the transaction. In Chapter 16, we'll talk about how to achieve these same results when buying from an institutional seller, like the government or a bank.

Renegotiating

The next phase of many real estate transactions involves *"renegotiation."* This part of the process is somewhat unique to real estate deals, and results from any *contingencies* that are likely part of the initial agreement.

Contingencies are actions that generally must occur before the transaction is finalized—for example, an inspection of the property. In many cases, the outcome of the contingency will require renegotiation of the contract, such as when an inspection turns up something troubling.

Contingencies can put deals at risk, and good negotiators will have a plan for handling this renegotiation process should a contingency issue arise. We devote the entirety of Chapters 13 and 14 to discussing all aspects of renegotiation, including how to ensure that it doesn't sink your deal, and even how—when necessary—to use renegotiation to get more out of the deal than you had originally negotiated.

Settlement

The settlement is the culmination of a real estate deal, where final papers are signed and the transaction is finalized. Typically, by this point, both sides are satisfied with the terms of the agreement and things conclude quickly and smoothly. But, occasionally, issues will arise at the conclusion of the transaction.

By the time you have completed this book, you should have an arsenal of tactics and strategies at your disposal to attack any last-minute issues head-on.

CHAPTER 1
INTRODUCTION TO NEGOTIATION

"Negotiation."

It's a simple word that, in many people, elicits a strong emotional response. For some, it strikes a chord of terror and anxiety; for others, it produces a gleeful sense of anticipation. For many people, the idea of *negotiating* is something that only takes place at UN Security Council meetings and in corporate boardrooms among high-powered business-men—though some of these people are reluctantly willing to embrace the idea of negotiating every few years by asking for a raise at work or buying a new car, if they really have to.

While negotiation does encompass all of these major life activities, in reality, we all engage in a variety of negotiations every day across all aspects of life—like trying to get the kids to eat their broccoli, convincing the faceless customer service person on the other side of the phone to send us a refund for the defective product we received, or coming to consensus with your spouse on a paint color for the dining room. And while negotiation may be most associated with big-ticket items—homes, cars, international peace treaties—developing your negotiating skills will serve you well in *all* walks of life.

After all, every transaction boils down to one simple fact:

When you're meeting another party at the negotiation table—whether that "table" is literally a boardroom table, a seller's kitchen table, or the paint aisle at Lowe's—both sides want something, and the goal is to reach a compromise that allows each side to walk away satisfied.

The big question is, "How can we best accomplish this?"

And that's the real goal of negotiation.

What We Mean by "Negotiation"

In an ideal world, after a negotiation concludes, each party is happy with the outcome and each feels he got everything he wanted... or at the very least, everything he needed.

But we don't live in an ideal world, and in most negotiations both parties aren't going to walk away feeling like they got exactly what they wanted. In the real world of negotiations, oftentimes the best we can strive for is to get everything we want or need, while giving the other party just enough to satisfy them. Obviously, we'd love for the other party to be thrilled about the outcome as well—especially if we expect that we'll have to negotiate with them again in the future—but, at the very least, we want them to walk away without any lingering animosity or regret.

In any negotiating situation, there are going to be some things that both parties really want. And there will be other things one side finds important but the other side doesn't particularly care about. A fair solution, generally speaking, is more than each party simply getting an equal amount out of the agreement.

This is where *perception* becomes important: In most cases, the parties won't consider the compromise to be a good one unless they also felt involved and empowered during the negotiation. If the other side felt humiliated or steamrolled during the negotiation, they won't be satisfied no matter how much they got.

In other words, negotiation is not just about the outcome, it's about the process.

A Simple Example

Consider, for example, two siblings fighting over the last piece of chocolate cake. Any wise parent knows that, while cutting the cake in half and giving a piece to each child may seem like the most reasonable solution, each child will inevitably end up complaining that the other one got a bigger piece, or more frosting, or less frosting, or... well, you get the idea.

As a parent, how can you negotiate an agreement where both children walk away from this situation satisfied and focused on stuffing their faces with delicious chocolaty goodness, rather than feeling slighted in some way?

Simple: You ask one child to cut the cake into two pieces, while the other child gets the first choice of these pieces. Knowing that his sibling will selfishly take the biggest piece, it's in the first child's best interest to divide the cake as equally as possible; the second child will feel empowered as well, as he is able to select whichever piece he deems the best. In the end, even if the pieces of cake aren't exactly the same, the kids are likely to be more agreeable to the outcome simply because they both actively participated in the outcome.

While this is obviously a very simplified negotiating situation, it's a perfect example of how negotiation can be used to allow both parties to feel they've received a fair deal and feel that they were empowered throughout the process.

Negotiation Outcomes

In negotiation-speak, such an outcome is known as a "win-win," as both parties receive a benefit. But, not all negotiations result in a win-win outcome. As you have probably seen in real life, there are several other possible results of a negotiation:

Win-Lose: Only one party perceives the result of the negotiation as positive. This is how many people feel after negotiating with a car dealer or other high-pressured sales situation. It typically results in the party who feels they have lost in choosing not to negotiate with the "winning" party in the future.

Lose-Lose: All parties are worse off after the negotiation. We typically refer to this as a "failed negotiation." Unfortunately, sometimes a negotiation is destined to achieve this result. For example, imagine a divorce or custody battle, where both parties end up in a worse position than when they started. In fact, in these types of negotiations, sometimes the optimal outcome is to ensure that both sides sustain equal loss—in other words, the most successful outcome is equal unhappiness.

Win-Plus: An outcome in which each party feels as they've gained more than they expected. While not all negotiations have the ability to achieve this result—especially when both parties want the exact same thing—this can happen more than you may imagine.

Here's an example of a win-plus negotiation:

⟩⟩ TALES *FROM THE* TRENCHES ⟨⟨

A couple years ago, I received a call from a seller who had responded to one of my direct-mail letters. She was selling her father's house, as he had recently moved into a nursing home. I asked her the address of the property, and because we had recently renovated two other houses in that little subdivision, I immediately knew which house it was.

Without even seeing the property, I had a pretty good idea of what it would cost to renovate. The house was 21 years old, which meant it almost certainly needed a new roof, new HVAC system, and a full cosmetic upgrade. Given the age, the electrical and plumbing were likely fine, and since I was familiar with the exterior of the house (I had driven past it dozens of times), I knew that there were no major issues with location or the exterior of the property.

It sounded like the house had a very similar layout as the other two I had done in that neighborhood. Based on my back-of-the-envelope rehab estimate and what I was fairly certain I could resell the property for, I was pretty certain that I could pay up to about $95,000 for the property—though I'd be more comfortable with a purchase price closer to $90,000.

The woman and I chatted a bit on the phone. Ultimately, she divulged that she would sell the house for $100,000 and not a penny less. Apparently, her father had picked this nice round number as his absolute lowest selling price, and she believed there was no way he'd go any lower than that. I believed her, and I didn't see any reason to argue or to try to convince her to go against her father's wishes.

Then I said to her:

Me: *"I've purchased several houses in your neighborhood. I bought [property address] in April for $86,000. And I bought [property address] last year for $93,000. You can look those sales up in the public records if you want to verify that.*

I don't believe any other investor would be willing to pay $100,000 for your house. It's just not worth that amount.

But, if your dad is anything like mine, I'm guessing he won't budge once he gets a price set in his mind. And I can respect that—I'd probably be the same way. This is what I'm willing to do...

I will give you the $100,000 for the property—full asking price—and I can have my attorney complete all the paperwork in the next ten days. You won't have to make another phone call, you won't have to clean out the house, you won't have to do anything.

But, if I'm going to pay a premium on this property, I need something in return to make this work for me—instead of paying you for the house the day I purchase it, I plan to renovate it and resell it and I will pay you the day I resell it. Probably in the next three to six months, but no longer than 12 months from now.

If I'm willing to pay the premium price you ask, are you willing to wait a few months to get your cash?"

Why was I willing to go $5,000 above my highest purchase price?

I knew that if I were to buy the property, I'd probably get a loan from a local bank to cover much of the purchase price. I'd put down 35 percent as a down payment, and I'd be paying about $2,000 in upfront loan costs, plus about $4,000 in interest and other fees on the loan, for a total of about $6,000 in loan costs.

If the woman chose to accept my offer, my down payment would go away (less cash I needed to spend out of my pocket), and I'd be able to eliminate the $6,000 in loan costs. With $6,000 in costs gone, the $100,000 purchase price was actually equivalent to about $94,000, which was within the range I was targeting.

It turned out that her father wasn't in desperate need of the cash, so she was willing to consider the future payoff. Her biggest concern—rightfully so—was that she didn't know me and didn't trust that she'd ever get paid.

After some back and forth, we eventually agreed that, instead of waiting to get the entire $100,000 purchase price, I would pay $20,000 upfront (still less than the 35 percent I would have paid to the bank for a down payment), and I agreed to pay the remaining amount within six months instead of 12 months, which was still longer than I needed to complete the project. I also agreed to pay to have her attorney draw up the note and deed, so she could be confident I wasn't taking advantage of her.

This was a perfect example of a win-plus negotiation. The seller got everything she needed and wanted from the deal, as did I. In fact, each side actually got more than they would have gotten had they walked away and tried to negotiate the same deal with someone else who was less creative.

Keep in mind, not every real estate negotiation is that quick and easy. In fact, we've never done a single deal over the phone like that before or since. But, this is a great example of how we—using cooperation, compromise, and some creativity—were able to reach an agreement that likely never would have happened had I dug in my heels and refused to budge off my $95,000 purchase price.

Negotiation Strategies

Even a five-year-old knows that the manipulation techniques used on mommy probably aren't going to work on daddy. And vice versa.

Different situations—and different people—will call for different amounts of negotiating "force." You aren't going to deal the same way with someone who is timid and averse to conflict as someone who is argumentative and always feels the need to be right. Understanding common negotiating strategies and styles will help you apply the right method at the right time.

Most negotiations are going to fall into one of two specific approaches, driven by the styles, skills, and goals of those doing the negotiation:

Distributive (competitive) approach: This approach is most typical of negotiations around zero-sum outcomes. In other words, "There's only so much cake to divide between us, and I want to win by getting the biggest piece." In these types of negotiations, one party's loss is the other party's gain.

While there are some situations when this approach is necessary—generally resulting from both parties wanting the exact same thing—it often ends in a win-lose or lose-lose result. A competitive approach to negotiating stifles creativity by limiting potential solutions that could lead to an outcome that would expand the benefits for all parties.

This type of negotiation is most common when making a simple purchase. The negotiation struggle is over a single issue—money. One side wants to receive more of it and the other side wants to spend less of it. In the end, the best outcome is one where both sides are not unhappy.

That said, these types of negotiations often end with one side feeling like they were taken advantage of, or in some cases, both sides left feeling like they lost.

Integrative (collaborative) approach: In contrast, the integrative approach to negotiation doesn't view the cake as finite. Instead, this strategy looks for ways to actually create *more* cake, so that all parties can get a bigger piece. The key to creating "more cake" is building a relationship of trust that involves asking questions, listening to answers, offering solutions and sharing just the right kind and amount of relevant information—not too little and not too much.

Also, understanding exactly what the other party really needs—as opposed to what they say they need—is integral to creating additional value that can benefit both sides. This is an extremely important topic when it comes to negotiating real estate and we'll delve more deeply into this concept throughout the book.

How Real Estate Negotiation Is Different

We've spent the first part of this chapter talking about the basics of negotiation. All of this information can be found in dozens of other books and—so far—we haven't provided much in terms of unique ideas (though this stuff really is important to understand before we get further into the book).

If there are plenty of other negotiating books out there, why do we need another one? Why did Mark, Carol, and I decide to spend more than a year of our lives putting this book together when we could have just found another book on negotiation to recommend to investors?

The answer is simple:

There are some very important differences between real estate negotiations and other types of negotiations. While there are plenty of books out there that will teach you how to be a better negotiator in general, there are none that we're familiar with that will make you a better *real estate* negotiator.

What are those differences in real estate transactions that make negotiation more complex than with most other transactions? Here are just a few of the differences:

- Real estate deals tend to be very expensive transactions. This means that the ability to successfully negotiate even relatively small details can result in large financial gain. Conversely, the inability to negotiate can lead to large financial loss.

- Along with the big money comes a longer transaction cycle—most real estate transactions take at least a month, and sometimes several months, from the time an initial offer is made to the day when the deal closes. A lot of things can happen during that time that can make or break the deal.
- There is often a big emotional attachment with real estate. Home sellers may have grown up in the house they're selling, or may have raised their family there. While you may be valuing the property purely based on market conditions, you can bet that many sellers will be viewing the value of their home from a much more emotional standpoint.
- Real estate negotiation often involves several parties, as it's frequently conducted with, or even through, intermediaries. Real estate agents commonly negotiate transactions, but mortgage brokers, inspectors, appraisers, and other stakeholders may also be involved in the negotiating process.
- A real estate negotiation may contain many separate smaller negotiations. A single deal may require multiple negotiations between parties such as buyers, sellers, inspectors, appraisers, agents, lenders, and title companies.

Along with everything above, it's important to realize that every real estate transaction is going to be unique. Some deals are hammered out between buyer and seller over drinks at the bar, while other deals take months to negotiate and the buyer and seller never exchange a single word—they let their real estate agents or attorneys handle the communication.

In fact, some deals seem to not involve any negotiation at all!

To illustrate this point, here's a story of a house we purchased in 2012:

⟩ TALES FROM THE TRENCHES ⟨

One Saturday, back when we were still pretty new to this business, I received a call from a friend who also happened to be our closing attorney at the time. While walking in his neighborhood he had stumbled across a garage sale. He spoke to the woman running the sale, and apparently, the woman's mother had lived in the house and had passed away a few months earlier. The daughter was selling the household possessions.

My friend asked if she was planning to sell the house, and she responded that she hadn't really gotten around to thinking about it yet. That's when he called us.

We loved the neighborhood and immediately drove to check out the estate sale, though our real motivation was to meet the woman running the sale, as she was likely the one who inherited the house and now owned it.

It turns out we were correct. My wife spoke with the woman for about an hour, got a tour of the house and listened to the woman talk about her mom's legacy. Eventually my wife asked about the house and the woman reiterated that she hadn't really thought about what she was planning to do with it. My wife left her a business card, collected her information, and we left.

About three months later, just after New Year's, my wife came to me and said, "Remember that house we saw at the estate sale a few months ago? It's ours if we want it!" It turns out my wife had sent the woman a Christmas card over the holidays, with a nice note about how hard it must be to celebrate a first Christmas without her mom.

The woman was so touched that she immediately called my wife to thank her, and in the midst of the conversation, decided that she was ready to sell the house, and did we want to buy it?

About a month later, we purchased the house. We got a great deal, and the woman who sold it to us seemed to be even happier to be able to sell it to us. Never did this transaction feel like a negotiation, which was part of the reason it was so successful.

Negotiate Everything!

Most of us aren't born negotiators, but the good news is that anyone can learn. Learning to negotiate is just like learning a new sport, the game of chess, or a musical instrument—the more you practice, the better you get. Similarly, your negotiation skills are like muscles; the more you work them, the stronger they'll grow.

As a real estate investor, it's especially important to both develop your negotiation skills and keep them honed by practicing negotiation whenever you can. Why? Because successful negotiation is just as much—actually, even more!—about practice and preparation as it is about "toughness." And the last thing you want is to be unprepared.

The best negotiators get that way because they are always practicing.

Why is practicing so important? In real estate transactions, skilled negotiators can make small financial gains across many situations. While these may not seem like much at the time, they can quickly add up and make a considerable difference in the outcome of a project. In fact, the cumulative gains from small negotiations may ultimately overshadow the gains from the big negotiations.

For example, imagine flipping a house and negotiating a mere $20 savings every time you purchase materials or pay a contractor. If you have 50 such transactions on your project, that's $1,000 in savings. If you do 20 projects per year, that's $20,000 extra in your pocket at the end of the year!

Good negotiation can mean more dollars in your pocket. But, it's actually more than that. Smart negotiation can provide you with extra control over your deals, resulting in easier and less stressful transactions. This, in turn, can make your entire business easier and more profitable.

TAKE ACTION

Next time you walk into Home Depot or Lowe's try to negotiate the price of your purchase. If you're buying an appliance with a big scratch in it or some poor-quality lumber, you should find it easy to get 10 to 20 percent off.

Are you willing to buy a floor model? If so, you can generally get a 10 to 15 percent discount. And, once you get comfortable haggling, there's no reason why you shouldn't be able to negotiate discounts simply based on the fact that you're a good customer or because you feel like you deserve a discount.

Win-Win Isn't Always Possible

While we'd always like to have win-win and win-plus outcomes, the truth is that it isn't always possible or practical.

This is particularly true when buying or selling real estate, where both sides typically want one thing more than anything else: money. In many cases, deals involve 1) an investor, who needs to get the lowest price to make a profit, and 2) a desperate seller, who needs to make enough money from the sale to pay off their mortgage or other bills.

For a buyer to pay the lowest price and the seller to receive the highest price for that same thing just doesn't work. The two scenarios are incompatible, so a win-win based purely on financial gain typically isn't possible.

You shouldn't expect to always be able to achieve a successful outcome in every real estate negotiation.

There are many times when the best strategy in a particular negotiation is to just walk away. Later in this book, we'll discuss the best way to do that.

CHAPTER 2
PRINCIPLES OF NEGOTIATION

We all essentially know how negotiations work: One side throws out an offer, the other side suggests a counteroffer, and they go back and forth until they either come to an agreement or give up.

From a 10,000-foot high view, that's a good summary.

But, when you *really* dig in, you'll find that there is a set of principles to successfully doing what we just described. In this chapter, we're going to review many of these basic, but not necessarily obvious, principles behind the negotiation process. Understanding them will give you a framework from which you will be able to analyze the various aspects and stages of the negotiation, and will give you the context necessary to understand the strategy and tactics we'll cover throughout the rest of the book.

Negotiating Mechanics

We're going to try to minimize the amount of new terminology we introduce in the book, but there are some basic negotiating concepts and terms that are important to understand before we get too far into the details. In order to truly understand the dynamics that go into a negotiation, we need to be able to step back and take a higher level view of what a typical transaction looks like.

With that in mind, here is some basic terminology that will help you think about the mechanics of a typical negotiation. For this discussion, we're going to assume the buyer and seller are negotiating the sale of a property valued between $150,000 and $200,000.

Target Point

The *target point* (or just "target") is the deal that each party would be thrilled to get out of the negotiation. The buyer is going to have his target (generally lower price and better purchase terms) and the seller is going to have her target (generally higher price and better sale terms). While the targets of the buyer and seller could be identical, in most negotiations, this won't be the case. This makes sense, as the buyer typically wants to purchase at the lowest price and the seller typically wants to sell at the highest price.

For this example, let's assume that the buyer would be happy purchasing a seller's property at $170,000 (buyer's target) and the seller would be happy selling the property at $180,000 (seller's target).

Here's what it looks like in visual form:

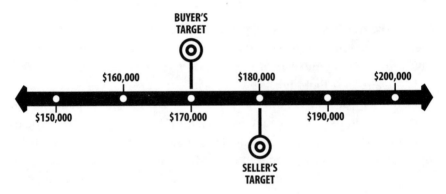

DIG DEEP *We use the term "wants" many times throughout this book as a way to describe those things that each side desires to get out of the negotiation (i.e., "The buyer wants to buy the house for $150,000"). While we tend to use this term very loosely, consider that the idea of a want equates nicely to each side's target (their best-case outcome of the negotiation).*

Minimum Acceptable Offer (MAO)

The *minimum acceptable offer* ("MAO") is the most extreme point (the worst deal) that each party would reluctantly accept out of the negotiation. The buyer's MAO is going to be a higher number than his target point, because he wants to pay as little as possible. Conversely, the seller's MAO is going to be a lower figure than her target point, because she wants to receive as much money as possible.

Let's go back to our example above and let's assume that the buyer would reluctantly agree to pay $190,000 for the property (buyer's MAO). Further, let's assume that the seller would reluctantly agree to sell the property for $160,000 (seller's MAO).

Here is what that would look like overlaid onto the same visual chart above:

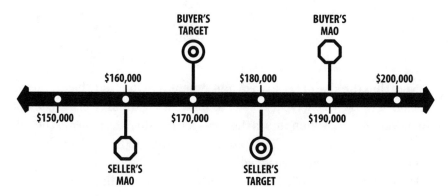

DIG DEEP *We use the term "needs" many times throughout this book as a way to describe those things that each side requires to get out of the negotiation (i.e., "The seller needs to get at least $200,000 out of the sale"). While we tend to use this term very loosely, consider that the idea of a need equates nicely to each side's MAO (the minimum each is willing to take in order to agree to a deal).*

Area of Agreement

The *area of agreement* is the range of prices where the buyer and seller would both accept a deal, even reluctantly. This area extends from the seller's MAO (the low end of the range) to the buyer's MAO (the high end of the range). It's within this area where a deal can potentially be reached.

Here is what the area of agreement would look like for our example transaction:

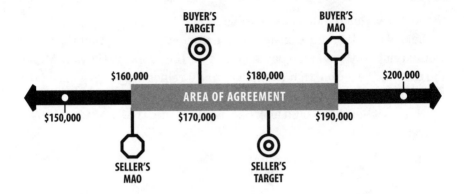

Note that the size of the area of agreement will fluctuate based on the location of the MAO each party sets. In some cases, the area of agreement can be very small. When this is the case, it's possible that—even though there is a range in which both parties would be willing to settle—an agreement may never be reached.

Here's an example of the area of agreement being small:

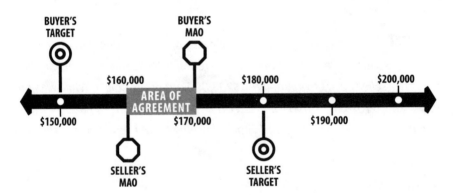

In this example, there is no chance that the buyer or the seller will get everything they want (their targets).

In fact, if a deal is to be reached in this situation, it's likely that both sides will need to be willing to settle for much less than they really want. When the area of agreement is small, this is when trust, rapport and cooperation are most important, as each side must believe that the other side is also making big sacrifices to get the deal done.

DIG DEEP *If you can get a deal at the other party's MAO, you've likely gotten the best deal possible. For this reason, one of the most important jobs of a great negotiator is to gather the information necessary to try to determine (guess!) the other party's MAO.*

Distance from Agreement

In some cases—and this is actually quite common in real estate transactions—there will be no area of agreement whatsoever. That occurs when the buyer's MAO is below the seller's MAO.

For example, modifying our example a bit, our negotiation might look something like this:

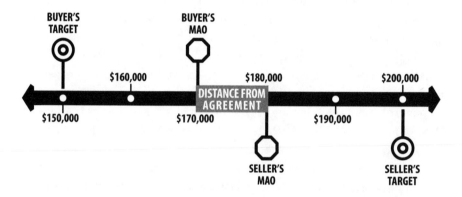

In this case, we have no overlap in acceptable price—the buyer isn't willing to pay even the lowest amount the seller is willing to accept. And there is actually a gap (our distance from agreement) that would need to be overcome in order to reach a compromise. Given that the buyer is unlikely to have a change of heart and go above his MAO and the seller is unlikely to have a change of heart and go below her MAO, this situation will often result in a stalled negotiation and no deal being made.

As we saw in the story of the woman who was selling her father's house, if the distance from agreement is small, we can often bring into the negotiation other terms besides price, which can help one or both parties get over their resistance and reach an agreement.

For example, perhaps the seller isn't going to be ready to move for a few months, and is willing to sell a little bit below her MAO if the buyer was willing to wait a few months to complete the purchase; and perhaps the buyer is willing to spend a little above his MAO if the seller would be willing to finance part of the deal herself. If both sides are willing to give and receive incentives other than price, it's sometimes possible to overcome a gap between MAOs.

DIG DEEP *If both you and the other party are solely focused on price, most of your real estate negotiations are going to fail. Good negotiators are able to focus on terms other than price. Great negotiators are able to get the other party to do the same thing.*

Concessions: The Currency of Negotiation

All negotiations, no matter how large or small, are built on a common "currency." This negotiation currency is known as *concessions*.

To illustrate this, imagine a negotiation as a big pot filled with things that both parties want, sitting between them on the table. The concessions are all the shiny, glittering things inside that pot. In many cases, the most important concession is money (price), but good negotiators realize that the pot is actually filled with many other things as well, depending on the specific nature of the negotiations.

As a negotiation progresses, either party may take things out of the pot and give them to the other party ("making a concession"). A party may also put things back in the pot that had previously been taken out. Great negotiators will continually find new things to add to the pot as the negotiation progresses.

When both parties agree on how all the stuff in the pot is distributed, a deal has been reached. A skilled negotiator realizes that the more concessions they can add to the pot throughout the negotiation, the more likely it is that both parties will feel like they got a lot out of the negotiation.

TALES FROM THE TRENCHES

When building my personal residence, I had a specific HVAC contractor that I really wanted to use. The company was experienced in new construction, they were local, and they came highly recommended by other investors in the area.

My original bid for my HVAC work was just under $15,000—about $3,000 more than I had budgeted for or wanted to pay. Unfortunately, they were a large company with plenty of work, so when I attempted to negotiate the price down, I didn't get very far. Because they didn't care much about getting my business and I cared too much about using them, I was in a bad negotiating position.

Ultimately, I decided that it was unlikely I could make any additional headway on getting the price down, so I started to focus on concessions instead. Long story short, I still paid the $15,000 price tag, but in return, I was able to get:

- Upgraded equipment (with extended warranty)
- Three years of free HVAC tune-ups
- 40 air filters
- Priority scheduling to avoid waiting to get my work done

In total, I received about $1,200 in "perks," plus they agreed to schedule my work on the exact days I wanted (this was a big bonus given their schedule was backlogged). While I was still not close to hitting my budget, I was very happy with what I was able to receive with how little leverage I had.

And even though I didn't hit my price target, the concessions I was able to negotiate allowed us to come to an agreement that ultimately worked for both sides.

Once you start to think of a negotiation as just a big pot of needs and desires (concessions), and once you understand how best to trade those needs and desires, you will find that your negotiations tend to result in much more successful outcomes for all involved.

Leverage: The Power of Circumstance

In the physical world, we use the word leverage to describe a system where a little bit of force can be multiplied to create a relatively large action. The more leverage the system has, the larger the result of the small amount of force. For example, tools like bolt cutters create enough leverage to allow you to cut through steel with only the power of your hands!

In the financial world, leverage is used to refer to loan products that allow you to multiply your return on investment (ROI). Under the right circumstances, borrowing relatively small amounts of capital for an investment can significantly increase the ROI of those investments. Like in the physical world, financial leverage allows you generate a proportionately greater outcome than the force put into the system.

We also talk about leverage in the negotiating world. Like in the physical and financial worlds, leverage refers to the ability to generate relatively large results from one or both party's relatively small circumstances. In other words, in the negotiating world, leverage generally refers to the power one side has over the other side, based on their current situation.

As an example, imagine a property seller is facing foreclosure in the next ten days. Imagine also that you are the only buyer. The seller is in a desperate situation—she must sell her property immediately for whatever she can get, or risk losing it, getting nothing, and potentially taking a big credit hit. In this situation, you would have a lot of leverage in the negotiation.

Specifically, you have the ability to make significant demands, and unless there are other buyers making offers, the seller is not in a very good position to push back on those demands. As long as you're willing to give the seller a deal that puts her in a better position than the alternative (the foreclosure, in this case), you can pretty much demand anything you want.

While leverage typically results from personal and financial issues, it can also be the result of other situations that create a strong need for one side to reach an agreement.

QUICK TIP *The party with the most leverage in a negotiation will generally be the one with the best alternatives should the negotiation fail. What is the alternative for the other party if an agreement is not reached? Answer this question to get insight into how much leverage you have.*

Power: A Balancing Act

Just like in any relationship, when it comes to negotiating, it's important to always be aware of the balance of power between the parties, and to correct for any imbalance that may put negotiations at risk.

Power will naturally shift between the parties throughout the negotiation process—it's rarely evenly balanced—but when one party has too much power, or for too long, the other party may react negatively. If one party is timid, this imbalance of power may result in their wanting to withdraw from the discussion and walk away from a potential deal. If one party is insecure, this imbalance may result in their lashing out and making crazy demands in attempt to regain control.

While there are ways to restore this balance of power when it shifts too far to one side or the other, it's typically easier to just focus on not letting the balance get too far out of whack in the first place.

The party that has the most leverage in the negotiation will typically have the most power. And in many cases, not caring about the outcome is the most powerful piece of leverage. If one party neither wants nor needs a deal, that party will typically have the most power throughout the negotiation. Further, if *both* parties need the deal, the one that needs it *less* will typically have the most power.

While this may be common sense, that doesn't mean it's easy to manage. When dealing with someone who doesn't care about the outcome of the negotiation, you must be willing to accept that you will almost always be in a weaker position. Can you handle that?

When you're in a position where you don't care about the outcome of the negotiation and the other party does, you must work to not take too much advantage of the situation. This often means providing the other side enough concessions that he doesn't get demoralized before the conclusion of the deal. You may need to give more than you otherwise would, or else risk the other party walking away.

Even when both parties care about getting a deal completed, the balance of power is rarely equal. When discussing an aspect of the deal that is more important to one side than the other (for example, a seller needs to sell by next week, but you're in no hurry to buy), power will transfer to the less invested party during that part of the discussion.

Momentum: Negotiations in Motion

A concept often overlooked in negotiation is *momentum*. Momentum is the idea of how forcefully something is moving forward. You've probably heard Newton's First Law of Motion: An object at rest tends to stay at rest; an object in motion tends to stay in motion.

This is the same with a negotiation. Keeping a negotiation moving forward toward a resolution is much easier than getting it going again after it slows down or stops. We call this slowing or stopping of a negotiation a *stall*. Good negotiators work hard to avoid stalls, as this gives the other party the opportunity to walk away or to decide they want more time to pursue other options.

Having momentum in a negotiation keeps both sides engaged, keeps both sides optimistic about an outcome, and generally keeps either side from looking for other options. In fact, tough negotiations with lots of momentum are more likely to be successful than easy negotiations without momentum.

That said, momentum doesn't necessarily mean that things are moving quickly—it just means that they're moving forward and both sides continue to be motivated to reach a conclusion. To this point, there are even times when one side can slow down a negotiation to increase momentum.

Here's a non-real estate story that will illustrate this point.

Back in 2002, the online auction company eBay made an offer to purchase the online payment company, PayPal. (One of the co-authors of this book was working for eBay at the time.) eBay offered $200 million to purchase PayPal outright. PayPal demanded $500 million to agree to the buy-out. Despite serious negotiations between the companies, no agreement was reached, and the sides deferred conversations for a couple months.

A couple of months later, eBay came back to the table, this time offering the $500 million PayPal had asked. But, PayPal had continued to grow during this time, and now demanded $1 billion. eBay couldn't bring themselves to spend that much for the fledgling company, and again, no agreement was reached.

A few months later, eBay recognized the amazing growth and potential of PayPal, invited the company back to the negotiating table, and offered the $1 billion PayPal had demanded. But, by this time, PayPal knew they were worth even more, and countered with a demand for $1.5 billion.

eBay, not wanting to risk even more than the $1 billion they had lost by not accepting the first offer, agreed to the $1.5 billion price.

While this entire negotiation took many months (perhaps a year or more from the time each side started their research and planning), there was strong momentum throughout the entire process. Each side remained engaged, saw the value and potential of an agreement, and continued working toward that eventual agreement.

Negotiation speed and momentum are two very different things; momentum is important, speed generally isn't.

Price & Terms

In negotiation, you'll often hear the phrase, "*price & terms.*" In real estate, "price" refers to the agreed upon amount for which a seller is willing to sell her house and the buyer is willing to pay for the house; "terms" are all the other details agreed upon as part of the deal.

Inexperienced negotiators—including many of the buyers and sellers that you're likely to be working with—focus much more on price than they do on terms. But, in your quest to become a master negotiator, you will come to realize that terms can often be just as important as price, and in some cases, mastering the ability to control terms can turn a failing negotiation into a successful one.

Many investors go into a negotiation with a fixed price in mind. They run the numbers, figure out what they need to make the deal work, and that's their price. They tell themselves—and the seller—that they can only pay $80,000 (or whatever the amount is) for the property, not a penny more. If the seller can't agree to sell at that price or better, the investor's only alternative is to walk away from the deal.

I'll be honest: We used to think that way as well. Then we met an investor who showed us the error of our ways...

TALES FROM THE TRENCHES

A friend of mine named Jeff, a buy-and-hold investor in Georgia, used to brag about how good he was at getting great deals.

One day I was sitting at lunch with Jeff and he told me about a meeting he had coming up that afternoon with a local landlord who was looking to sell off his portfolio of eight single-family houses in the area. I asked Jeff how much he was going to try to get the houses for, and he said:

"I'd love to pick up the entire portfolio for $300,000."

That was under $40,000 per house, and based on the rents in the area, that seemed like a really good deal to me.

A few days later, I saw Jeff at a local investors' meetup, and asked him if he had been able to buy the houses. He had and said he got an even better deal than he wanted. I responded with:

"Wow, you were able to get all eight for less than $300,000?!?!"

His response, said with a little grin, was:

"Nope, I paid $480,000."

I was still a novice, and I could tell he was just prodding me to ask more questions to learn his "secrets." And of course I did. I asked him how $480,000 was "better than the deal he wanted," when just a few days earlier we had talked about him wanting to pay no more than $300,000.

Jeff went on to explain:

"I offered the seller $300,000, but quickly realized that he was set on getting at least $400,000. I knew that if we just kept haggling over the price, there was no way we'd ever reach an agreement. After talking to the guy for a bit, I found out that he owned the portfolio outright [no loans on the properties], and that he wasn't selling because he needed the money for anything—he was just tired of dealing with the properties.

Instead of wasting time arguing over price, I told him I'd pay him his $400,000 price, but instead of paying all cash, I offered him $1,667 per month for 20 years. We went back and forth a bit, and we finally agreed on me giving him $30,000 as a down payment, and then $1,875 per month for the next 20 years."

I already had my phone out with the calculator app running. Between down payment and monthly payments, I quickly determined that Jeff really was paying a total price of $480,000 over 20 years—$180,000 more than he originally wanted to pay!

Before I could ask him to explain his rationale, he continued:

"If I had purchased the deal for $300,000 in cash, I was planning to get a commercial loan with the same down payment, and I'd be paying about $2,000 per month for 20 years to the bank. This way, I'm paying $125 per month less, plus I don't have to deal with the bank."

Ultimately, Jeff was saving $125 per month for 20 years and the landlord was making a total of $80,000 more than he wanted for the property. Sure, the landlord didn't get all the money upfront (which was a downside), but he apparently didn't need all the cash at once, and there were also some tax advantages to doing it this way.

What we learned that day from Jeff, and what we hope you learn as you read this book, is that smart negotiators recognize that there is a lot more to a good deal than just a great price. By using terms—both payment terms and other non-price considerations—great negotiators have the ability to find creative solutions to problems.

DIG DEEP *According to a recent Zillow study, over 20 million homes (nearly 30 percent of all homeowners in the U.S.) are owned free-and-clear, without a mortgage.*

Successful Negotiation = Solving Problems

As any truly formidable real estate investor will tell you, success doesn't come from knowing how to negotiate—it comes from knowing how to *solve problems*. Your best deals won't come from exerting leverage over the other party or from charming a buyer or seller with your charisma. Your best deals will come from solving the problems that are motivating the other party to want to enter into the transaction in the first place.

There will be times when the problem the other party is facing will be far more overwhelming than you can reasonably solve. (For example, a seller owes $500,000 to the IRS and is trying to sell a house worth $80,000 to pay it off.) But, there will be other times when solving their problem will cost you very little, or can be achieved by means other than forking over lots of money.

Here's a good example of that:

TALES FROM THE TRENCHES

Back in 2008, when we first started investing, we had had each of our properties inspected by a professional home inspector before our purchase. We found a great inspector who came highly recommended, and he charged a reasonable fee—$300 per inspection. On our third house, I asked him if he'd be willing to drop his fee to $250, since we were giving him a lot of repeat business.

He very nicely said something along the lines of:

"I'd love to be able to do that, but business is slow these days, and I really can't afford to discount my services."

Instead of his just saying "no" (which would have led me to believe he was just being stingy and unreasonable), he justified his answer with a reason. And not just a reason, but the specific problem he was facing that wouldn't allow him give me what I wanted.

Instead of continuing to try to negotiate the price down—for example, I could have said, "How about $275 instead?"—I decided that a better strategy would be to try to solve the problem he had expressed.

So, I said to him:

"How about this... Will you give me a $10 credit toward future inspections for each new job I refer to you?"

His response was simply, "Hell yeah!"

Over the next several months, I referred that home inspector to dozens of my investing colleagues and friends, and I literally cut the cost of my own inspections by about half with the credit he gave me for the referred work.

Keep in mind, in our story above, I would have been happy to refer my inspector to all the other investors I knew for absolutely nothing in return. In other words, this was a concession that literally didn't cost me anything.

But, the value of this concession to my home inspector was huge.

How huge? *It solved his problem.*

Every referral was $300 in his pocket (okay, $290 after giving us our referral fee), and enough referrals could make the difference between his barely making enough money to survive and earning a nice lifestyle. Because we focused on his problem, and not just our own, we created an opportunity to solve both his problem (not enough business) and mine (paying too much for inspections).

If you want to be a great negotiator, don't focus on negotiating—focus on solving problems!

CHAPTER 3
THE POWER OF INFORMATION

It's well known in the negotiating world that the party who enters the negotiation most prepared is far more likely to walk away with the better deal. Information is power. It can provide leverage over the other party (for example, finding out that a seller just lost his job and can't make his payments); it can help verify the value of what's being negotiated (for example, finding out that the property is built on top of an oil field); and it can help you avoid nasty surprises that cause you to overpay for a property.

As an example of that last point, let's say you're trying to buy a house and the seller knows that there's a loud train that runs behind the property every night at 3 a.m. Or perhaps there's a flight pattern from a local airport that routes planes directly overhead when the wind is blowing in a certain direction.

Unless you're visiting the property at 3 a.m. or happen to be there when the wind is blowing in the right direction, you may not know about these things until after you've completed the purchase. And depending on the disclosure laws in your state, when you resell the property, you may have a legal obligation to disclose this negative information to your end-buyer (even if the seller broke the law by not informing you). These types of things can have a dramatic impact on your resale value, and could even result in your losing money on the deal.

All because you didn't have some basic information before you purchased the property.

Back when we first started in this business, we purchased a rehab in a neighborhood where we had done a number of previous projects. We were comfortable with our purchase price, knew exactly what our rehab costs would be, and because we had sold other properties in this neighborhood, we were confident about the resale value.

We closed on the house on a Tuesday, and started work the next morning. The first thing I noticed when I pulled up to the house on that Wednesday morning was two large and somewhat intimidating Dobermans from the house next door. They were running to the fence-line between the houses, barking like crazy at us and our contractors. We're dog lovers, so normally we wouldn't mind, but the barking didn't stop all day. And the next day, the dogs were out barking at us again. And the same thing again on Friday.

It turns out that the neighbors would let the dogs out at 8 a.m. each weekday before leaving for work, and leave them out until they got home around 6 p.m. We had only visited this house once—on a weekend—before making our offer. Because it was a weekend, the dogs were inside, and we had no idea the surprise in store for us when we started working on the house.

Selling this house took about three times longer than average, as we had to avoid doing any showings on weekdays, knowing the dogs would scare many potential buyers. On top of that, the first buyer who placed an offer (after seeing the house on a Saturday and again on Sunday), showed up to his inspection the following Wednesday with his three-year-old son. When he saw the menacing dogs running to the fence and barking like crazy, he immediately canceled the inspection and the contract.

We were unsuccessful at getting the neighbors to cooperate and keep their dogs inside, and instead ended up selling the house for about 10 percent below market to another investor who kept it as a rental. Luckily, we still made a profit on the deal, but our lack of due diligence could have easily caused us to lose money.

This is why, early in the process—before a first offer is made—you should gather as much data as possible, both from external sources and directly from the other party. This might take a couple hours; or if it's a large deal with many potential risks, you may spend weeks on this part of the process.

We like to think about due diligence on three scales:

We'll discuss each of these layers in more detail below, along with strategies you can use to complete your due diligence and best prepare your negotiation strategy using the information you find. Keep in mind that all of this research can be performed without having to talk to the other party in the transaction—that's a completely separate area of due diligence that we'll tackle in the next two chapters.

Information about the Market

Information about the current local and national real estate markets will not, in and of itself, give you enough ammunition to dominate a negotiation—market data, by definition, will be generalized and not specifically related to the deal at hand. But what it *will* give you is a reasonably good barometer of how much leverage you realistically have as the buyer or seller of the property.

Market data will also provide you with some perspective on the alternatives the other party will have if the deal doesn't get done with you. Specifically, if you're a buyer, it will give you an idea of whether there are other buyers, potentially competing with you. Likewise, if you're a seller, you'll gain a sense of how many other alternatives your potential buyers have when considering your property for purchase. (As we discussed earlier, the alternatives that each party has is a key driver of the leverage they have.)

Your main goal for analyzing the national and local real estate markets is to determine whether you are operating in a *buyer's market* or a *seller's market*. This will give you an idea of which party will have the best alternatives—and the most leverage—in the negotiations.

Buyer's Market/Seller's Market

To understand the concept of buyer's and seller's markets, we first need to understand how we talk about real estate inventory on a large scale.

Real estate professionals often refer to the amount of *supply* in a real estate market. Measured in months, supply is the amount of time it would take to sell all the available houses using the monthly average number of sales.

For example, if in a particular area 20 houses sell per month, and that location currently has 100 houses listed for sale, we would say that that area has five months of housing supply.

If you look at the data over a long period of time, you'll find that in many parts of the United States, the average housing supply is about six months. In other words, six months of housing supply is about what we would consider equilibrium in many real estate markets across the United States. Your market may have a higher or lower average than this (that's something you need to work with a good agent to determine), but we're going to use six months as our example.

When our market has lower supply than average (for this example, fewer than six months), we say that sellers are in control. There are more people looking to buy houses than there are people selling houses, which means buyers are competing for the same properties and sellers are able to increase their prices because of this competition. This is what we call a *seller's market*.

When our market has more supply than average (in this example, more than six months), we say that buyers are in control. There are more houses for sale than there are buyers looking to buy and the lack of interested buyers means that sellers are going to have to compete against one another to get their properties sold. This often means lowering prices to attract buyers. This is what we call a *buyer's market*.

We could write an entire other book on market cycles, buyer's markets, and seller's markets, but here's a quick summary as it relates to real estate negotiation:

SELLER'S MARKET	LOW INVENTORY, MANY BUYERS	BUYER'S MARKET	HIGH INVENTORY, FEW BUYERS
BUYER	• Less leverage • Must be willing to compromise • Fewer options for purchasing • Underdog in the negotiation		• More leverage • Can be more aggressive with demands • Many options for purchasing • Has upper hand in the negotiation
SELLER	• More leverage • Can be more aggressive with demands • Many options for purchasing • Has upper hand in the negotiation		• Less leverage • Must be willing to compromise • Fewer options for purchasing • Underdog in the negotiation

Information about the Property

Once we have a general sense of the market, it's time to dig into data related to the property we're considering buying.

While we like to think the seller is going to disclose to us most of what we need to know, that's not generally the case. Perhaps the seller neglected to mention something that didn't seem relevant; perhaps they truly forgot to point out an issue from long ago; or, worst case, perhaps they are trying to hide information about the property that you might consider negative or alarming.

Regardless, as the buyer, it's your responsibility to do your own due diligence and ensure that you eliminate as many potential surprises as possible. This involves not only the most obvious route of getting information from the seller. You will often discover just as much, or even more, relevant information by chatting with neighbors, visiting county offices, researching public records and online community resources, and perhaps even calling around to contractors.

To some people, this may sound like a time-consuming and cumbersome process, but when making large purchases that can create substantial profit but also carry substantial risk, it's just part of the job.

Look at Public Records and Online Community Resources

Before we even visit a property, we like to gather as much information as possible from public records and online community resources. In some geographical areas, public records are available on your county's website or some other online portal; in other areas, you'll need to visit the clerk of the local court to access this data.

There is a wide variety of information available through public records. In general, it should serve two purposes:

1. The info will help confirm that there are no major "surprises" with the property you are considering for purchase.
2. In some circumstances, you just might discover there are some potential upsides to the property that aren't obvious at first glance.

Here are some of the public records sources you should take a look at, along with the type of information you need to consider within each:

PUBLIC RECORD	QUESTIONS TO ASK
TAX ASSESSMENT: Valuation by local municipality, used for tax purposes. (Note that this valuation is unlikely related to actual market value.)	What are the annual taxes? *Land and structure are typically calculated separately when determining overall value.*
	Are there any tax exemptions that could affect the property later? *This could mean your (or your buyer's) taxes will go up or down in the near future.*
	What year was the structure built? *You might be surprised how often original owners "forget" this info.*
	What is the square footage? *Does it accurately reflect any additions to the property?*
PROPERTY DEED(S): Real property records filed with the court each time ownership is transferred and each time a loan is taken out on the subject property. A summary of previous owners is often also listed on the tax assessment.	How long has the current owner owned the property? *A long-time owner may have substantial equity and, therefore, more flexibility in the sale price.*
	How did the current owner pay for the property? *Was it a cash sale? If not, what kind of financing did they use?*
	How many previous owners have there been? *A pattern of short ownership is likely a red flag you should explore further.*
	Are there any deed restrictions? *Restrictions can impact future use—the settlement officer will typically find these later as part of the title search, but it's also useful upfront in your negotiation.*

PLAT MAP/SURVEY: A scale drawing of the piece of land, indicating boundaries, access rights, easements, roadways, etc.	What are the exact boundaries of the property? *Plat maps give substantially more accurate information than a simple address or birds' eye view.*
	Are there any access rights or easements on the property? *Easements for utilities, driveways, etc. may impact potential plans.*
	What are the property setbacks? *Setbacks delineate where additions, garages, exterior structures, and other improvements can be built.*
BIRDS' EYE VIEW: Accessible online at Google Maps and most real estate sale sites.	Is the property near power lines, railroad tracks, or a busy highway? *These are not necessarily deal breakers, but should be considered in your offer price.*
	Which direction does the house face? *This may be a consideration for gardeners, artists, and members of certain religions.*
NSOPW.GOV: U.S. Department of Justice public resource for sex offender public registries.	Are there registered sex offenders living nearby? *To a savvy buyer or tenant, especially since this information is easily accessible online, this will have impact on the on the perceived market value.*
GREATSCHOOLS.ORG: Ratings on a scale of 1-10 of most public and many private schools.	Were the assigned schools once coveted, but their ratings have declined in recent years? *Use that to your advantage in your negotiation.*
MSC.FEMA.GOV: FEMA Flood Map Service Center.	Is this property in a flood zone? *Flood zones affect insurability, and can impact resale value.*

ZONING REGULATIONS: Local ordinances that define what may be built upon a particular parcel.	For what use is the property currently zoned? *In some circumstances, zoning regulations will reveal that the property could also be used for multifamily housing or commercial use, both of which could potentially increase property value.*
	What do the regulations state about property and structure specifics? *These documents will help you determine things such as the legal overall height of a potential addition, or what kind of fence is allowed.*
HISTORIC PRESERVATION GUIDELINES: Outline requirements for alteration of properties with a designated historic district.	Is this property in the National Register of Historic Places or a local historic preservation district? *If yes, approval may be required prior to any modifications, in order to maintain architectural integrity.*
	Are any tax incentives available? *Some jurisdictions offer tax credits for property owners to restore or preserve historic properties.*
HOA COVENANTS AND BYLAWS: Conditions and restrictions for properties with a home owners' association.	What types of modifications may be made to the property? *HOA requirements vary greatly—many require committee approval before painting an exterior, repaving a driveway, or changing landscaping.*
	Are there any regulations that would impact future use? *Some considerations are limiting the number of FHA buyers or Section 8 tenants, for example.*

That's a lot of information, right? But this list is just the tip of the iceberg. Want to be armed with all the *really* good stuff to use in your negotiation? Then get out there and talk to some key people.

Talk to the Neighbors

One of the best ways to gain information about a property and neighborhood is often overlooked: simply talk with the neighbors. When we're considering purchasing a new property, we go out of our way to chat with people who are mowing their lawn, strike up a conversation with someone sitting on their front porch, and even knock on doors to "introduce ourselves."

As one example, our friend and fellow investor, Jordan Thibodeau, has a routine of picking oranges from his orange tree and walking around the neighborhood handing out fresh oranges. He calls it "orange juice diplomacy."

Regardless of how you make the introduction, we've found that people typically appreciate the gesture and that more often than not, the conversation quickly turns into the other person divulging all sorts of information about themselves, their family, their house, the neighborhood gossip, and so on.

As we'll discuss in the next chapter, people *love* to talk about themselves. When you give them an opportunity to do so, you begin to bond and build a trusting relationship, which ultimately leads to them subtly—or not so subtly—giving you far more information than you asked for.

So introduce yourself as someone who is considering buying in the neighborhood (don't lie about moving in if you don't plan to!) and then ask some simple questions such as:

Then let the conversation lead wherever it leads. As you build trust over the course of the conservation, it's likely they will divulge more important information than you'd ever garner from the property seller or from public records.

QUICK TIP *Check out NextDoor.com—this free community-based social network can help you learn about the neighborhood and keep up to date on the local gossip and issues.*

For example, they might tell you about the kid around the corner they suspect of vandalizing mailboxes; they might tell you about the prolonged power outages in the neighborhood "because the electric company doesn't care about our little cul-de-sac"; they might tell you about the time the house you're considering buying had a major termite infestation and how they had to tent the house for three days to remediate the problem. (By the way, we've actually heard all these things and plenty more!)

All this information will not only help you make better buying decisions, but will also give you leverage in your upcoming negotiations.

QUICK TIP *These three magic words will encourage the other party to keep giving you information: "Really! What else?" Remember, people like to feel helpful. Let them know you appreciate their candor.*

Talk to County Employees

Does the property you're considering purchasing have a substantial addition, a post-construction basement finish, or any significant repair work? Or perhaps your public records search turned up a few questions about the current or proposed zoning of the property?

If so, head on over to the county offices and get some answers.

Department of Planning & Zoning

In addition to answering your questions about zoning specifics (the current and future use and development of a particular property), the folks at the department of planning & zoning office can usually offer insight to all kinds of factors that might influence the value of the property.

For example, if you're looking to purchase and then hold as a rental a large house that has been converted to a three-family unit, the zoning department can tell you whether the property can legally be used as a triplex. (If not, there may come a time when the property is required to be reconfigured back to a single family. This would likely decrease your rental income, in turn making the property a bad investment.)

The staff at planning & zoning can often also tell you about upcoming development projects nearby, such as proposed housing subdivisions, shopping center construction, school redistricting, or road widening projects. Depending on the circumstances and timing, new projects such as these could positively or negatively impact the value of the property you're considering—all of which is excellent information to use in your purchase negotiation.

Permit Office

The permit office should be able to pull up any permit applications on file for work on the property. This will help give you some insight into what work might have been done, which can often indicate past or current issues. For example, perhaps the homeowner pulled a permit to fix a sewer malfunction. If so, it's probably worthwhile to do some extra due diligence to ensure the problem was fixed correctly and is no longer an issue.

While you're at the permit office, there are two important questions to ask:

1. Did the current or any past owner pull any permits that haven't been closed? Permitted work should have eventually been inspected and the permits subsequently closed. However, if permits are still open due to non-completion of work or still awaiting final inspection, this is a big red flag that you need to discuss with the property owner before entering negotiations.

2. Was any significant work done at the property that wasn't permitted? If it's obvious that a previous homeowner finished the basement but you can't find any permits on file, it's quite possible the work was done without permits or inspections. Let's say you proceed with the purchase anyway. Now let's suppose a local jurisdiction, a building inspector, or even a future buyer or tenant were to find out. Guess what? You run the risk of being fined, being required to rip open walls to get everything inspected, retrofit as necessary, and potentially even having to start over to ensure all the work adheres to building codes.

Talk to Contractors

Do a bit of treasure hunting and you'll often find that contractors leave evidence of their work in the house. For example, installation companies usually leave a sticker on the furnace, hot water heater, or breaker box, indicating their contact information along with date of install and any maintenance they subsequently completed.

When you have questions about the condition of any mechanical systems, pick up the phone, call the contractor who left the sticker, and have a conversation that goes something like this:

Investor: *"Hi there. I'm considering buying the house at 123 Main Street and I noticed that you did maintenance on the HVAC system* *back in August of 2015. Can you tell me exactly what work you completed and if there were any additional work items you recommended, but that the homeowner didn't have you complete?"*

We've found that the vast majority of the time, reputable contractors are happy to go back through their records and give you any information they have. In fact, on several occasions, we've learned of homeowners having a contractor come out to the property to only do the bare minimum amount of repair work required to pass the system through a buyer inspection. Once you find out about deferred maintenance items—especially if the homeowner was trying to hide them—it's typically pretty easy to get concessions for those things during the negotiation process.

Here's a relevant situation in which making a couple of easy phone calls saved us over $13,000.

TALES FROM THE TRENCHES

Back in 2014, we were under contract to purchase a house. During our inspections, the only issue we found that concerned us was evidence that there had previously been some water in the basement. We asked the homeowner about it, and he said that while there was some water getting into the basement a few years prior, they had done some repairs to some exterior downspouts and it had fixed the problem.

Unfortunately the water stains were old and we were in the middle of a long dry spell, so it was impossible to determine if the owner was telling the truth. There were three big waterproofing companies in town, and I figured that if the homeowner had ever sought to have this problem looked at by a professional, it's likely he would have called one of these companies.

I called all three and asked them if they had ever inspected this house or given an estimate for work. To my surprise, over the previous few years the owner had called *all three* of the companies to investigate the water intrusion, and all three had determined that the issue would cost between $13,500 and $18,000 to fix!

It appeared that the homeowner was hoping that he could get through the sale without any rain, so we wouldn't know about the issue until after the closing, at which point he likely would insist that it had never happened before. But because we knew about the contractor bids, we were able go back to the homeowner and renegotiate the price.

Information about the Buyer/Seller

Now that you have a good grip on the market, the neighborhood, and the property itself, it's time to put the final pieces of the puzzle together: Figure out everything you possibly can about the other party in your negotiation.

This can mostly be accomplished by learning and mastering some stealthy online detective skills. This research will help you paint an over-all picture, generating the "story" behind the buyer or seller's motivations—and potentially their desperations.

"Google stalking" people takes creativity, and every situation is going to be unique, but here are some basic tips to start your investigations:

Google Search

Enter the other party's name and, at minimum, city, and state.

- If you're the buyer and don't have the seller's complete info, check out the property's tax records to get the seller's full name (and also determine if her primary residence is elsewhere).
- If you're the seller, the buyer's information should be on the purchase contract. Cross-reference this with the name and address on the earnest money check. Many mortgage lender pre-approval letters also include this info.

QUICK TIP *If you're selling, never assume the maximum approved price on a pre-approval letter is accurate. Many buyers will have their lender provide a letter listing the offer price, not the amount they're actually approved for.*

Scan the search results. In addition to directing you to several common sites, which we'll explore below, you may find links to info about the other party such as:

- A business journal spotlight featuring a recent promotion at work or a charity event in which they've participated
- Family pics uploaded to a photographer's online portfolio
- Sports affiliations, such as coaching their kid's soccer team, becoming a certified fitness instructor, or playing in the town softball league
- Community ties—perhaps they're PTA president, a member of a local woodworking club, or they own a small business nearby
- Public financial information, such as a recent vehicle purchase, past foreclosure, short sale, or bankruptcy

Does any of this really matter, you might ask? *Yes, it all matters.* It helps you paint an overall picture about the other party. You can use this information to build trust and rapport (as we'll discuss in the next chapter) and help the other person identify with you, which is ultimately useful in reaching a successful outcome to the negotiation. (You discovered the seller ran a marathon last summer and you happen to be training for a half? Show up in your running gear, mention the big race this weekend, and see where the conversation leads!)

LinkedIn Search

Find the other party's employer and company location, and then do some more research to fill in the blanks by seeking out answers to questions such as:
- Is the other party a high-level executive, an entry-level customer service representative, or somewhere in between? What is their income and how much disposable income might they have?
- What is their job history? If they change jobs to climb the corporate ladder every few years, does the employer provide financial assistance for relocation? Or does the company offer its employees first-time homebuyer help as a benefit?
- Where is the other party's workplace located? If you're the seller, is your property nearby? If you're the buyer, could the seller's motivation be that the commute is too long? Does the person have a job that likely requires travel and is proximity to an airport or major highway important to them?

Realtor.com Search

Enter the other party's address and determine:

- *If you're the seller*—is the buyer renting in an apartment complex or residing in a house? If a house or condo, do they own or rent? (Verify the owner's name on the tax records.)

  Is the buyer's current residence for sale? If yes, what's the asking price and is there a sale pending? What do the listing photos look like? You might find clues about the buyer, such as kids' bedroom photos (schools are likely important); pet bowls (that huge fenced yard in your newly renovated house would be perfect!); or familiar-looking furniture (we've had several situations in which our staging inventory coincidentally looked much like the furniture and accessories in a buyer's current home!)

- *If you're the buyer*—Has this house been listed for sale before? What did past photos look like and how do they compare to the current state of the property? Could this reveal something like a fire in the past, or a pool that's been filled in (that explains the big sinking spot in the back yard!), or any improvements that have recently been made?

  Where is the owner moving? You can sometimes narrow down this info with your or your real estate agent's access to the MLS. For what price is the seller's new property under contract? How much money does it look like they need to get out of your deal for purchase or a down payment on their new place?

  Are you looking at a property as part of an estate sale? Go to Legacy.com and find out whether there are other surviving family members who may play a part in the decision-making process.

WhitePages.com Search

Enter the buyer or seller's first and last name along with city and state and look for info that reveals:

- What is the approximate age of the other party? Who else lives at the residence?
- Does the other party have other current addresses listed? Do they also own those properties as second homes or investment properties?

Social Media (Facebook, Instagram, Twitter, Blogs, etc.)

People love to post about themselves, making many aspects of their life public through social media. Use this to your advantage! Dive right in to their photos, status updates, and likes to discover all kinds of juicy nuggets such as:

- Any noteworthy life events? Did the other party recently get engaged or married? Visit TheKnot.com to find out more. New set of twins, or a grown kid recently graduated and accepted to a prestigious university? The other party might now be empty nesters or needing to pay for a hefty college education, both of which can be motivators for a purchase or sale.
- Something noteworthy in their career? Celebrating a big promotion at work? Perhaps their small business finally moved into a real office space? Or maybe they've realized that their entrepreneurial venture needs to finally call it quits. Maybe they're retiring?
- The questions that can be answered are virtually endless. Are they avid golfers? Did their child recently enroll in a new private school that's far away from their current address? Did they grow up in the neighborhood you're selling in, but are now drawn back to the area because of its nostalgia? Do you know anybody in common? You got it—these all help round out the profile of the other party you're dealing with in your real estate negotiation.

Here's a story that will illustrate our point, and to this day, we're still amazed at how perfectly this worked out for us.

⫘ TALES FROM THE TRENCHES ⫘

We were selling a house in Baltimore, Maryland, and despite a hot market, we weren't getting as much traction with buyers as we had expected. The house had been listed for nearly four weeks without an offer, which was a good bit longer than average in this area.

We were getting ready to drop the price when a young woman visited the house with her real estate agent on a Sunday morning. The next day, we had an offer at $172,000, nearly 15 percent below our $199,000 list price.

We were pretty certain the buyer's agent knew that after almost a month without an offer we'd likely consider something a good bit below full asking price. So, offering low was actually a smart move on their part. Under normal circumstances, we might have countered at $190,000 or $195,000 and perhaps negotiated down to $185,000— the point where we were confident we could get other offers.

But with just a bit of internet stalking, we changed our strategy. The contract listed two buyers with different last names, and we were quickly able to find both of them on Facebook, where it was clear they were engaged and preparing for their upcoming wedding. In addition, their Facebook pages made it obvious that the guy was just finishing up grad school in Wisconsin, while the woman was in Maryland for the week, looking for a house where they could settle down.

Then came the most interesting post on her Facebook page. Here's the screen shot (and, yes, we actually cut-and-pasted it specifically with this book in mind):

January 25 at 9:16pm ·

Was getting ready to give up on this trip, but I think I found our house today! Made an offer this morning, and waiting to hear back from the agent. hasn't seen it yet, but I know he's going to love it! Best part is it's only a couple blocks from ! We could be neighbors!!! Fingers crossed!

Like   Comment   Share

By posting this publicly, the buyer may as well have told us, "I'm willing to pay a lot more than I offered!"

So, instead of countering below list price, we instead countered at full price and –because we knew they were moving half way across the country to "start their new life"—we offered to include upgraded appliances and as much of the staging furniture as they wanted.

Ultimately, we settled at $196,500, with about $2,500 in other concessions, or a net sale of about $194,000—nearly $10,000 more than had we not found her Facebook page and used the information she posted publicly to craft our response.

CHAPTER 4
PSYCHOLOGY OF RAPPORT

When most people think about negotiating, they assume that the key to success lies in being tough, standing strong, and never budging an inch. Those who watch a lot of TV drama shows probably assume that an effective negotiation is one that's defined by big, dramatic gestures, made specifically to elicit a similarly dramatic response from the other party. And some people believe that winning a negotiation is simply about using any means necessary to get what you want.

In reality, none of these tough-seeming strategies provide the most consistent negotiating results. The best predictor of overall success in a negotiation is how much the two parties respect and trust one another.

While it may seem intuitive that the other party is your *opponent* during the process, treating them as an adversary is the surest way to encourage them to dig in their heels and refuse to come to a mutually beneficial agreement. Instead, using social skills to build rapport, trust, and respect are how great negotiators position themselves for successful outcomes.

As veteran foreign correspondent Robert Estabrook so succinctly put it, "He who has learned to disagree without being disagreeable has learned the most valuable secret of a diplomat." While Estabrook may have been referring to his latest interview with some high-ranking government official or foreign dignitary, his words ring true across all fields of negotiation, including real estate.

But why is it so important to build rapport? Negotiation is about getting what you want, not making friends... right?

It all boils down to one simple fact:

If someone likes you, they will want you to succeed.

This is true even if you are sitting opposite them at the negotiating table.

Think about the last time you worked with someone you'd describe as pleasant, reasonable, or just plain nice. Now remember a time you had to deal with a total jerk. If you had to deal with each of those parties again, to whom would you be more likely to grant a little leeway or to give a little break? And whom would you be more likely to really try to screw over?

Hopefully, we don't have to work too hard to convince you that creating a trusting relationship is usually a better way to get what you want out of a negotiation than trying to steamroll the other party.

Here are some specific things you can do in order to build rapport and create trust with those you're trying to do business with.

Business *Is* Personal

"It's only business... It's not personal!"

This is a common refrain from those who think that steamrolling the other party in a negotiation is a winning strategy. Not a week goes by that we don't find ourselves in negotiating situations where the other party thinks that they need to act like a billionaire CEO, using intimidation and brute force to try to "win" the negotiation.

I once saw the owner of a very small business rent a corporate office, so he would have a big table around which the parties could negotiate. He had probably watched too many TV dramas and thought the environment would be intimidating and would give him a psychological edge. And, while it may have given him a small edge, his advantage was easily wiped out by his large ego and his belief that he needed to *win* the negotiation.

Don't get us wrong—at the most basic level, negotiations are about battle. They are a struggle for resources. When a cooperative agreement can't be had, one side may win and one side may lose. But, despite that, good negotiators realize that making a negotiation personal can be a great way to get what you want. In fact, great negotiators will always try to make things as personal as possible. They will take advantage of pre-existing relationships. They will find people or things they have in common with the other party. They will do whatever it takes to form a bond—a relationship—with the other party, to encourage the other party to treat them with respect and consideration.

In fact, as this story demonstrates, making a negotiation personal is sometimes the only way an agreement will be made.

TALES FROM THE TRENCHES

I was in the process of negotiating the licensing rights to a product I had created. Of all the companies to which I could license the product, my first choice was a company owned by a long-time friend of mine, and we'd always had a good relationship. I had licensed previous products to his company, and he had indicated he wanted this one too.

Because our starting positions were far apart, I had assumed the negotiation would be long and involved; but I also expected that based on our long-standing friendship, in the end we'd both be willing to make reasonable concessions and get the deal done.

We had scheduled a time to chat on the phone to discuss how we could move forward together. But instead of receiving a personal call from him, as I had anticipated, one of his employees called me. She informed me that she was going to be in charge of the negotiations for this deal, and that any discussions should go through her, because her boss—my personal friend—wasn't going to be involved.

I'm sure my friend didn't intend it, but his move damaged the negotiation. First, instead of making me feel important and special, which obviously would have been a good move when asking me to give concessions, he made me feel insignificant. Instead of a friend and long-time colleague, I was now just a business deal to him and his company.

Second, the woman he instructed to negotiate with me entered the negotiation by making an offer that she called their "standard offer," and presented it as a take-it-or-leave-it deal. She acknowledged neither the pre-existing relationship I had with the company nor the work her boss and I had done together. Again, had she made even a slight effort to make me feel like I wasn't just getting the "standard offer," I probably would have been more apt to consider something close to what she was demanding.

But, instead, I was pissed. I felt slighted. I didn't feel like I was getting the special treatment I deserved (whether I *actually* deserved it or not is a different question). And because of that, I dug in my heels and demanded a *better* outcome than I was originally planning on accepting. Not only did I demand a better outcome but I decided at that moment that I'd sooner walk away from the negotiation than give them anything close to the deal they wanted.

You see, my friend hadn't taken advantage of his biggest piece of negotiating leverage—our *personal relationship*. This was a deal worth a lot of money over many years. For less than $1,000, my friend could have hopped on a plane, flown the 2,000 miles to come see me, taken me to lunch, and finalized our deal. Had he done that, I surely would have felt obligated to make the deal work, and likely would have been much more flexible in the deal I would accept.

We spent eight months trying to negotiate that deal. Never in that time did my friend pick up the phone and say, "Hey, let's figure this out, you and me." And the longer he didn't do that, the more I dug in my heels and decided that if I couldn't "win" the negotiation, I was happy to walk away. Even if it cost me some money as well.

Unfortunately, he never did pick up the phone. And we never did come to a deal.

Whether they're long-time relationships or brand new relationships that you're cultivating specifically for the deal at hand, personal relationships are great leverage toward getting a deal done and getting the concessions you need. Use them to your advantage.

Face to Face

When it comes to building rapport in a new relationship or reigniting it in an existing relationship, there's nothing that beats face-to-face contact. While many people these days prefer communicating through email and text, face-to-face interaction forces the parties to engage on a much more personal level. Things such as taking turns while speaking, showing engagement through eye contact, nodding, and offering verbal responses all work to increase a feeling of understanding and closeness.

Studies have indicated that a high percentage of communication effectiveness is based on body language and non-verbal cues. Studies have also indicated that a face-to-face discussion can serve to build trust between the parties, resulting in greater levels of cooperation.

This makes sense. Without the ability to communicate tone or intent, email and text discussions run the risk of misunderstandings and—as anyone who has engaged in an internet debate knows—it's much easier for impersonal communication to escalate to argument or heated debate. Finally, it's much easier for someone to say "no" over email, text, and even a phone call. And a good negotiator never wants to give the other party an easy opportunity to say "no."

To help build feelings of rapport and trust, and increase the chances of building a cooperative relationship, try to speak in person before the negotiation process begins.

QUICK TIP *People are more receptive to others who are confident. Simply acting confident (even if you don't feel confident) will make you a much better negotiator. Why you do you think self-help gurus are so charismatic? A very big part of it is their self-confidence.*

Name Recognition

Want people to like you more? There's plenty of research indicating that frequently using someone's name during face-to-face communication can go a long way toward making that happen.

There are two reasons for this.

First, people like hearing their own name. A 2006 study (among many others) by Dennis P. Carmody and Michael Lewis placed subjects into MRI machines and determined that hearing one's own name—versus other names—activated several regions of the brain, including the middle frontal cortex, which is responsible for decision making. This shouldn't be surprising given that our own name is perhaps the first sound we ever hear, and is likely the most common sound we hear during the first couple years of life, while we are developing our sense of self.

The second reason why using someone's name can improve rapport is even more basic: It sends the message that you paid attention to them when they introduced themselves and that you care enough to have remembered who they are. Imagine the last time you were in a gathering and ran into someone you didn't remember, but they remembered you! How did it make you feel? Perhaps a bit uncomfortable, since you couldn't remember them; but, it probably also made you feel important, as a random person had previously taken enough notice of you that they bothered to remember personal details about you.

TAKE ACTION

Next time you're at a party or social gathering, make a point to learn as many names as possible and use each person's name as often as possible during your conversations. Not only will you likely create better rapport with those you meet but you're also more likely to remember their names the next time you see them.

Mirroring

In psychology, "mirroring" is the behavior where someone—typically subconsciously—imitates the actions of another person. This can include gestures, mannerisms, posture, and speech patterns. Psychologists have noted that people often mirror others in social situations, and studies have proven that when someone is being mirrored, it tends to lead to feelings of connectedness and closeness.

In other words, simply mirroring another person during a casual conversation or encounter can create a rapport between you and that person, without them even realizing it. Two people displaying similar gestures when communicating will start to feel that they share a common belief system. "Mirror neurons" in the brain will react to (and will in turn cause) these movements, allowing the individuals to feel a greater sense of engagement and belonging within the situation.

Good negotiators use mirroring to their advantage. Instead of relying on mirroring to occur naturally during a face-to-face negotiation, they purposefully—subtly!—mimic the other party to elicit the feelings that come when being mirrored.

For instance, when talking to the other party, try to mimic their voice speed, volume, and word choice. Is their speech pattern rapid and loud?

Speed up your speech and adjust your volume. Do they tend to speak slowly and quietly? Tone it down and match their calm pace. Do they use the same phrases over and over? Try using those same phrases when it makes sense.

Here are some other things you can look for and mirror in your next negotiation or the next time you're in a situation where you are trying to build rapport or influence someone:

- When they talk, do they tend to look away or make eye contact? How about when they're listening?
- Do they tend to blink a lot?
- Do they gesture with their hands while talking?
- Are they leaning in? Or out? Or to the side?
- Do they make physical contact during the interaction? Make a similar level of contact.

Keep in mind that any intentional mirroring should be subtle and respectful, with the goal of maximizing similarities and minimizing differences. It should never come across as mocking, and of course, you don't want to make it obvious what you're doing.

QUICK TIP *Try to use the other party's "language" when negotiating. For example, when having a financing discussion, if you're talking in terms of "interest rate" and they're talking in terms of "monthly payment," you should start talking in terms of monthly payments as well.*

Talk about *Them*

It shouldn't be surprising that the thing people most like talking about is themselves. If you've ever gotten dating advice or corporate networking advice, it's probably started with something along the lines of, "Ask them about themselves."

Not only does this make sense, but neuroscience tells us that it's true. The average person spends 60 percent of their conversations talking about themselves, and the reason for this is simple—it makes them feel good!

Remember how we discussed that when someone hears their own name, an MRI will show parts of their brain lighting up? When people talk about themselves, some of the same areas of the brain tend to light up. In addition, areas of the brain associated with feelings of reward are activated as well. These are the same areas of the brain that respond during sex, when ingesting cocaine, and when eating high-sugar foods.

In other words, talking about yourself is practically an addiction. And by asking people to talk about themselves, you are feeding their addiction. Makes sense that someone will like you when you do that, right?

So, whether you're on a date, networking at a business event, or trying to build rapport with someone at the negotiating table, asking the other person about themselves is a great way to strengthen the relationship.

QUICK TIP *Want to be the life of any dinner party? Use the following phrase as often as possible:*

"Interesting...tell me more about that."

Because you give them the opportunity to talk about themselves, people will flock to you.

Make an Upfront Concession

As we'll discuss later in the book, when negotiating, you typically don't want to give any concessions without getting something of equal or greater value in return. But, there's one exception to this rule: It's often worthwhile to give a concession at the beginning of the negotiation, while asking for nothing in return.

There are many psychological studies that indicate that even a small gift or gesture creates a feeling of indebtedness in the receiver of that gift. Not only that, but that a simple act of giving will create a discomfort in the receiver that can only be extinguished by reciprocating the gesture, oftentimes with a larger and more meaningful gesture.

In addition, by freely giving a concession to the other party very early on, you're sending the message that you're invested in their well-being, you're willing to compromise, and you're not looking to dominate in the negotiation. A small gesture of goodwill can prove your commitment to building a trustful relationship and to a cooperative negotiation. It can also highlight your understanding of the other party's needs and wants.

Here's an example of how I recently used this tactic:

}} TALES FROM THE TRENCHES {{

I was negotiating the extension of an important product distribution contract with one of my distributors a few months back. The existing contract had the distributor paying us commissions on a monthly basis, but I knew with their new partners the distributor had gone to quarterly payments. They hadn't yet come to us to ask if they could move from monthly to quarterly, but I suspected it would be a benefit to them.

At the beginning of the first renegotiation phone call, right after the pleasantries had been exchanged, we had this exchange:

Me: *"I heard you were planning to move to quarterly commission payments for some of your other partners."*

Distributor: *"Yes. To make it a bit easier on our accounting and accounts payable departments, we're trying to move our new customers to a less frequent payment schedule."*

Me: *"You know, if it makes it easier for you guys, I'm happy to restructure the current contract to move to quarterly payments until we can get a new contract hammered out."*

Distributor: *"Yeah, sure, that would be awesome. I'll have our legal team write a rider [a change to the contract] and get it over to you. Thanks!"*

It was a small gesture on my part, but it set the tone of the renegotiation—I wasn't coming into the discussion prepared for battle, I was entering the negotiations looking to be cooperative and to find a win-win for both sides. Also, it put them in a position where they psychologically "owed me one."

Ultimately, this renegotiation went very smoothly, and I believe that setting the tone of the discussion with the early concession was a big factor.

And Brag about It

If you followed our advice above and made a no-strings-attached concession, now is your chance to get a little something out of it yourself. While now isn't the time to ask for a concession in return (remember, this one was free), you should take an opportunity to remind the other party how nice you were to provide that no-obligation concession.

There are two goals here.

First, you want to ensure that the other party is aware of the concession. More specifically, they must be aware that you are making a concession. There are times when we say or do something so nonchalantly that it's hardly recognized. We don't want that to be the case here. If the other party doesn't fully realize that you have made a sacrifice on their behalf, they won't feel a need to reciprocate later.

Second, we want to ensure that the concession you gave isn't under-valued or discounted. Unfortunately, giving and not asking for something in return is a great way to send the subconscious message that what you gave wasn't very important. This would achieve the opposite of what we're trying to achieve. We want the other party to be as appreciative as possible about that concession we gave. This way they're more likely to reciprocate, either immediately or in the future.

Here's an example of that from a recent property we were negotiating to purchase:

In response to a letter we had sent to a local family, the husband indicated that they might be interested in selling their property. We arranged a time for us to see the property and chat. We looked at the property and we liked it.

We sat down with the husband and wife and I started the discussion by asking:

Me: *"So, are you excited about the opportunity to sell your house?"*

(We like to ask this question upfront to ensure that they are psychologically committed to making a deal before we get into the details.)
The wife jumped in with:

Wife: *"The most important thing to us is that our son can finish out the school year at [his current middle school]. So, we wouldn't want to move until at least mid-June."*

It was late March at the time of the conversation, so this meant that we wouldn't be able to take possession of the house for at least two and a half months. Because we'd miss the hottest part of the selling season by the time we rehabbed it and got it back on the market, this wasn't optimal for us, but we thought we could make that work. Her demand would be a big concession, but one that we'd have been willing to make at some point during the negotiation.

Typically, we would use this concession later in the negotiation when we hit a sticking point around some other detail, but in this case, we decided to make this concession immediately, and without asking for anything in return.

We did this for two reasons:

First, because she jumped to this point so quickly, we got the feeling that not moving until June was going to be completely non-negotiable for them. In other words, the concession was going to come at some point or another and without me making it, the deal would stall.

Second, we knew that until we agreed to this stipulation, the mom wasn't going to be able to focus on the rest of the discussion. She would have this issue in the back of her mind and wouldn't seriously consider any other details until she was confident that her school concerns were addressed.

So, I replied with:

Me: *"Of course! We have two kids in school ourselves, and my wife and I would never consider moving in the middle of the school year. Under no circumstances will you guys have to move out of the house until after school ends."*

(We used this opportunity to mention some additional commonalities—that we had a similar family and that we shared the same values with respect to schooling.)

Note that *selling the house* and *moving out of the house* are two separate and distinct issues. We made certain not to address any other details around this concession. Would we hold off closing the deal until June? Would we close quickly and let them rent the house back? Would we close quickly and let them stay for free until the school year was over? These are all terms that were still on the table to be negotiated, but the important part is that the mom got her assurance that they wouldn't have to move until after school was over.

Once we made that concession, it was time to reinforce it—to remind the husband and wife that we had just made a sacrifice and that it was a big one for us. I said:

Me: *"Okay, so we agree, you guys stay in the house until the school year ends. This is going to make it hard for us to make a profit on this deal, as the house needs a good bit of work, and we wouldn't be able to get it renovated and back on the market until after the selling season. But, that's now our problem—it's a risk we're just going to have to take.*
How much cash are you guys looking to get out of the sale?"

Notice a couple things from my follow-up comment:
- I reinforced both the fact that I had given a concession and that it was a big sacrifice for us;
- I subtly mentioned that the house needed a good bit of work, planting

the idea in their head that their house may not be worth what they expected;

- Immediately after bragging about my sacrifice and lowering their expectation for what their house would be worth, I ask them to throw out a price (now is a first opportunity for them to reciprocate, potentially asking for less than they otherwise would have).

Long story short, always take the opportunity to point out the value of your concessions to the other party.

QUICK TIP *In addition to pointing out the value of your concessions, strong negotiators will also try (again, subtly!) to devalue the concessions the other party is giving you. Simply saying something along the lines of:*

"That isn't going to make a huge difference to my bottom line, but I really appreciate you offering that up!"

Send the message that you appreciate the concession, but that it's not worth as much to you as they might think it is.

When You Cannot Get Face-to-Face

Unfortunately, there are going to be times when you're ready to negotiate a deal, but for some reason—perhaps real estate agents are involved, the deal is long distance, or the other party is unavailable—a face-to-face meeting isn't possible. Real estate agents will typically be the biggest barrier to a buyer and seller meeting, but remember, even though there are agents involved, *you* are still the one who is negotiating and controlling the negotiation.

While it may not be possible to talk to the buyer or seller in person, there are other alternatives that can allow you to build rapport and trust. Even though you can't meet, you can still make meaningful gestures that indicate your interest in cooperation, such as including a handwritten letter with your offer or even creating a video presentation to go along with your contract.

Even small actions and gestures of goodwill go a long way toward building a relationship and allowing the other party to get to know you and care about you. While face-to-face meetings are best, even a quick chat on the phone or a brief email can help build rapport. It's essential to start the rapport-building process as early as possible—ideally before the negotiations even start—but many good investors will take the opportunity to find something in common with the other party and highlight that at the time they make an offer.

For example, did you attend the same school? Do you root for the same sports team? Do you share any interests or hobbies? Use whatever affiliations you can find to help create rapport as early as possible. That way, as the negotiation starts and progresses, you'll already have established common ground—and the other party's empathy—that can be used to pave the way toward a more favorable discussion.

TALES FROM THE TRENCHES

We were helping our friends—a married couple with one daughter and a second baby on the way—find a house that they could move into, renovate, and then sell after two years, the time it would take to get the maximum tax advantages. The market in our area was hot and our friends were finding it difficult to get any of their offers accepted.

We found them a great little house that had tremendous opportunity for renovation. It was a small "starter home" with great potential for adding some square footage and optimizing the layout. I asked the listing agent (the agent who represents the sellers) why they were selling. She said that they were getting ready to have their third child and needed something bigger. This was perfect!

My wife helped our friends create a short video of themselves, introducing their family, mentioning that they were looking for a starter home, mentioning that they had a daughter and another child on the way, and discussing how excited they would be if the sellers would accept their offer. The point of the video was to appeal to the sellers' emotions and to remind the sellers that our friends were just like them. We wanted the sellers to say to themselves, "They remind us of ourselves," which we hoped would lead them to accepting our friends' offer.

And it worked. We submitted their offer with the video, and a couple of days later the sellers asked for a face-to-face meeting. While the deal took a good bit more negotiation because the sellers had several competing offers on the table, ultimately they accepted our offer. While we still don't know the details of the other offers, we suspect they were a bit better than ours, but the video created an emotional bond that made them want to work with our friends over the other potential buyers.

Leave Your Ego at Home

While this can be difficult for some of us, if you want to be a great negotiator, you must be able to leave your ego at home. Many of us like to prove how much we know, how powerful we are, and how good we are at winning, but at the end of the day, you have to care more about getting a successful deal than you do about proving how awesome you are.

While it's tempting to view every negotiation and transaction as a test or validation of your prowess and abilities, remember that the middle of a negotiation isn't the time for you to build your self-confidence. Instead, it's the time for you to *prove* your self-confidence by not having to control every aspect of the situation.

Why is it so difficult for many of us to leave our egos off the table when it comes to negotiating? A cognitive bias called "egocentrism" may just be the culprit. Egocentrism means that we tend to interpret the same information in ways that support positive views of ourselves. In negotiation, this translates into us interpreting the other party's demands as self-serving and an attempt to cheat us out of something. Of course, the other party is interpreting *our* demands in the same egocentric way.

Egocentrism can cause a negotiation to spin out of control. It can cause each party to question the motives and means of the other party, eroding trust and breaking down any bonds that had previously been created between them. But by remaining cognizant of these tendencies, it's possible to control your ego and focus on the goals at hand: finding benefit for both sides.

How do you do this? First, try to put yourself in the position of a third party to the negotiation. Be objective, and see the other party's view of the overall situation.

To use a cliché: "Try to put yourself in the other person's shoes."

Leverage Their Ego

On the flip side of keeping *your* ego in check, there are times when you'll be dealing with someone who seems to care more about their ego than about getting the most out of the deal. When you're in that situation, use it to your advantage.

We often assume that the other party is looking for something tangible in the outcome of a negotiation (more money, better terms, etc.), but there are many people who are more interested in having their egos stroked than they are in measurable outcomes. For them, compliments and deference can often substitute for making concessions. Instead of giving them something in the deal, try complimenting them instead.

For example, when you're nearing a deal and you're looking to get one last concession without giving anything else in return, try saying something like this:

> **Investor:** *"I have a feeling I'm going to regret accepting this deal— I've never been a good negotiator and you clearly do this a lot. Perhaps I should ask you to throw some free negotiating lessons in the deal! Okay, just so I don't feel like you completely took advantage of me, how about if [insert your request here] and we've got a deal..."*

You'd be surprised how often that final request is accepted without protest, simply because your compliment was taken as fair compensation for that final concession you requested.

DIG DEEP *Make sure that your compliment is reasonable, so as not to come off as condescending. For example, if the person you're negotiating with* *clearly isn't a good negotiator, don't tell them they are—they'll know you are just trying to butter them up.*

Instead, find something else to compliment them on that will resonate with them. For example, telling a contractor how highly recommended he comes; telling a potential investor/buyer how good she is at rehabbing on a shoestring budget; or admitting to your real estate agent how much you love working with him because he "can sell anything!"

Keep Building Rapport Throughout

One final thought on building rapport and trust: This isn't something that you should only focus on at the beginning of the negotiations. Good negotiators will take every opportunity to continue to build the relationship, every step of the way, until the deal is completed. You never know when you might run into a snag just before a deal closes, and a small relationship-building gesture or discussion you had the previous day just might convince the other party to stick it out.

Not only that, but as most long-term investors will tell you, there's a good chance that the relationships you build today will have a way of coming back to benefit you in the future. To this day, by exchanging Christmas cards and sending birthday wishes my wife still keeps in touch with many of the people who have purchased our houses over the years. We have had several occasions where someone who purchased one of our houses has come back to us several years later looking for their next house.

Remember, real estate isn't just about "sticks and bricks"—it's about people, too.

CHAPTER 5
SELLER MOTIVATION & LEVERAGE

In Chapter 3, we focused on completing due diligence around the market, the neighborhood, the property, and the other party. And we did all of that independently, without ever utilizing the most important resource at our disposal—the other party.

Whether you're negotiating an off-market property directly with a seller, or you're making offers through real estate agents on MLS-listed properties, your greatest opportunity for gathering useful information will come by speaking directly with the seller (or her agent).

This process might start over the phone, when a seller contacts you from a direct-mail piece or a bandit sign. It might start on the front steps of a seller's house after you've knocked on their door. It may occur at a party where a discussion with a random stranger turns into a discussion about buying their house. It could occur at a meeting you've scheduled with a potential seller in her kitchen. Or perhaps you've found a great deal on the MLS and you have your agent get in touch with the seller's agent to get more information.

Regardless of the circumstances, an early discussion with the other party is your opportunity to accumulate information that can be used to your advantage later in the negotiation.

But, at this point, we're not looking to gather random information. We want certain, specific information.

The Information We're Looking for

This is our opportunity to seek out the critical information that will allow us to create a competitive first offer and provide us the greatest amount of leverage later in the discussions. Specifically, the initial interaction with a potential seller should be focused on three things:

1. **Determining the seller's source and level of motivation.** There are several factors that influence how favorable a deal you can get from a seller, but the one that stands far and above all the rest is her level of motivation.

   If the seller has circumstances in her life that make her highly motivated to sell, you will have much greater leverage throughout the negotiation and, generally speaking, you will have an opportunity at a much better deal. On the other hand, if the seller's motivation is low—perhaps she is only talking to you because you wouldn't stop pestering her about selling her house—you will be entering the negotiation in a weak position and are unlikely to achieve a remarkable outcome.

   The seller's source and level of motivation are going to be driven by current circumstances in her life. Is she going through a divorce, job relocation, or death of a spouse? Is the seller a senior citizen who is moving to assisted living and the house is being sold by a relative? Is there some specific financial circumstance driving the sale—for example, the seller has a large medical expense or needs to fund a business opportunity?

   These types of motivators will often create an urgency that will encourage a seller to accept an offer far below retail price—and perhaps far below a price that she would otherwise accept.

2. **Determining the seller's MAO.** As we'll discuss in the following chapters, the next step in our negotiating process will be putting together our initial offer. There is a lot of guesswork that goes into determining an optimal offer price, but much of that guesswork can be removed if we have a reasonable idea of what the seller's minimum acceptable offer (their MAO) will be.

   In most cases, while we can certainly ask, the seller isn't going to just tell us her MAO. And, in fact, even if she is willing to tell us, there's a reasonable chance that she'll be lying to us or, more importantly, that she might go even lower under the right circumstances. So, in addition to just asking, we need to use other strategies to determine the seller's MAO.

3. **Finding additional leverage for our negotiation.** The third goal of interacting with the seller prior to a negotiation is to assess the leverage you will have once the negotiation begins. Remember, leverage is just a fancy word for all the things that give you power over the other party in the negotiation. Like with motivation, this will generally be driven by current circumstances and situations in the seller's life, but there may be other, more nuanced, factors at play as well.

   For example, maybe the seller wants to leave town but can't sell her house until she can sell her business as well. Perhaps you have some connections to help with that. Armed with this information, you might now be able to help the seller solve two problems at once, which makes you very valuable to her (and provides you additional leverage).

As we discussed earlier, a deal where you can speak with the seller directly is going to be much different than a deal where there are agents involved and speaking directly with the other party is unlikely to happen.

Luckily, there are ways to get the information we are looking for regardless of whether you have the ability to speak directly with the seller or there are agents working as intermediaries. We'll examine each of those situations separately below as we dive into some tactics you can use to start gathering the three types of information that will determine how much leverage you'll have in the upcoming negotiation.

Getting Information Directly from the Seller

It may seem obvious, but the best way to determine the motivation of the other party in any negotiation is to talk to them. We discussed building rapport in the last chapter, and all of the techniques we mentioned there can be used to foster a relationship with the seller, to build trust, and to start gleaning information that can be used to assess the strength of your negotiating position.

But it's going to require more than just building rapport to get the information we're looking for. Here are a number of tips on how to approach your initial discussions with the seller.

Ask Good Questions

Your first goal during your discussion with the seller should be to determine the reason she wants to sell her house. We're not just looking for a general response such as "I need the money" or "I'm ready to move," but a specific reason, such as, "My child is starting school at Stanford next fall, and I need $80,000 for tuition."

Obviously, the seller is unlikely to give you that level of information from a simple question, which is why building rapport prior to delving into her motivations is so important. For example, you might start the discussion with the simple question:

Investor: *"Why are you looking to sell your house?"*

You should then be prepared to follow up that question with more detailed questions. The conversation could go something like this:

Seller: *"My wife and I are just looking to downsize and use the equity in the house to pay for some upcoming expenses..."*

Investor: *"I can understand that. I'm looking forward to the day my kids head off to college so that my wife and I can downsize and do some traveling. What kind of expenses are you dealing with?"*

Seller: *"My daughter is getting married next year, and weddings aren't cheap these days."*

Investor *(in a half-joking manner):* *"Ugh. I can just imagine. I have two boys, so luckily I won't be facing that particular expense. That's part of the reason my wife and I just eloped. How much do weddings cost these days?"*

Seller: *"We're looking at a minimum of $30,000—maybe more! But, she's my little girl... she's worth it."*

At this point, the seller has just told you that he needs at least $30,000 out of the sale of the house. It could be much more, but it's unlikely to be much less. Once you know how much they owe on their house, you can add $30,000 to that amount, and you now have the bottom range of their MAO!

To glean information from a seller, here are some other questions we like to ask:

"How long have you owned the property?"

"How long have you been thinking about selling the property?"

"Have you already found a new place to live?"

"What do you plan to do with the money from the sale?"

"Are you under any pressure to sell?"

"Are the payments current?"

QUICK TIP *The key to getting detailed information from the other party is to avoid asking "yes" or "no" questions. Instead, ask open-ended questions that require back-and-forth discussion.*

Gauge the Seller's Expectations

It's important to gauge the seller's expectations and to determine upfront whether she has a reasonable grasp on what to expect from your offer.

One great way to do this is to ask the questions about the condition of the property—this can either be done over the phone during an initial conversation or in person after you've already had the opportunity to evaluate the property for yourself.

Here are a few questions we might ask:

"On a scale of 1-10, how would you rate the condition of your house?"

"If you were going to renovate the house to sell yourself, about how much would you expect that you'd need to spend?"

"If you were given $50,000 to renovate your property, which items would you fix or renovate?"

While this line of questioning is a great way to get information about the condition of the property before you see it, that's not the main goal. The main goal is to determine how realistic the seller is with respect to her property's condition and the amount of work and money required to bring it up to full value.

For example, if the seller thinks her house is a "9 out of 10" in terms of condition and that it would only cost $5,000 to renovate—but you determine it's about "3 out of 10" and would cost $80,000 to renovate, then you can expect that the negotiations will go a lot differently than if the seller recognizes her house is in major need of work.

Having this information will determine how much you need to educate the seller throughout the process, and will ultimately help guide you in presenting your initial offer.

Determine Motivating Factors Other than Price

In addition to determining motivation and trying to get as much information as possible from the seller, you'll also want to use this discussion to determine if there are motivating factors other than price, or other requirements the seller has.

For example, you might ask:

Investor: *"Assuming we can agree to a price, is there anything else you want or need out of this deal?"*

This gives seller the opportunity to give you more information about her situation—information that could be used to help formulate an offer and then later be able to better negotiate that offer.

For example, the seller might respond in a half-joking manner with:

Seller: *"Price is the most important thing... But, if you know anyone who can haul all of our furniture to Nebraska for us, that would help too!"*

Now, the seller has not only given you more information (they're moving to Nebraska), but she's also expressed a pain point she has—she is stressing over how she'll get her furniture from here to there. At some point prior to submitting your offer, you could investigate the cost of shipping a houseful of furniture from here to there, and then during the negotiation, you could potentially use that as a concession.

Let's say that you find out it's going to cost $11,000 to move the furniture. At the appropriate time during the negotiation, you might say:

> **Investor:** *"You had mentioned earlier that you needed to get your furniture to Nebraska. I happen to know a great moving company that I've used for several years now. If you'll agree to take $15,000 off the price, I'll pay to have your furniture moved. I'll coordinate with the movers, schedule the dates for you, and you'll never see a bill."*

In this example, a simple question and a bit of follow-up investigation gives you an opportunity to solve one of the seller's problems and at the same time, would save you $4,000.

Listen Aggressively

We often don't listen as intently as we should. Instead of listening, too many of us think about what we're going to say next. When we do this, we tend to miss small—but important—cues that the other party may be giving us.

For example, our brain naturally filters the words that give us the most meaning and context—typically, these are the nouns and verbs. Because they give us the basic gist of what's trying to be conveyed (the most bang for our listening buck, you could say), we often don't give enough attention to the descriptive words—the adjectives and adverbs.

For example, let's say a seller tells you that she needs to walk away with $50,000 in cash at closing. You ask her if she'd consider walking away with less, and she responds with:

> **Seller:** *"Well, uh, I'd really like to walk with $50,000. I kinda need that amount and I'd be reluctant to walk with much less than that."*

The important words and phrases here are, "really like," "kinda need," "reluctant to" and "much less."

Each of those words weaken the main message that she must walk away with $50,000. While she's not admitting to being willing to take less, her choice of words makes it very obvious that she *would* be willing to take less.

Listen to What They Don't Say

Sometimes you can get more information from what someone *doesn't* say than from what they *do* say. Which is why it's important to be able to read between the lines when trying to get information from the other party in a negotiation.

Here's a quick example:

⟩ TALES *FROM THE* TRENCHES ⟨

A couple of years back, I (Carol) was selling a property for one of our friends (I was the listing agent). The sellers had filled out a property disclosure statement, listing all the issues that they knew about with the house. One question on the disclosure was, "Does the property have any underground oil tanks?" The sellers checked "no" to that question.

A week later, I got the house under contract and the buyer had his inspection. The inspector found evidence of a buried oil tank. The buyer's agent called us, livid about the fact that the sellers had "lied" on the disclosure statement. (In reality, they didn't know about the tank—it had been there since long before they had bought the property.)

For ten minutes, the buyer's agent ranted and yelled about how the sellers were liars, how I was a liar, how his buyer was angry, and felt betrayed, etc. But, the one thing he never said was, "The buyer doesn't want the house," or "The buyer is backing out."

Most listing agents would get concerned about losing the deal, make excuses, and then offer concessions to make up for the mistake. But because the buyer's agent didn't make any demands or threats, I was pretty confident that he simply needed to blow off some steam. In fact, I thought there was a pretty reasonable possibility that the agent was doing this in front of his client, just to put on a show and prove to his client how dedicated he was.

I was confident that the buyer wasn't going to back out, and I didn't want to shift the balance of power into his favor based on a misunderstanding. For this reason, I simply said, "I'm so sorry about that misunderstanding. I feel horrible and I'm sure the sellers will as well. They didn't know about the oil tank, but if you can forward me

the inspection report, we'll update the disclosure statement immediately with that new information."

We never heard another word about the oil tank.

Determine Their Motivation to Work with *You*

One more thing to keep in mind when trying to determine a seller's level of motivation. It's not just important how motivated they are to sell, but also how motivated they are to sell to *you*. A seller may be desperate to sell, but if she's talking to several different investors who are interested in buying, you're no longer just competing with the seller for the deal—you're now competing with a bunch of other investors as well.

While you don't necessarily want to come right out and ask a seller if she's talking to any other investors—you don't want to remind her that she has other options—there are ways to glean this information more subtly. I like to ask sellers this question:

> **Investor:** *"If we can't come to an agreement for me to buy your house, what do you think you'll do?"*

This gives the seller an opportunity to discuss her alternative options (she's talking to other buyers, she doesn't really need to sell, etc.), which is what will ultimately drive her level of motivation. The better her alternatives, the more careful you need to be about an aggressive offer; the fewer alternatives she has, the lower your offer can be without her jumping ship and going after another option.

Determine Property Payoff Amount

The payoff price of the property is often going to be a major determining factor of the seller's MAO. Because you can often assume the seller will not be willing to accept an offer below the payoff amount, this is a number you should be getting as quickly as possible. During the very first conversation, most investors will ask how much the seller owes on the house.

If you find out that a seller owes far more than you know you could possibly purchase the property for, the next step would be to dig deeper into whether she would be willing (and able) to sell below the payoff price. If the answer is an unequivocal "no," you can often move on from the deal right there—the seller has set her MAO (her minimum acceptable offer) at well above your MAO (your maximum acceptable offer), leaving little room for any chance at a compromise.

In addition to asking the seller what she owes on the property, it's also a good idea to verify this number before putting together your initial offer. Not all sellers are going to be honest, and even those who have the best of intentions might not have all the facts. For example, if a seller is delinquent on their mortgage payments, it's possible that penalties and fees are accruing and their payoff is much higher than they realize.

In addition to finding out what's owed on the property, make sure you also ask about any unpaid back taxes, liens, or other obligations attached to the property. We can't tell you the number of times we've heard about investors who ask a seller what they owe on a property, only to later find out that because the investor didn't ask the right questions, the real payoff amount is more than double the amount the seller indicated.

By the way, asking the seller for a copy of their most recent mortgage statement or an online printout of the current loan status isn't unreasonable. If they are unable or unwilling to provide this information, you can generally find out the date and amount of the initial loan and any refinancing from public records. Using this public data, you should be able to determine a reasonably accurate payoff amount.

Ask the *Most Important* Question

The information we've gathered on motivation and property payoff amount are likely enough to allow us to generate a reasonable opening price bid. But, given that we're great negotiators, there's one more tactic that will often provide an even clearer picture of the seller's minimum acceptable price.

And that's asking the seller flat out, "What is the lowest price you'd accept?"

Now, you may be thinking that's a bit too direct and any reasonable seller is going to be unlikely to give you an honest answer. And I'd agree with you. But if you phrase that same question just a little bit differently, you can get the information you're looking for, while at the same time sending the message to the seller that she'd benefit from answering the question.

Instead, what if we asked the question:

Investor: *"If I were to offer you all cash and close as quickly as you'd like, what is the best price you could give me in return?"*

Do you see what we just did there?

We changed the discussion from, "I want you to give me information that will allow me to get the best deal for myself," to "I want to offer you the things you likely most want—cash and quick close. What can you do in reciprocation?" You're now doing *her* a favor by asking this question!

If the seller had indicated that there was something else tremendously important to her as part of the deal, you can simply replace (or add) these items instead of the cash and quick close. The key question is, if you were to provide the seller her dream scenario, what is the lowest price she'd be willing to accept in return?

You may be thinking, "What if I can't offer all cash or close quickly (or whatever terms you suggested)?" That's okay. You're not making any promises at this point; you're merely gathering information. You're only saying, "What if?" If the seller later expresses frustration that, for example, you want to get financing instead of paying cash, you can simply say:

Investor: *"I asked that question in the hopes that I would be able to offer cash and a quick close. Unfortunately, since our discussion, I've entered discussions with two other sellers as well, and while I still hope to be able to pay cash, I take my promises seriously, and I don't want to overcommit to you."*

This not only sends the message that it was just a misunderstanding (you didn't lie about anything), but it also allows you to send two subtle messages: Should the two of you not reach an agreement, you have other alternatives—and the fact that you are serious about your commitments.

Assuming the seller is willing to answer your question, you now have another important data point that you can use to evaluate about where the seller's MAO might be.

Getting Information from Seller Sources

When you don't have the ability to talk face-to-face with a seller, it can be much more difficult to determine both a source of motivation (why they are selling) and a level of motivation (how badly they need to sell). That said, it's not impossible. You just need to be more resourceful and it helps to have an agent on your side who's resourceful as well.

Talk to the Listing Agent

Your real estate agent is a powerful ally in the offer process, and you should be leveraging him as much as possible and as often as possible. In the case of determining motivation, the first thing your agent should do before you even think about putting in an offer is to call the listing agent and ask directly why the seller is selling.

It's possible that you won't get any useful information, especially if the listing agent is a good negotiator herself; but many listing agents are happy to divulge motivation of their sellers if they think it will help them sell the house. In fact, many listing agents are just too timid to refuse to answer a question when asked, and will give a response, even if they know they shouldn't.

You must encourage your agent to ask as many questions as the listing agent will answer; and just like you would use good follow-up questions and aggressive listening skills to get information from your seller in an off-market deal, you should ensure that your agent is doing the same with the listing agent.

Here are a few examples of questions you should encourage your agent to ask:

Agent: *"Why is your client choosing to sell at this time?"*

Agent: *"Have you received any other offers on the property?"*

Agent: *"My client would love to make an offer. Unfortunately, for it to work for him as an investment, the offer would likely be a good bit below list price. Is that something your client would still consider?"*

At the end of the conversation, your agent should ask one more very important question:

Agent: *"What else should my client know about the seller or the property?"*

You'd be surprised at the type of information a listing agent will give if a buyer's agent asks that one open-ended question and then just sits back and listens.

If your agent isn't willing to call the listing agent and attempt to get as much "inside information" as possible, you probably want to consider finding a new agent. Remember, your ability to negotiate the deal is going to hinge on your agent's ability to negotiate, and if your agent doesn't like to negotiate, you'll be putting yourself at a big disadvantage.

Use MLS Information

In addition to having your agent attempt to get information directly from the listing agent, in most cases, the MLS listing itself can provide a great number of clues as to the motivation of the seller.

Here are some specific things we look for in a real estate listing:

- **Price:** If a house is priced *below* market value, that is the best indication that the seller is motivated. They are willing to give up at least some profit in return for a quicker sale. On the other hand, when a house is listed *above* market value, this typically indicates that seller is not desperate to sell and is more interested in a high sale price than a quick sale. Additionally, once a seller lists a property above market value, they will become anchored to that above-market price, and—barring any major realizations by the seller—it will be difficult to break that anchor and get a great deal on the property.

- **Days on Market (DOM):** The second piece of information a listing can provide with respect to motivation is the number of days the property has been listed for sale. Typically, when a seller first lists a property, they are confident (or at least optimistic) that they will get an offer close to list price. For that reason, it's generally difficult to purchase newly listed properties much below list price. But as a home sits on the market without arousing buyer interest, sellers often get dejected and pessimistic about selling, at which point they are more likely to consider a lower offer. What constitutes a high DOM? That depends on the market—your agent should be able to tell you average DOM for your area; any properties listed longer than that average may have sellers who are becoming more motivated.

- **Price Changes:** If a property has had a price drop, that indicates that the seller has accepted the fact that the list price was incorrect. While they may be anchored to the new list price, some level of trust in their agent has been broken, and the seller is less likely to be anchored to the new list price. The more times a seller drops their price, the less likely they will tend to be anchored to the current price. Additionally, sellers who drop the price quickly (as opposed to letting a property linger for months before dropping the price) are more likely to be realistic about the value of the property and are less likely to be anchored to the current list price.

- **MLS Comments:** Another great indicator of seller motivation is the language in the listing. If the listing uses words like "needs TLC," "all offers considered," "cash only," "quick closing," "will not qualify for financing," etc., you are likely dealing with a seller who is more motivated. Remember our discussion from earlier in this chapter about "listening aggressively"? This strategy works for written communication as well.

- **Agent Commission/Bonus:** Listing agents realize that buyer's agents have a tremendous amount of influence over their buyers. If a buyer's agent tells his buyer to consider a property, the buyer is more likely to consider the property; if a buyer's agent tells a buyer to avoid a property, the buyer is more likely to avoid the property. For this reason, when some listing agents believe a property will be more difficult to sell or when they're trying to induce a faster sale, they'll provide a buyer agent bonus in the form of a higher commission or flat fee. If you see a listing offering the buyer's agent an incentive to convince his client to purchase the property, that's a good indication that the seller and the listing agent are motivated to get the house sold.

- **Pictures:** If you can look at the pictures in a listing and determine that the property is in bad condition, other buyers can too, and they are more likely to avoid setting up a showing or making an offer on that property. Most buyers looking at MLS listed properties are going to be homeowners interested in a move-in-ready house, and will be less likely to be interested in a property that needs considerable renovation. And if a listing has no pictures whatsoever, or no interior pictures, that's an even better indication that the property is in such bad condition that the seller or agent believes the pictures would discourage most buyers from setting up a showing. Any retail property that is in distressed condition is going to get less buyer interest, and retail sellers are typically going to be more motivated to take a reduced offer on these types of properties.

Visit the Property

Just like looking at pictures will give you a good idea of the condition of the property—and the likelihood of other buyers being interested—visiting the property will allow you to confirm the condition and also get an indication of how much interest the seller is getting from other buyers.

If you walk into a property that is dirty and unkempt, but functionally looks to be in good condition, there is a reasonable chance that other buyers won't be averse to making an offer. But if you visit a property and it's obvious that it will require costly maintenance, you can be reasonably certain that many retail buyers will choose not to submit an offer.

For example, if there is an obvious roof leak (such as discoloration on the ceiling), potential structural issues (cracks in the wall or foundation), off-putting odors (urine, cigarette smoke), or any of a number of other obviously costly issues, there's a good chance most other buyers will avoid making even a low offer on the property. Unlike many investors, most retail buyers aren't interested in a big renovation project when they purchase a home.

Once you see the condition of the property and can gauge the first impression the property is making on other potential buyers, this should give you an idea whether the seller is likely getting other offers and what their level of motivation may be. If their property is in poor condition, most sellers are going to be aware of this and they will often have accepted the fact that they will need to consider a well-below-market offer if they want to sell the property.

Expect Lower Motivation

While a seller of a listed property may have some very specific motivations, they are less likely than off-market sellers to be willing to slash their price. Remember, a seller with a real estate agent will have already agreed to pay 4 to 6 percent of the sales price in commissions, and except in extreme circumstances most listing agents will highly discourage their sellers from accepting very low offers.

We typically recommend *against* focusing on private MLS sales for the reason that great deals tend to be too few and far between. But that doesn't mean they aren't available. You'll just need to look at more properties, make more offers, and accept the fact that most of the sellers you will be dealing with won't be motivated enough to agree to a price where the property will make a great investment.

DIG DEEP ⟶ *While sellers who have a listing agent are likely to be less motivated than sellers working on their own, one big advantage of working through agents is that you won't have to deal directly with any repercussions of insulting the seller with a low offer. For this reason, many investors are emboldened to make lower offers on listed properties than they would on unlisted properties.*

Determine Property Payoff Amount

Similar to when dealing with non-listed properties, the payoff amount of the house may play a big determining factor in the seller's MAO. But, since you're unlikely to be able to ask the seller who has an agent how much they owe on their house—and you're almost certainly not going to be able to request proof of this from the seller—you're going to have to rely on public records to get this information.

If the seller purchased the property with financing or has refinanced since purchasing it, there was most likely a closing transaction where a promissory note and deed of trust (or mortgage) was signed. These documents were also almost certainly filed or recorded at the local courthouse. Using these documents, it should be possible to determine the original loan amount on the property, the interest rate, and the payoff timeline.

With that information, a good online mortgage calculator should allow you to generate an amortization schedule for the loan, which you can use to determine a reasonable estimate of the current payoff amount. It won't be possible to get an exact amount—the seller could be making extra payments (in which case the payoff would be lower) or could have accrued penalties or fees (in which case the payoff would be higher). But, it should give you a good starting point for your analysis.

Also note that in many cases, this information can be found online—either through local government public record websites or even using sites such as Zillow or Trulia, which often publish financing and re-financing information for the properties they list.

If you've done a good job of gathering information, you should now be well prepared to start thinking about your opening offer. We'll start that discussion in the next chapter.

CHAPTER 6
OPENING BID CONSIDERATIONS

Now that we've gathered key information, both directly from the other party and from a whole host of other reliable sources, it's time to put that information to use in what is often the most difficult aspect of any negotiation—determining an initial offer, also called the "opening bid."

We're going to spend several chapters talking about how to prepare and deliver the opening bid. Why? Because we can't stress strongly enough just how important your first offer is. It sets the tone for the entire negotiation moving forward, and shouldn't be taken lightly.

A first offer that's too high and doesn't leave you room to give much during the bargaining process can lead to a stalled negotiation. A first offer that's too low can discourage the other party from even entering into negotiations with you and can damage the relationship over the long term.

Define Your Target Point and MAO

Before we sit down with the other party to start negotiating—or even start thinking about putting together an opening bid—it's important that we figure out what, specifically, we want and need from the deal.

If you recall from Chapter 2, when we say "wants" and "needs," what we're specifically referring to is your target point (your ideal deal) and your MAO (the worst deal you'd accept).

Define Your Target Point

It's important to define your target point before putting together your first offer, for two reasons:

1. First, you will want your opening position to be designed to best position you to achieve your target. If you don't know what your target is, it will be impossible to define an opening position that makes sense. On too many occasions, I've seen real estate investors make an opening offer that—even if accepted as-is—provides them less than what they really want, because they haven't given considerable thought to what they want or why.

   Given that the final deal will nearly always be worse than your first offer, this virtually guarantees that the investor isn't going to get a deal that he really likes. In many cases, this also leads to the negotiations stalling, as the investor has chosen an opening position that is too close to his MAO, which doesn't give him enough room to make concessions during the bargaining process.

2. Second, defining your target point will prevent you from conceding too much—or too little—during any negotiation round. When you don't know your target, it's difficult to judge whether a particular concession, or set of concessions, might be giving too much or too little. If you give too much early on, you will set a precedent, and you may find yourself giving too much throughout the haggling process. Likewise, if you give too little early on, you risk sending the message to your counterpart that you're not serious about compromise.

   By clearly defining your target point upfront, you will always know exactly how far your current offer is from your target, and you can make appropriately sized concessions that ensure you are staying as close to your target as you feel is appropriate.

Define Your MAO

While defining your target point will help you in your attempt to achieve your best-case goals, defining your MAO will actually serve to do the opposite—it will keep you out of trouble. During the course of a negotiation, in the heat of battle, it's easy to lose track of your goals and let your emotions take over.

During a tedious negotiation, sometimes the desire to reach an agreement becomes so strong that you're willing to compromise your needs.

When dealing with a seller who is in a difficult financial position, you may find yourself feeling bad for her and willing to sacrifice to help her to achieve her goals. Or when up against a tough negotiator, the stress may induce you to give too much just to bring the negotiations to a conclusion.

Regardless of the reason, too many negotiations end with one side or the other waking up the next morning and realizing that they accepted a deal that didn't really work for them. Defining your MAO before the negotiations start will protect you from this risk of "buyer's remorse" when the deal is done. It will also help you throughout the haggling process by:

- Reducing your stress by not wondering if you're giving too little or much.
- Increasing your appearance of strength by never appearing "wishy washy."
- Giving you a clear indication of when the deal isn't good enough and you need to dig in your heels or walk away.

How to Determine Your Target & MAO

We discussed above *why* it's important to define your wants (your target) and your needs (your MAO), but we didn't discuss *how* you go about doing that. While it's outside the scope of this book to delve deeply into analyzing real estate deals, we'd be remiss not to touch on the subject, as your analysis of the deal is ultimately what will determine what you want and need to achieve from the negotiation.

It doesn't matter if you are flipping houses, buying and holding, wholesaling, buying commercial deals, or specializing in any other strategy. And it doesn't matter if you're focused on single-family houses, apartment buildings, mobile homes, skyscrapers, self-storage facilities, or land.

Every deal is going to be different, and the criteria for determining a good deal is going to vary from strategy to strategy, from property type to property type, and from specific deal to specific deal. When it comes to figuring out what your target and MAO are for a specific deal, we highly recommend finding a good reference guide for how to analyze the type of deal you're looking to do.

Write It down

Now that you've determined your specific target and MAO, you must document it. Our brains have an uncanny way of selectively misremembering (that's a nice way of saying "forgetting") information—this is especially true when we are stressed or when we are trying to trick ourselves into believing something else.

We don't know about you, but it seems like every time we decide to cut sugar out of our diet, we're good for a day or two. Then, without even realizing it, we find ourselves standing at the freezer with a half-gallon of ice cream in one hand and a spoon in the other. In other words, our primitive brain takes over and decides that it knows more than our logical brain—and the decision it makes isn't necessarily a good one for us.

Likewise with negotiating. You can find yourself in a situation where you have firmly decided what your minimum acceptable offer is, and then in the next moment, find yourself unconsciously agreeing to something even worse. Writing down your target and MAO won't completely eliminate that situation from happening, but it will go a long way toward keeping you out of trouble.

Target & MAO Example

So, you're ready to write down your target and MAO for your upcoming negotiation.

What does this actually look like?

Let's take a look at an example of how we might document our wants (target) and needs (MAO) while we're preparing to negotiate a property we're looking to purchase and flip:

Address: 123 Main Street, Anytown, USA
Target Point
Price: $120,000
Earnest Money Deposit: $1,000
Closing Date: May 23
Financing: Combination Cash & Seller Financing
Contingencies: 10-Day Inspection Period
Other Terms:
- Use my title company
- Seller pays closing costs
- Seller provides 20 percent seller financing (36 months, 8 percent interest)

Minimum acceptable offer
Price: $145,000
Earnest Money Deposit: $10,000
Closing Date: ANY
Financing: ALL CASH
Contingencies: 5-Day Inspection Period
Other Terms:
- Use my title company
- Buyer takes possession at closing

As you can see, there are some aspects of the deal that we would be very negotiable about (purchase price, financing, closing date) while there are other aspects of the deal where we're not willing to budge very much (having an inspection period, using our title company).

By writing down our specific target and MAO, we can better focus on hitting that target while also ensuring that we never get into trouble by accidentally agreeing to a deal worse than our MAO.

Who Offers First?

It's often debated among serious negotiators whether it is generally in your best interest to put out the first offer or to try to coerce the other party to make the opening bid.

There are actually pros and cons for each side. And luckily, when it comes to real estate negotiations, there typically won't be a struggle over who opens; in most of your real estate discussions, the determination of who throws out the opening bid will be made long before the negotiations begin. In other words, you likely won't have a choice one way or the other.

For example, when you list a house on the MLS—it's unlikely that your real estate agent, your broker, or the people who run the MLS are going to allow you to list the house without including a price. Likewise, when you're buying a house off the MLS—it's pretty much certain that the seller will have chosen a list price; this is the opening bid and when listing a house for sale, the seller always makes it.

On the other hand, there are going to be plenty of times when you contact a seller about buying her house and she says to you, "Hmmm... I'm not sure I'm interested in selling, but make me an offer..." It's unrealistic to expect someone in that position to be making *you* an offer when she's not even sure she's interested in a deal.

Given that you generally won't have a choice about whether to make the first offer or not, we're not going to continue the debate over which one is better or worse. Instead, we're just going to discuss the benefits of each, so that when you find yourself in one situation (you having to offer first) or the other (the other party offering first), you'll have an idea of how best to use this situation to your advantage.

Having the Other Party Make the First Offer

Let's say you're in a position where the other person puts out the first offer. Again, this could be a purchase off the MLS (or an FSBO), where the first offer is the list price of the property. Or, it could be an off-market deal where you've asked the seller how much she wants for the property, and she's given you a number.

Having the other party make the opening bid can put you in a tremendously powerful position. There are two reasons for this:

1. You Can Define the Mid-Point

The first benefit of having the other party put out the opening bid is that it allows you to define a *mid-point* for the negotiated price.

Let's take a look at an example to see what we mean by this:

Let's assume two parties (a homeowner and a contractor) are negotiating the price for some handyman work. The conversation may go something like this:

Homeowner: *"I have $800 to spend on this project. Can you do it for that much?"*

Contractor: *"That's gonna be a lot of work. I'd normally charge $1,000 for that."*

Homeowner: *"Well, I guess I could pay a little more. How about $850 instead?"*

Contractor: *"That still barely covers my costs. Will you do $950?"*

Homeowner: *"How about if we just split the difference and go with $900?"*

Contractor: *"Okay, I guess I can do that."*

Given the lack of negotiating skill exhibited by either side, it's not surprising that the final agreed price ended up at $900—the exact mid-point of the first offer ($800) and the first counteroffer ($1,000).

This is typical for inexperienced negotiators—once the extreme positions are set, each side continues to give in a little bit at a time, until they eventually end up somewhere between where each party started. They, in essence, find themselves "splitting the difference." This is human nature—most people do not to want to give any more or any less than they're getting, so people tend to increase or decrease their offers by the same amount as the other party.

Now, when you can force the other party to state their position first, you have the ability to define the mid-point of the negotiation. Let's see how that simple change in dynamic could have helped our homeowner in the example above.

Homeowner: *"How much do you want to do this job?"*

Contractor: *"I'm thinking $1,000 to complete everything."*

Homeowner: *"I have $600 to spend on this project. Can you do it for that much?"*

Contractor: *"That's too little. I could probably go down to $900."*

Homeowner: *"Well, I guess I could pay a little more. How about $700 instead?"*

Contractor: *"How about if we just split the difference and go with $800?"*

Homeowner: *"Okay, I guess I can do that."*

In this case, the contractor still makes the same initial offer to do the work for $1,000. But, our homeowner took the opportunity to define a lower mid-point with her counteroffer. She offered $600 (instead of $800), thereby reducing the mid-point of the two negotiating positions down to

$800 (where she wanted to be in the first place).

Assuming the contractor would agree on a price around the midpoint (as many inexperienced negotiators will), she was able to reduce the likely price from $900 to $800 simply by asking the other party to make the first offer.

On the other hand, had the homeowner just opened the negotiation with an offer of $600, the contractor could have increased his ask to, say, $1,200, thereby increasing the midpoint back to $900. As you can see, the person who states the first position is at a disadvantage to the person who waits, as the person who waits can define the mid-point.

2. Their Opening Bid Might be Even Better than Yours

The second benefit to getting the other party to open the negotiation is that it's quite possible that the other party will surprise you by making a first offer that is better than the first offer you would make.

Using our example above, the homeowner was happy to pay $800, and that was her goal in the negotiation. Knowing what she knows now, if she were forced to state her offer first, she'd likely start somewhere around $600, expecting the contractor to counter at $1,000, and settling at $800.

But, what if the contractor was only planning to charge $500? By throwing out the first offer of $600, the homeowner has now told him that she's willing to pay at least that amount and possibly more, so the contractor has little reason to quote her anything less than that. By stating her position first, she's given away valuable information to the other party (in this case, her minimum price), and he will use that information to extract the most money possible from her.

As you can see, having the other party put out the first offer provides two big opportunities for you to come out on top of the negotiations.

QUICK TIP *If the other party puts out the first offer, take extra caution to avoid your first counteroffer being too low. Too often a first offer from the other party will anchor us (see below) much lower than our target and we'll give in too much on this first counteroffer. Don't do it!*

You Offering First

After discussing the two big advantages of having the other party make the opening bid, you may be thinking that having to open always puts you at a severe disadvantage.

Luckily, that's not the case!

When you need to make the opening bid, you have one major advantage, and if you leverage that advantage appropriately, you can tip the scales in your favor. Specifically, offering first will allow you to set the foundation for the entire bargaining process. The first offer in any negotiation will generally serve as an *anchoring* point for the rest of the negotiation.

This idea of anchoring is very important, so let's look at it a bit more closely.

In many negotiations, one or both parties have no idea what a reasonable compromise looks like. For example, let's say you walk into a car dealership, and the salesman comes up to you and says:

"Hey, we just got this brand new model in, you should take a look."

He walks you over to a car you've never seen before, and then he asks:

"How much are you willing to pay for it?"

What do you say?

If you're like me, you'd probably just stare at him, thinking to yourself, "How the heck should I know what to pay for this car? It could be worth $20,000 or $200,000!"

Most of us expect to pay a certain price for a car because the manufacturer has already set an expectation in our mind. Sure, the list price might be $30,000 and we might want to try to negotiate down to $26,000, but because the manufacturer set the suggested retail price (MSRP) at $30,000, we don't expect the car is worth $80,000 (or $15,000).

By setting the MSRP, the manufacturer has *anchored* us to the $30,000 price, and we now expect that particular make and model of car to sell for somewhere around $30,000.

If in the following year the manufacturer comes out with a newer model of the same car, we will still expect it to cost about $30,000. And the manufacturer knows that. They won't add a whole bunch of new features and try to raise the price to $40,000, as they know that their customers are anchored to the $30,000 price tag, and—even if the new features warrant the price increase—customers won't accept it. Instead, the manufacturer is more likely to release the car under a different name at the higher price point, as customers aren't yet anchored to a price for this new, more full-featured model.

Just as the MSRP serves as an anchoring point when buying a car, typically it's the first offer thrown out in a negotiation that sets the anchoring point for the entire negotiation. When we are forced to throw out the first offer in a negotiation, we have the ability to create this anchor point in the mind of the other party. This is especially powerful when the other party doesn't know what a reasonable price might be (like me, in the car example above).

For example, when talking with a potential seller who has no idea what his house is worth, you have the ability to define—in his mind—the relative value of his house. If you tell him the house is worth $100,000, he's going to think of his house differently than if you tell him it is worth $500,000—even if he later finds new information that suggests you were not being truthful. He is likely to be anchored to the general value you suggest; and it will typically take a good bit of work to later get him to accept something different.

This explains why, during the Great Recession after 2008, it was common for me to walk into the home of a seller, ask him what he thought his house is worth, and get the response that showed me they thought the house was worth twice as much as it actually was. The sellers had bought (or perhaps refinanced) the house a few years earlier, when prices *were* twice as high, and they were still anchored to *that* value of the house. Getting them to accept the sad truth that their house was now worth much less took a lot of work.

Getting back to how you can use anchoring when you have to throw out the first bid, remember that there is a high correlation between the first offer and the final negotiated price, especially when the other party doesn't have a value in mind. So, as a buyer this is your opportunity to throw out the lowest price you can justify.

While it won't always work, you can often anchor the other party to your extreme first position, and they will be hesitant to move too far away from that anchor point, for fear of being unreasonable or insulting you.

Avoid Round Numbers

In many of the examples we present in this book, for convenience we use nice round numbers, like $100,000 or $150,000. But in the real world, there are two good reasons for avoiding round numbers in your opening offer, as well as often avoiding them during the counteroffer process.

1. Non-Round Numbers Are Better at Anchoring

Choosing a round number will send the message—especially to experienced negotiators—that you have no specific rationale for that price. And, if you have no rationale for a price, it's reasonable to assume that you aren't committed to that price.

For example, if a house is listed at $250,000, and you offer $200,000, a smart seller will realize that it's unlikely that $200,000 number has any specific meaning to you, and that you're likely just fishing to see if the seller will budge on their price.

On the other hand, if you were to offer, $204,200 on that same house, the seller will assume there was thought put into that offer, and will likely believe that the number has some specific meaning. You could reinforce this belief by communicating additional information to the seller when making the offer.

For example, before offering $204,200, you might say to the seller:

> **Investor:** *"I'm glad I met you today... this is actually perfect timing. I just left a closing this morning where I sold a previous property, and I have some cash available to make another purchase."*

You haven't said that the amount of cash you have available is $204,200, but given that your offer is so specific, the seller will likely assume a connection. The seller is now anchored to your $204,200 number, subconsciously thinking that this number is important to your side of the negotiation, perhaps even a requirement for you.

Later in the negotiation, you can reinforce this anchor by saying something to the effect of:

> **Investor:** *"I only have a specific amount of cash available to invest right now. I may be able to increase my offer a little bit, but not much."*

Without saying it, you have reinforced the belief that $204,200 is the specific amount you have available to purchase the property, though you're willing to reluctantly try to find a few more nickels under the sofa cushion.

2. Non-Round Numbers Help You Beat the Competition

The other reason to avoid round numbers is to separate yourself from competitors, especially when buying from institutions, like banks. With many of these types of sales, you will only have one opportunity to submit your best offer, and since most buyers like to use round numbers, it's often not too difficult to predict the amount other buyers might bid. If you can predict your competitor's offers, choosing to offer a little bit more can provide a substantial advantage.

For example, let's assume a bank-owned property is listed at $100,000, and the bank demands that all final offers be submitted by the following day at 5 p.m. Your MAO on the property is $90,000 and you know there are other buyers out there who are interested in the property as well. You suspect that you will beat out any offers below $90,000, though you'd likely lose out to any offers above $90,000.

But, what about those buyers who are thinking exactly like you—with $90,000 being their MAO? If they are typical buyers, their offer will be at the nice, round figure of $90,000. If you offer slightly higher—for example, $90,150—and there are no higher offers, you are likely to beat out the other investors who had the same MAO as you.

The one downside is that you will be offering a bit over your MAO, but if the extra $150 or so is going to compromise your deal, it's probably too thin of a deal anyway.

Offer Low—But Not Too Low

It's often said, "If you're not embarrassed by your first offer, you offered too much." While we don't completely agree with this sentiment, we understand the point—a lower first offer is going to give you a better chance of eventually hitting your target point.

But, just how low should you go?

The general principle behind the opening bid in any negotiation is that it should be low enough that you have plenty of room to come up to your target, but not so low that the other party rejects your offer out-of-hand

and refuses to continue the negotiation. The optimal initial offer price is one that the seller is willing to counter, but had it been even a dollar lower, the seller would have told you to take a hike.

While there is no scientific way to determine what this price—that point just high enough that the seller doesn't rip up your offer—may be, there are a few factors that will help you generate a good estimate:

1. The seller's source of motivation (their reason for selling) and level of motivation (their desperation to sell).
2. The amount the seller owes on the property.
3. Some additional market data (when offering on a listed property).

We spent the previous chapter discussing the best ways to talk to the seller to determine her source and level of motivation. In general, the more motivated a seller is, the lower your initial offer should be. High levels of motivation will often create an urgency that will allow a seller to accept an offer far below retail price—and perhaps far below a price that she would otherwise accept.

QUICK TIP *The stronger the seller's motivation, the less likely you are to insult them with a low offer. The more motivated they are, the lower your initial offer should be.*

We also discussed how to find out the seller's mortgage payoff amount in the last chapter. The amount owed on the property is important because, if a seller is truly motivated, it generally means she is not in a particularly strong financial situation. If she were, she'd likely have options that would generate a higher sale price. A seller who isn't in a strong financial position is often going to be limited by the payoff price of the house. If they owe $100,000 on the property, they aren't going to be able to sell much below $100,000, as it would require them to come up with the difference in cash.

While the payoff price of the property shouldn't necessarily drive your opening offer, you should realize that in most cases, the payoff price of the house will be the seller's worst-case MAO (this is what they *need* to get from the sale). In many cases, their MAO will be higher than the payoff (they want to walk away with additional cash from the sale), but rarely will it be lower.

As for additional market data, we'll address that in the next chapter when we talk about putting together offers for MLS-listed properties. These offers tend to be more difficult because you will have agents intermediating the negotiations, and listing agents will often use market data to help drive the seller's decisions.

Of course, every situation is unique, but in most cases, you're going to find that the cause and level of motivation, coupled with the payoff price of the house and potentially some additional market data, are going to be the biggest determining factors of how low a seller is willing to sell, and therefore how low your initial offer should be. We'll discuss in a lot more detail exactly how to gather all this information and how to use it to create your best opening price bid in the next chapter.

But first, there's one more important aspect of your initial offer that you need to consider: What *won't* you be offering?

Hold Back Some Concessions

One of the most important considerations when creating an initial offer is what aspects of the deal do you want or need, and what aspects of the deal do you believe the other party wants or needs, but that will *not* be addressed in the initial offer?

We realize this might not make much sense, so let's dig in a little deeper. Back in Chapter 2, we described a negotiation as "a big pot filled with things that both parties want, sitting between them on the table. The concessions are all the shiny, glittering things inside that pot."

Many people assume that all the concessions (all the things both sides want) should be introduced during the initial offer—in essence putting everything out on the table (or in that pot). But when you're making the first offer, it's often a better strategy to completely avoid introducing some potential aspects of the deal.

For example, let's say that during your early discussions, the seller mentioned to you that she would like to be able to stay in the house for a couple of weeks after closing to finish up some packing and moving. When you make your first offer, you could include a term that allows her to stay for three days. Since you know she actually wants two weeks, this would give you plenty of room to negotiate this particular term and get concessions from the seller when she asks you for more time.

But it may be a better idea to not include that term at all. Instead of offering to allow the seller to stay for three days in your initial offer, you could just ignore the fact that this term was ever discussed in the first place.

There are several reasons why this might be more advantageous to your position.

First, perhaps this term isn't very important to the seller, and if you don't bring it up in the initial offer, she may never ask for it again. Instead of agreeing to give her three days to stay in the house, you might get away with giving her none.

Second, if this term isn't important to the seller, and if she's a good negotiator, she could use it against you. For example, she could offer to take the three days you proposed *out* of the contract, while asking for a concession from you in return!

When making an initial offer, include in the contract only those terms that are beneficial and important to you, and ignore any terms that would provide benefit to the other party. Allow the other party to "remind you" of these terms during the negotiation, and then use those reminders as an opportunity to get concessions from the other party in return for adding those terms into the contract.

Good negotiators will enter the bargaining phase of the negotiation with a secret list of concessions that they didn't include in the initial offer but they know can be offered and traded later. This way, if the negotiation should lose momentum or stall, these concessions can often be used to get things moving forward again.

The Real Estate Contract

Depending on whether real estate agents are involved in the transaction, and depending on the type of property being bought or sold, the specific format of the offer could range from a single page fill-in-the-blank document to a hefty file folder containing many obscure legal documents.

If there's even one real estate agent involved in the transaction, it's safe to say that the transaction will involve a standard state contract in addition to other documents or contracts. A standard state contract will most likely contain a dozen or more pages of boilerplate contract terms geared toward protecting the buyer, the seller, and the real estate agents or brokers involved in the transaction.

If there are no real estate agents involved in the transaction, you may find yourself using a custom contract generated by a local real estate attorney. These contracts typically contain many of the same clauses as the state contract, but are often much shorter and more easily readable.

Both state contracts and custom contracts typically contain a bunch of common fill-in-the-blank sections. It is how you fill in these blanks—what we call the *offer terms* and *offer contingencies*—that defines your offer.

Offer Terms

Offer terms are the fixed details that the buyer and seller promise to each other as part of the transaction. Each term of the contract provides one or both parties a legal obligation they must fulfill, and if either party fails to fulfill one or more of terms, they run the risk of the deal breaking down or, worst case, getting sued by the other party.

The most obvious term you'll find in a real estate contract—and most other contracts—is the price. The contract states the price at which the seller agrees to sell a property and at which the buyer agrees to buy the property.

Simple real estate contracts may contain as few as a half-dozen terms; complex real estate transactions may contain hundreds of terms.

Offer Contingencies

In addition to all the fixed details (offer terms), your offers will likely include one or more contingencies as well. A contingency is a statement (sometimes called a "stipulation") that is added to your contract saying that if something negative happens before the transaction is completed, one or both parties has some recourse.

Contingencies basically say:

If X occurs (or doesn't occur) before closing, the result is Y.

Very often, the "X" describes major issues, like a bad inspection or the buyer being unable to get his financing. And "Y" gives the buyer the ability to renegotiate or back out of the contract without penalty. In fact, some contingencies immediately and automatically invalidate a contract if they ever occur.

Contingencies are often used by buyers who aren't 100 percent convinced they're ready—or able—to buy the property, and want some extra time to "get their ducks in a row." For example, one of the most common types of contingencies is called a *financing contingency*. Basically, it says that your offer is contingent on you being able to procure financing for the property.

Your offer may contain any contingency you want, and there are some very common contingencies used in many offers. In Chapter 8, we'll discuss some of the contingencies you may find advantageous in your negotiations, and we'll also discuss some best practices for using those contingencies in your offers.

The Six Major Components of an Offer

As mentioned above, a typical real estate contract will contain all the basic building blocks of your offer. The fact that nearly anything can be negotiated as part of the offer is what makes every real estate transaction unique and allows for both the buyer and seller to get exactly what they need in a deal.

While there are countless things that can be negotiated as part of the deal, there are some basic aspects of every deal. Many of these are legally required to ensure the contract is valid, while others are just good practice.

With most real estate transactions, your offer will, at a minimum, have the following six basic components, which will be discussed in more detail in subsequent chapters:

1. **Price:** This is the most important term that any real estate contract will contain, simply because this is where both parties will start their negotiation.

2. **Earnest money deposit:** Earnest money is a good faith payment you make at the time an agreement is reached. The purpose is to give the seller confidence that you will complete the transaction. If you, as the buyer, don't follow through on the terms and contingencies in the contract, the seller may be entitled to keep this deposit. There is no legal requirement for how much earnest money you must provide, but as a buyer, the more earnest money you include, the stronger your offer may appear to the seller. But a larger earnest money deposit also means a larger loss should you break the contract.

3. **Closing date:** When will you officially buy the property? Many sellers would like to sell as quickly as possible, and given that a real estate transaction can take weeks or months, your promise of when you

will complete the deal could determine how attractive your offer is.

4. **Financing:** Are you paying cash or getting a loan? If you're getting a loan, what are the terms of the loan? While the seller will be getting all their money at the time of the closing, many sellers will care where you're getting the money from, as this will have some impact on the likelihood of you actually getting to the closing table. How you structure your financing can make a big difference in how attractive your offer appears to a seller.

5. **Contingencies:** As we discussed above, your contract may be contingent on various things happening. You need to provide a detailed list of those contingencies, along with the consequences of one or more of them not being met. To a seller, contingencies mean the deal is not certain and they create risk. To a buyer, contingencies provide security and often leave an "out" should they decide not to move forward with the purchase. Weighing the risk versus reward of your contingencies is an important part of creating a strong offer to the seller, but also keeping you safe as the buyer.

6. **Other terms:** In addition to the contract terms mentioned above, any additional terms (sometimes called "stipulations") that the buyer and seller agree to can be included in the contract. This is where creative negotiation can turn an average deal into a true win-win deal for both parties.

Over the next two chapters, we will discuss how to build your optimal opening bid by defining these six areas of your offer. Because price is so important, we'll spend the entirety of the next chapter focused on that component. And then, in Chapter 8, we'll discuss the remaining five components of your initial offer.

CHAPTER 7
YOUR OPENING BID PRICE

A seasoned real estate investor can walk into a house, look around for ten minutes, and determine how much it will cost to renovate the property. They don't have to write anything down, don't need to tear open walls, don't need to bring in a contractor or inspector. They're able to do this because after years of practice and experience the methodology of estimating costs is so ingrained in their brains that they can seemingly do it without much effort or thought.

It likely took years of experience before they were able to do that. They probably started their career by walking through houses with a spreadsheet, noting specific items, looking up costs, and then sitting down with a calculator and adding everything up. You may not see it, but now every time they walk a property, they're running through the same script in their heads that was previously on a detailed checklist.

It's the same way when an experienced negotiator is tasked with determining an opening bid price. It may seem that they can talk to a seller for five minutes and then magically come up with the perfect price to throw out to start the negotiation. But just like the investors who used years of experience going through a detailed methodology to come up with the rehab estimate, these great negotiators are using years of experience with a detailed methodology to come up with the perfect initial offer price.

In this chapter, we're going to lay out a methodology for how you can determine the optimal opening bid price for your real estate negotiations. Note that the methodology for determining an optimal offer price is going to change based on whether you have the ability to communicate directly with the seller or whether you're working through real estate agents. If you can't communicate directly with the seller, many of your offer decisions are going to be based off of information provided in the MLS listing and through market statistics your agent can provide.

We'll address each of these situations separately, as they each require a very different approach.

Opening Bid Price When Working with Sellers

We'll first look at putting together an offer without agents involved. This will generally be the case when dealing with a seller you've approached or a seller who has listed her house as "for sale by owner" (FSBO).

Our methodology for determining the right opening bid price relies on our ability to determine the lowest price at which the seller would likely agree to sell the house (her MAO), assuming that all other aspects of the offer met her needs. We're not saying that this is the price where you will want to start the negotiation—it's not—but having a good guess at the seller's MAO is key to determining what that opening price should be.

Once we have a good guess at the seller's MAO, we can compare that to our own target and MAO and come up with a reasonable price with which to start the negotiations.

Before we begin let's think back to Chapter 5, where we attempted to get the following three key pieces of information from the seller or the seller's agents:

- The seller's source and level of motivation.
- The payoff price of the house.
- The seller's stated lowest acceptable sale price.

We'll use these three pieces of information to make our best guess at the seller's MAO and then, along with our own target and MAO, determine a reasonable opening price bid.

Step #1: Create an MAO Range

The first step in guessing what the seller's MAO may be is to use the information we have to create a range where we're confident their MAO falls. To create this range, we'll want two pieces of information: the seller's property payoff amount and their stated lowest acceptable offer.

For example, let's assume the seller owes $155,000 on their property and when you asked how much they'd accept if you paid cash and closed quickly, they said their lowest acceptable price was $195,000.

We now know that—worst case for us—the seller is willing to go down to $195,000, and given that sellers often don't tell the truth, it's likely lower than that. How much lower? We don't know for certain, but barring any other information we have, we should assume their lowest acceptable price is their payoff amount, $155,000.

Based on this, it's reasonable to assume that the seller's MAO is somewhere between her property payoff amount (at the low end) and the amount she told you she'd accept under best-case conditions (at the high end).

To visualize this, let's look at what our example above would look like on a number line:

Step #2: Adjust the MAO Range

The MAO range above assumes that the only pieces of information we have are the payoff amount of the property and the seller's stated lowest acceptable price. But if you did a good job of getting information from the seller during your discussions, you should have a good bit more information.

For example, if the seller told you that she needed to walk away with $25,000 from the closing to pay the down payment on her new condo, it may be safe to assume that the MAO range doesn't really start at the payoff amount, but actually starts $25,000 higher. Or, if the seller indicated that they were flexible on their stated lowest sale price, you could assume that the top end of the range is lower.

Once we factor in this information from the seller, we should be able to narrow down our MAO range. Continuing the example from above, let's assume that the seller told us two things: She needed to walk away from the sale with $25,000 in cash as a down payment on her new place, and her $195,000 lowest sale price might have some flexibility.

From here, we can realistically narrow the MAO range to $25,000 higher (on the low end) and perhaps $5,000 lower (on the high end):

Step #3: Make a Best Guess at Seller's MAO

Now we're getting somewhere. We've narrowed down the MAO range a good bit based on information we've gotten from the seller, and now it's time to choose a price within that range that we believe is reasonably near the seller's MAO.

Yup, we said to make our best *guess*. Unfortunately, without a crystal ball or mental telepathy there is no way to know for certain how low the seller will be willing to go. She may not know herself. But to get negotiations started, we need to put a stake in the ground.

To help, we can think more about the source and the level of motivation the seller has. Based on the information you were able to get earlier, would you say that she is not at all motivated to sell, highly motivated to sell, or somewhere in between? If she's highly motivated, then we can reasonably assume that her MAO is at the low end of that range; if she's not very motivated, we can assume her MAO is at the high end of the range; and if her motivation is somewhere in-between, we can assume her MAO is somewhere in the middle of the range.

For the sake of this example, let's assume the seller is reasonably motivated, and let's guess that her MAO is right in the middle of our range, at $185,000:

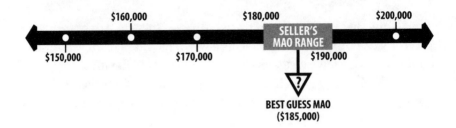

We now have our best guess at the seller's minimum acceptable price, and we can use this information to determine where our opening price bid should be.

Step #4: Compare the Seller's MAO to Your Target

It's now time to compare our best guess of the seller's MAO to our own target and MAO. This should provide us two important pieces of information: whether there's a reasonable chance that we can come to an agreement that will work for both parties and, assuming so, where our initial offer price should fall.

There are three potential scenarios we'll face at this point:

1. **Seller's MAO is below your target**

In this situation, we believe the seller is willing to accept a price lower than our ideal purchase price. For example, imagine a situation where you would be thrilled to pay $195,000 for a particular property, and if necessary go all the way up to $210,000. And as we previously determined, you believe that the seller would be willing to sell for as low as $185,000, given the right set of circumstances:

In this case, you're in a great position. Not only is there a good chance you can hit your target purchase price, there's a chance you could do a good bit better as well (anywhere in the "optimal deal for buyer" area above).

In these situations, our preferred approach is to be conservative and be willing to compromise more than we otherwise would. This is because we are in an almost no-lose situation, and the biggest risk to the deal would be insulting the seller or pushing her away by trying to suck every last dollar out of the deal.

When it comes to choosing an opening bid in these situations, we will tend to try to stay close the seller's MAO, and if there is a good bit of room between the seller's MAO and our target, we may even offer at the seller's MAO (or perhaps even higher!). The goal here is to come to an agreement between the seller's MAO and our target, while making the seller feel as though she's getting what she needs without much of a fight. You also want to indicate a little bit of flexibility to avoid the seller shutting down if it turns out you've picked a price a bit below her MAO.

In the example above, we'd likely pick an opening price bid somewhere in the $180,000 to $185,000 range.

2. **Seller's MAO is between your target and your MAO**

The next possible scenario is that the seller's MAO is higher than your target, but lower than the highest price you'd be willing to pay for the property. In this case, there's still a reasonable chance of coming to an agreement, though you're unlikely to get your target price.

For example, let's say your target price is $175,000, your MAO is $195,000 and, again, you believe the seller's lowest acceptable price is $185,000:

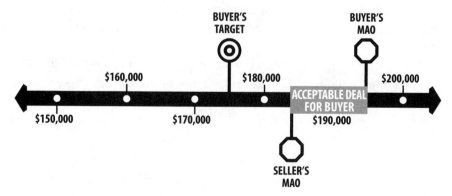

In this situation, you have less negotiating room to play with, and if you don't approach the situation aggressively enough, you run the risk of not ending up in the range of an acceptable deal. On the other hand, a deal is very possible, so you don't want to take too tough a stance, turning your likely deal into no deal.

This is the most difficult of the three situations we'll examine, because the margin for error is small, and the risk—going from a very possible deal to no deal whatsoever—is great. In other words, an offer well below the seller's MAO is likely to give you enough room to make concessions and still get a deal; but, at the same time, an offer well below the seller's MAO runs the risk of the seller saying, "No thanks!" and walking away.

In these situations, we generally find that too many investors err on the side of not being aggressive enough with their offers. They don't want to risk losing the potential deal, and they choose to open at a price too close to the seller's MAO. While they *may* end up at a successful compromise, it's generally going to be very close to their own MAO.

Instead, we generally recommend an opening offer closer to your target, with the goal of negotiating up to a compromise somewhere around the seller's MAO.

In the example above, we'd likely pick an opening price bid somewhere in the $160,000 to $175,000 range, depending on how aggressive you feel you can be with the seller without her walking away.

3. Seller's MAO is above your MAO

In our final scenario, we believe the lowest price a seller would accept is higher than the highest price we'd be willing to pay. These situations are all too common in real estate negotiations, and we will often have to accept the fact that these situations rarely result in a successful compromise, especially if there is a large gap between our MAO and the seller's MAO.

For example, imagine we were willing to pay up to $175,000 for the property, but we believe that the seller would be unwilling to accept anything below the $185,000 we determined earlier:

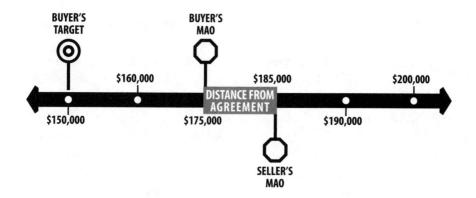

The only way we'll come to an agreement in this scenario is if the seller is willing to drop below her MAO and/or if we're willing to go above our MAO. Assuming neither party is willing to adjust their MAO, the only opportunity for a successful compromise would be if the parties could find concessions valued at the price difference that they were willing to trade.

For example, imagine a scenario where you and the seller are $5,000 apart in your MAOs, and neither is willing to budge. Perhaps the seller has a broken-down car in his garage that he plans to scrap. You have some experience restoring old cars, and you know that you could probably fix this car up, resell it, and make a $5,000 profit.

In this case, why not ask the seller to throw the car into the deal? He loses nothing (he didn't want the car and may save himself the trouble of having it towed) and you know that the car is worth $5,000 to you. You may now be willing to go $5,000 above your MAO knowing you'll recoup that $5,000 by eventually selling the car.

While great negotiators can sometimes turn situations where there is a gap between buyer and seller MAOs, in many cases, the price gap is impossible to overcome and the likelihood of a deal is small. For that reason, we typically like to take one of two approaches to these types of negotiations:

1. Go in with a very low offer (typically at or below your target price) in hopes of shocking the seller into realizing that his property is worth much less than he had thought. If he doesn't walk away and is still willing to negotiate, there is a chance that he is more highly motivated than you had anticipated, and he may reduce his MAO.

   If we wanted to go this route for the example above, we'd likely pick an opening price bid somewhere in the $140,000 to $150,000 range.

2. Communicate to the seller that you don't want to insult him with a low price and that you don't plan to make an offer. The seller will either thank you for your honesty (in which case there was no deal to be made), or the seller will ask you what your price would have been. If the seller is interested in what you would have offered, that's an indication that he may be more motivated than we suspected, and again, may be willing to move off his MAO.

If the seller asks you what your offer would have been, we typically will present the offer exactly as we did in the first example above, but indicate that we might have a bit of flexibility in that price.

QUICK TIP *In some situations—especially when you're not confident that your opening bid is reasonable—consider offering a range instead of a single value. For example, instead of saying, "I'll give you $100,000," consider saying, "How about somewhere in the $80,000 to $100,000 range?"*

Giving a range allows you to "feel out" the other party, indicates flexibility on your part and may make the other party feel as if they "won" should they accept an offer in the part of the range that most benefits them.

Opening Bid Price When Agents Are Involved

You may be wondering why we need a different set of rules for an opening bid price when the seller has an agent. When working directly with the seller, we took a best guess at our seller's MAO and we compared that to our target price and our maximum purchase price to generate our opening bid. But for listed properties where the seller is represented by a real estate agent, that same strategy won't work.

There are three reasons for this:

1. The seller's acceptable price range is likely to be smaller and anchored around the list price.

2. If we make the wrong first offer, we may lose our chance at the negotiation.
3. We likely won't be able to get enough information from the seller.

Let's look at each of these important points in more detail.

Agent Anchoring

Most sellers are going to consider their real estate agent to be an *expert* on the market and on the sales process. Whether the agent truly is an expert on these things doesn't really matter—the seller is going to assume the agent knows the market well, and any negotiating advice the seller gets from the agent is going to be viewed as coming from an expert.

What does this mean for a buyer looking to get a great deal on the property?

Because sellers are going to trust that their agent is an expert, they will typically be anchored to the information they get from the agent. Specifically, sellers are going to believe that the price at which the agent recommends listing the property is the fair market price, even if the is too optimistic. So, unlike sellers working without an agent, sellers with agents are going to be more anchored to whatever price they have initially established—that is, the listing price.

DIG DEEP *Breaking the anchor the listing agent sets can be very difficult, which is why it's often difficult to purchase properties for much below list price when agents are involved in the transaction.*

You May Only Have One Chance

There is one other nuance to making offers on listed properties that you should be aware of, and consider, when deciding on your opening bid price. Because listed properties will often get multiple offers at the same time (especially when it's priced well), there is no guarantee that the seller will choose to negotiate with you.

For example, you might submit a low offer with a willingness to pay a good bit more, but if someone else submits a higher offer than yours, the seller could choose to negotiate with the other buyer, and never give you the opportunity to raise your price. For example, you might initially offer $50,000 on a house where your maximum offer would have been

$100,000 after negotiations, but if another buyer were to offer $80,000 at the same time, the seller could accept that offer without any notice to you.

In other words, you were willing to pay $20,000 more than the offer the seller ultimately accepted, but you never got the opportunity!

QUICK TIP *Always consider the likely competition you'll have when making your offers, and adjust your offers accordingly based on your desire to get the deal and the likelihood of the seller receiving other simultaneous offers.*

Using our example above, if you believed there would be significant competition for the property, instead of making a first offer of $50,000 (close to the seller's MAO), to avoid losing out to another buyer if the seller chooses not to negotiate with you, you may want to consider making an offer closer to your MAO of $100,000.

We rarely recommend making an opening price bid at or near your MAO, but there will be situations where that will be your only opportunity for a deal, and if your motivation is high enough, it may be your best option. Keep this in mind as we discuss our methodology below for selecting an opening price bid when agents are involved in the transaction.

Difficulty Getting Information from the Seller

With agents involved in the transaction, it's unlikely that you will have the luxury of being able to talk directly to the seller. This makes determining her level of motivation more difficult, which in turn makes determining her MAO more difficult.

While it's certainly possible to glean some of this information by reading the MLS listing, visiting the property, and having your agent talk to the seller's agent (all the things we discussed in Chapter 5), at the end of the day, the amount of information we'll get about what the seller is willing to sell her property for is going to be relatively small. Even the simple fact that we can never directly ask the seller, "What is the lowest price you'd sell your property for?" makes the entire process of trying to nail down the seller's MAO nearly impossible.

For all of these reasons, our strategy for determining an optimal opening bid price needs to change when agents are involved in the deal.

Instead of trying to guess the seller's MAO, in these cases, we will instead work to establish the seller's MAO *range*—similar to how we did earlier—and then compare that range to our MAO.

But, in order to establish an MAO range for a seller who has an agent, we need one more piece of information.

Sales Price to Listing Price Ratio (SPLP)

A listing agent involved in the transaction will be familiar with the local real estate market, and she will be advising the seller based on that local market data.

For example, if the listing agent knows the market is "soft" (things aren't selling quickly), she may advise the seller to consider lower offers to get a quick sale. On the other hand, if the market is hot, the listing agent may try to convince the seller not to respond to any offers for a period of time to create competition among the likely multiple interested buyers.

Good real estate agents try to set list prices for their seller's properties right about where they expect the property to sell. In a typical market where the agents are doing a good job, it's not uncommon for houses to generally sell between 95 percent-100 percent of list price. But in a hot market, agents are often not aggressive enough on their pricing, and it's not uncommon for properties to tend to sell above list price. Buyers compete for properties, and drive prices up. Alternatively, in softer markets, agents often overestimate the pace of the market, price houses too high, and then those houses tend to sell for a lower percentage of list price.

At any given time in a market, there will be a ratio of average listing price to average sales price. If houses tend to be selling for about 90 percent of the listing price, we would say that the SPLP is about 90 percent. If properties tend to be selling above list price, the SPLP would be over 100 percent.

SPLP will give you an idea of what the listing agent and seller realistically expect to sell the property for. Again, while agents should be listing properties right where they expect the sales price to fall, many will tend to be over-aggressive or under-aggressive in their price for various reasons. If SPLP is currently about 90 percent in your market, it's not unreasonable to assume that the listing agent knows this, and will expect that the seller will have to discount a sale at least 10 percent below list price.

When making offers on listed properties, we highly recommend asking your agent to provide you this data. You're going to need it in the next step when formulating your opening bid price.

Determining Our Opening Bid Price

Now that you have the SPLP data for your area—and assuming you know your target and MAO for the property and the list price on the property—you now have enough information that you should be able to determine a reasonable opening bid price for your offer.

Let's take a look at how to do that.

Step #1: Create an MAO Range

Our first step is to create a range in which we believe the seller's MAO falls. Remember, because there is an agent involved, the seller is likely anchored to a price somewhere near list price, even if that price is far above or below fair market value. We will generally assume that the high end of the seller's MAO range is the list price of the property. In other words, if we were to offer the seller full list price, she would probably accept our offer.

In addition, we assume that the seller may be willing to come down on her price depending on how soft the market is—the softer the market, the more the seller will likely be willing to go lower than list price. And that's where the SPLP comes in.

Here's an example:

Let's assume the seller has a property listed for $200,000 and let's further assume the market is currently a little bit soft—specifically, houses tend to be selling for about 5 percent below list price, giving an SPLP of 95 percent).

We've already determined that the list price of $200,000 is likely the high end of the seller's MAO range. We will also assume that for a typical seller who isn't tremendously motivated, the low end of the MAO range will be the SPLP price—in this case, 95 percent of list price, or $190,000.

Further, if the seller is motivated, the MAO range could extend down to 10 percent below the SPLP price, depending on how motivated she is. For this example, let's assume the property was in subpar condition and the market is declining, so we believe the seller is reasonably motivated. We can make a guess that the bottom of the seller's MAO range is 5 percent below SPLP price.

To visualize this, let's look at what our example above would look like on a number line:

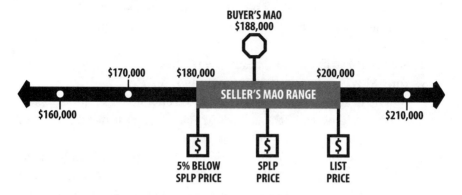

Let's review what this picture is telling us:

- For a seller who is not any more or less motivated than an average seller, you can expect that the lowest price the listing agent would recommend the seller accept will be somewhere between SPLP price (where the agent would expect the final sales price to fall in this market) and list price (if the listing agent is aggressive).

- If the seller is more motivated than the average seller, she may be willing to accept an additional discount below SPLP price, up to about 10 percent (we assume 5 percent in this example). This additional motivation may be due to the seller's situation, the condition of the property, the trajectory of the market, or some other factor. You will use the information you collected in Chapter 5 to determine how motivated the seller likely is.

Keep in mind that the 10 percent below SPLP price is the lowest you should ever expect the seller's MAO to be, not the payoff price of the house like when working directly with the seller.

Why is that?

Because most listing agents are smart enough to realize that dropping the price and creating more buyer competition is a better strategy than taking an ultra-low offer. In other words, the listing agent would generally recommend to their seller to drop the price a moderate amount before suggesting that they accept your extremely low offer.

Step #2: Compare Your MAO to Seller MAO Range

It's now time to compare your MAO to your best guess of the seller's MAO range. This should tell us whether there's a reasonable chance that we can come to an agreement and, assuming so, where our initial offer price should fall.

There are three potential scenarios we'll face:

1. **Your MAO is *above* seller's MAO range**

    The first scenario we'll look at is when your MAO for the purchase is higher than the seller's MAO range. In other words, you are willing to pay more than list price to get the deal.

    This is not going to be tremendously common for listed properties in most markets, but it does happen. While this may seem like a great opportunity, consider that, if you have a realistic MAO for this property to be used as an investment, it's likely there are other investors in your area who have also determined that there is potentially a great deal lurking here as well. That competition will often push the sale price above the seller's MAO range and the list price, closer to your MAO.

    In other words, in these situations, you should always expect the seller to get other offers in addition to yours. As an example, imagine a property that is listed for $200,000. And imagine that it would make a good flip deal if purchased at anything below about $210,000. At this point, the seller's MAO range doesn't matter—if the property will make a good investment even above list price, there's a reasonable chance other investors in the area will take notice and make offers at or above list price.

    Here's how that would look:

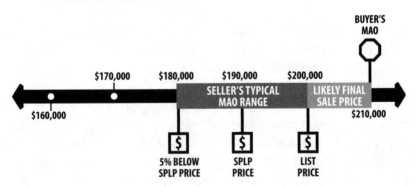

In these situations, our strategy wouldn't be to offer much below list price. If you were to offer, say, $190,000 (an otherwise perfectly reasonable offer), and the seller then gets three offers at $200,000 (from other investors who realize it's a good deal, even at list price or above), there's a chance the seller will ignore your offer completely and continue negotiations with one or more of the other buyers.

It's also not uncommon in these situations for the seller to call for "highest & best" offers. Highest & best is a tactic sellers often use in multiple offer situations where they ask each potential buyer to submit their best offer by a pre-defined date and time. This tactic will often allow the seller to get near optimal value from the sale with minimal negotiation. (Of course, as a seller, there are risks to this tactic, which we'll discuss more in Chapter 15.)

If the seller calls for highest & best in this scenario, we will generally offer near or at full price, hoping that we can come to an agreement with the seller before any other offers come in—and before the seller realizes that she may have priced the property too low. If you live in an area where there isn't much investing activity and you don't believe you'll be competing with other investors for the property, then it may be better to open a little bit lower; but if it's still a good deal at list price, we prefer to lock in the deal than to get greedy.

2. **Your MAO is *within* seller's MAO range**

The next possible scenario is that the highest price you'd consider paying falls somewhere in the seller's MAO range. Continuing the seller example above, let's say that in this case, your MAO is $188,000:

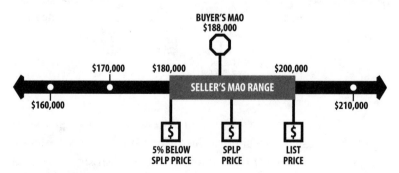

In this case, there's a potential for a deal, assuming you can get the seller off her list price. We want to ensure that our opening price bid gives us enough room to be able to negotiate up to a deal below our MAO, but not start so low that the seller refuses to engage in a negotiation with us.

In these situations, we will often open a little bit below the bottom of the seller's MAO range. As long as the seller believes she can get us into her range, there's a reasonable chance she'll engage in negotiations at this price, and it also gives us a bit of negotiating room to get a price better than our MAO, or worst case, at our MAO.

In this case, we're likely to set our opening bid price somewhere in the $170,000 to $180,000 range. Assuming the seller isn't getting other offers, that should be high enough to encourage a counteroffer but low enough to give us an opportunity at a successful deal.

3. **Your MAO is *below* seller's MAO range**

In our final scenario, our MAO is below the lowest price we believe a seller would accept. In any reasonably vibrant real estate market, you'll run into these situations with most MLS properties. Which is why most MLS listed properties don't provide much opportunity for investors.

Let's use the seller example from our previous scenarios and assume that our MAO for this deal is $170,000:

In this case, there's a $10,000 gap between the most we could pay and the least we believe the seller would accept. Unless there are enough other concessions that one or both sides can make to bridge this $10,000 gap, it's highly unlikely that there's a path to a successful negotiation here.

In addition, if the listing agent did even a half-decent job of pricing the property, it's likely that there will be other, non-investor buyers who will be willing to pay more than the seller's MAO, which is already more than you are willing to pay. Unless you and your agent enjoy writing up offers all day, these are the types of deals that you typically won't want to waste your time with.

Now that we've determined the price we'll be making with our opening offer, it's time to look at the rest of the terms we'll include in our contract.

CHAPTER 8
TERMS & CONTINGENCIES

In the previous chapter, we took a deep dive into how to select an opening bid price for our offer. As we discussed earlier, while price is often the most important component in our real estate offers, it's far from the only one.

In this chapter we're going to delve into the other five major components of our offer, and will lay out a plan for completing our initial offer and creating a list of additional terms and concessions we can use later in the deal.

Earnest Money

As discussed earlier, an earnest money deposit is a good faith payment made to the seller (though typically held in escrow by the title company) once an agreement is reached. If the buyer doesn't fulfill his contractual promises, the seller typically gets to keep this payment. While earnest money deposits are a common part of nearly all real estate transactions, there is no legal requirement for including earnest money in a deal.

That said, if there are real estate agents involved in the transaction, it's nearly certain that the listing agent will require an earnest money deposit, or at least heavily recommend to their seller that they demand an earnest money deposit. Even though many state contracts can make it difficult for the seller to keep the earnest money deposit—even in cases where the buyer defaults on the contract—the notion of not including any earnest money as part of the deal is a non-starter for many agents.

In these situations, you should expect to include at least $500 in earnest money, and typically at least $1,000. For higher priced properties, some agents will require more earnest money, and in the case where a buyer is offering to pay cash for a property, some listing agents will recommend to their sellers that they should collect up to 10 percent of the purchase price in earnest money.

When offering on listed properties, we typically recommend starting with an earnest money deposit of either $500 or the lowest amount that is customary in your area. If the seller is uncomfortable with that low of an amount, we are usually willing to go higher in return for some concessions from the seller.

When working with off-market sellers who are not represented by an agent, there is, more often than not, much more flexibility when it comes to earnest money payments. Some sellers—especially those who are very motivated—may not ask for or require any earnest money. Other sellers are going to be happy with a nominal payment of $50 or $100, just to be assured that you are acting in good faith.

Typically, we will always include some earnest money deposit with every offer. We like to start at $100—a small, but reasonable number that will give the seller some confidence that we're serious about the deal. In fact, in many cases, the seller won't ask for more. If they do, this is a good opportunity to trade a higher earnest money deposit for other concessions from the seller that benefit you.

There are situations where a high earnest money deposit can be a very strong concession to the seller, as it removes some of the risk that you'll back out before the closing and nearly guarantees them that they'll get the agreed-upon money, since the earnest money payment is made at the time the contract is signed.

As an example, we once made an offer on a listed property priced far below market. After receiving six offers, the seller asked each buyer to submit their highest & best price. We didn't budge on our offer of $39,000, but we did offer the entire purchase price (the full $39,000) in earnest money. They accepted our offer, and the next day, we wired $39,000 to the title company.

The sellers had a few slightly higher offers than ours, but by offering the full purchase price in earnest money, they knew that even if we were to back out of the deal, they'd still get all the money. Reducing risk was worth accepting a slightly lower purchase price.

Closing Date

Most likely, it's your source of financing—whether you'll be getting a loan on the property or using your own cash—that will determine how quickly you can close a transaction. For example, depending on how things work in your state and how diligent your closing agent is, if you're paying cash, and barring any issues with clean title, it should be possible to close on a purchase within about five business days of signing a contract.

But, if you're getting a loan, it can often take several weeks for the lender to complete his due diligence, get an appraisal, complete the paperwork, and get everything ready for the closing. Depending on the type of loan you plan to get, you may need a closing date up to five weeks past the date the contract is signed.

Before putting together your offer, it's important that you talk to both your lender and your closing agent about how quickly you can close the deal. They should be able to give you a general time frame for how long they will need to complete their tasks and get the closing scheduled.

We typically recommend taking the longest period of time they indicate it could take, adding a week or two, and using that date as your closing date on your initial offer. For example, if your lender says he'll need between two and three weeks to prepare for the closing and your closing attorney says he'll need three to five days to prepare once he gets all the documents from the lender, we'll normally assume that our best-case closing date is four weeks from the signing of a contract.

We'll add another week or two as a cushion, making a total of six weeks in our example, and that will be the closing date we initially propose. Worst case, something will come up and we'll need the extra time. Best case, this will give us one or two weeks that we can offer to pull in the closing date as a concession, in return for something from the seller.

Financing

If you're making an offer on a listed property using a standard state contract, it's almost certain that the contract will require the buyer to indicate how he will be paying for the property. Even if you are using your own contract and working directly with a seller, it's likely that the seller will want to know how you plan to finance the transaction.

Cash versus Financing

While there are many ways to acquire a piece of real estate, they all boil down to two main methods:

1. **Cash purchase.** A cash purchase of real estate typically involves the buyer having direct access to the cash necessary to close the transaction, and the buyer transferring those funds directly to the closing agent on or before the day of the sale. The buyer's cash may come from his own bank account or may come from friends, family, partners, or other investors. Regardless of the source, the funds are transferred to the closing agent without any promissory note or mortgage/deed of trust needing to be signed at the closing table.

2. **Financed purchase.** A financed purchase of real estate typically involves the buyer receiving a loan from a bank, private investor, or hard money lender and—while the lending party will still transfer the cash directly to the closing agent—the buyer will be required to sign loan papers (typically a promissory note and mortgage/deed of trust) at the closing table in order to release the funds to the seller.

From the seller's perspective, the end result is typically the same—at the completion of the closing, the seller will receive the proceeds of the sale in cash (actually, a check or wire transfer). But while the seller will receive their cash the same way regardless of whether the buyer is paying cash or getting a loan, many sellers are going to treat these two situations very differently.

If a buyer is getting a loan—whether from a financial institution or a private lender—there are likely a number of hoops the buyer will have to jump through to complete the loan. This may include the lender underwriting the buyer (verifying credit, income, financial history, etc.) as well as underwriting the property (completing an inspection, appraisal, etc.). Unless and until the lender is confident that both the borrower and the property are a safe investment, the lender isn't going to release the funds.

In other words, between the time the contract is signed and the transaction is closed, both the buyer and the seller are at the mercy of a third party: the lender. If the lender decides—for any reason—not to fund the deal, it's quite possible that the transaction will fall apart and both the buyer and seller will be back at square one. From a seller's perspective, a buyer getting a loan constitutes a big risk to the deal.

On the other hand, if a buyer is using his own cash, or cash that he has readily available from another source, there are no third parties involved that could potentially squash the deal. If the seller has verified the buyer has the funds and is acting in good faith, she can be confident that the deal will close successfully.

For this reason, a cash purchase is typically going to be a lot more attractive to a seller than a financed purchase. In fact, for a motivated seller who wants to reduce risk in a transaction, a cash offer will nearly always take precedence over a financed offer, most other things being equal. Even if another buyer is willing to pay a little more and make other concessions, most motivated sellers would prefer to work with a cash offer in lieu of a financed offer.

With that in mind, if you're facing competition from other buyers for the property, your method of financing will become important to the seller. If the seller has several offers on the table, it's likely she'll prefer offers that promise cash over financing.

On the other hand, if you're making an offer to a seller on an off-market property with no competition from other buyers, there's a good chance that the seller won't argue with your financing method—especially if that seller is motivated. Likewise, if you're making an offer to a seller of a listed property and you believe your offer is competitive with other offers the seller might receive, it's unlikely the seller will have an issue with a financed offer.

Cash offers tend to be most important when dealing with an off-market seller who is considering offers from several different investors. Cash offers are also going to be important when making offers on listed properties where your offer is below other offers the seller might be getting from retail buyers. Why would a seller accept a low financed offer from you when she could be getting a higher financed offer from another buyer?

QUICK TIP *When offering on a property where you don't think you'll have competition and where you plan to pay cash, make your offer with financing anyway. This way, when you need a concession to provide to the seller later, you can offer up a cash purchase instead. This was your original intent, but now, you will likely get something in return for it.*

Making a Cash Offer on a Financed Purchase

Making a cash offer will greatly improve your chances of getting a good deal on a property, especially when you have competition from other buyers. While you generally won't have much choice about whether you can purchase with cash or not, there are a couple techniques that some investors will use to make a cash offer, even when they plan to finance the property.

Here are the two most common techniques:

- **Refinance.** This strategy involves purchasing the property with borrowed cash that doesn't require any loan paperwork, and then doing a refinance after the purchase to pay back the loan. If you can come up with the cash for a short period of time—long enough to make the purchase plus the time it would take to get the refinance loan approved—this strategy may be viable. Obviously, you would have to be able to come up with the cash in the first place, such as borrowing from credit cards (an expensive choice) or from friends/family who don't require any loan paperwork.

   There are risks with this strategy as well. What if you borrow to purchase the property, but don't get approved for the loan? What if you get to the closing table and realize that the cash you were planning to borrow is now not available and you don't have the money to close? These are both situations we've seen happen, so if you're going to go this route, you will want to ensure that not only are you confident you'll have the cash at closing, but also that you'll have the ability to refinance after the closing.

- **Line of Credit/HELOC:** Instead of getting a mortgage against the property, some investors will work with their bank to get a line of credit or home equity line of credit (HELOC) that can be accessed like cash. Typically, lines of credit are like credit cards—they are a fixed line of credit that you can borrow from as you need and repay on a monthly schedule with a minimum payment required each month. A HELOC is similar, but the credit is extended against a piece of property—typically your personal residence.

   The biggest risk with a line of credit is that the interest rate may change based on outside economic factors, so you may find that you're paying more per month on a line of credit than you had anticipated.

   Remember, when you're making a cash offer some sellers are going to want to see a "proof of funds," which is essentially a bank letter or statement proving you have the cash available for the transaction. If you make a cash offer, you should be prepared to demonstrate that you actually have the cash, even if it's being borrowed from a friend or family member.

Contingencies

To protect your interests in your transactions when making an offer you'll often use at least one—and maybe several—contingencies. In the following sections we'll discuss some of the most common contingencies you may find useful, and how to use these contingencies to maximize your chance of negotiating success.

Contingency Examples

While there are literally dozens of common contingencies—and we've probably seen and written hundreds more—there are some that are most common when making offers on investment properties. Here are three of the contingencies you may consider using when making offers, and that you should expect to see when you're receiving offers on houses you sell.

Note that while we've included some sample contingency language in our examples below, we are not attorneys, these are not meant to be legal recommendations, and it's quite possible that the specific verbiage we provide may not hold up in court in your state. So, please don't copy and paste the examples below without consulting a local real estate attorney for advice. These are only used for example!

Also keep in mind that if you're making an offer through a real estate agent and are using a standard state contract, it's nearly certain that the contract will already have many of the most common contingencies written into the contract. You will likely have the option of making that contingency part of the contract by checking or initialing a box, and the specific wording of the contingency will then apply.

Make sure that if you're using a standard state contract, you work with an experienced real estate agent or attorney to help you understand the limitation of the contingencies you are including in the contract, as they may be very different than those we suggest below. The point is, if you're using a state contract, ensure that you know exactly what you are agreeing to (and not agreeing to); and if you are not happy with the contingency as it's written, revise it or work with your agent/attorney to write in a new one that satisfies your needs.

Inspection (Due Diligence) Contingency

Also known as a "due diligence period" or a "due diligence contingency," an inspection contingency typically says that the buyer has a set amount of time (between one week to two weeks is common) where he can do whatever he needs to do to ensure that he wants to buy the property. This might include inspections, appraisals, and contractor walk-throughs.

If at any time within that pre-defined period the buyer chooses to back out of the deal for any reason, he can. This is a common contingency for anyone who is not intimately familiar with inspecting properties and coming up with rehab cost estimates. The buyer can use this time period to get a full property inspection and get bids from contractors to do any necessary work. If any surprises turn up, he can then either ask for a discount or repairs, or just back out of the deal.

One of the benefits of a well-written inspection contingency is that it can allow you to back out of an agreement for any reason, not just bad inspection results. When writing our own due diligence contingencies into the contract, we typically write them very generically—something like this:

> *"All parties agree that Buyer has the right to terminate this contract for any reason and with no penalty within seven days following binding agreement ("Due Diligence Period"). All parties further agree that, should Buyer deliver notice of termination in writing to the Seller prior to the expiration of the Due Diligence Period, Earnest Money shall be refunded to the Buyer."*

Note that many standard state contracts include much narrower inspection/due diligence contingencies. For example, the contingency may require the buyer to do an inspection, and may only allow the buyer to back out of the deal if there is a verifiable inspection issue that would cost more than $1,000.

Financing Contingency

The second most common contingency you'll see in real estate contracts are financing contingencies. These contingencies allow the buyer to attempt to get financing (a loan) for the property, and should the buyer be unable to get financing, will give him the right to back out of the deal.

If you are including a financing contingency in your own contract, we typically recommend something generic, such as:

"All parties agree that Buyer will attempt to secure his preferred financing for the property within 15 days following binding agreement ("Financing Contingency Period"). If for any reason, Buyer is unable to secure financing within the Financing Contingency Period, Buyer has the right to terminate this contract with no penalty. All parties further agree that, should Buyer deliver notice of termination in writing to the Seller prior to the expiration of the Financing Contingency Period, Earnest Money shall be refunded to the Buyer."

While that generic contingency might work when you're dealing with a seller of an off-market property, if the seller is represented by an agent and you are using a standard state contract, it's unlikely the agent will allow her client to accept that kind of contingency.

More likely, you will be required to include a financing contingency that details specifically what type of financing you are trying to secure and under what terms. For example, the contingency in many state approved contracts may look similar to the following, with fill-in-the-blank terms:

"Buyer shall have _____ days from Binding Agreement Date to determine if Buyer has the ability to obtain the Loan described below:

Loan Amount: _____ percent (%) of purchase price of property

Term: _____ years

Interest rate at _____ percent (%) per annum

Loan Type: _____

Rate Type: _____

Source of Loan: _____

The term "ability to obtain" as used herein shall mean that Buyer, as of the end of the Financing Contingency Period, is qualified to obtain the Loans described above based on the Lender's customary and standard underwriting rules."

The first contingency (above) is generic enough that you could likely use it to back out of the deal for other reasons—for example, you could make up some impossible-to-get loan and then say that it was your preferred financing but you couldn't get it.

The state approved language is likely to be much more specific, and simply states that you *could* qualify for the loan, not that you did. Which means that, unless you make a good faith effort to get the specified loan, you have no grounds on which to back out of the contract without risking your earnest money and, in some cases, being sued.

Appraisal Contingency

Another common contingency, especially when there is financing involved in the purchase, is an appraisal contingency. This contingency generally says:

- If the buyer gets an appraisal on the property and it doesn't come in at least as high as the agreed upon purchase price, the buyer can ask the seller to drop the purchase price to the appraised price; and
- If the seller refuses to drop the price to the appraised price, the buyer can back out of the deal.

The appraisal contingency often goes hand-in-hand with a financing contingency, as most conventional, portfolio, and hard money lenders will require an appraisal and will refuse to lend at a higher amount than the property appraises for. So even if a buyer has the ability to get funding, the appraisal contingency will ensure that he gets the amount needed to actually purchase the property.

An appraisal contingency might read something like the following:

"All parties agree that within twenty-one (21) days of Binding Agreement ("Appraisal Contingency Period"), the Buyer may, at his sole discretion and expense, order an appraisal on the property. If the appraised value is less than the agreed upon purchase price, the Buyer may, at Buyer's sole option, request that Seller reduce the purchase price to a value no lower than the appraised price. If Seller rejects the request to reduce the sale price, the Buyer may terminate this contract without penalty prior to the completion of the Appraisal Contingency Period."

Again, if you are submitting an offer on a state approved contract through real estate agents, there will almost certainly be a standard appraisal contingency that may be included with the contract. You will want to work with your agent or attorney to ensure that the contingency provides the protection you need in your contract.

Additional Contingencies

In addition to the contingencies discussed above, here are some other contingencies you may find useful when making offers, or that you may see when receiving offers on your properties. In some cases, especially when entering into contracts where real estate agents are involved, some of these contingencies may be required by law:

- **Legal description contingency**: allows for review of the legal description of property.
- **Survey contingency**: requires satisfactory property survey results.
- **Termite letter contingency**: allows for termite inspection.
- **Lead paint test contingency**: allows for lead paint inspection.
- **Deed contingency**: stipulates what type of deed is expected from the seller at closing.
- **Radon testing contingency**: allows for radon testing.
- **Mold inspection contingency**: allows for mold testing.
- **Sewer inspection contingency**: allows for inspection of sewer line.
- **Private well inspection contingency**: allows for inspection of a well.
- **HOA documents contingency**: requires seller to provide HOA docs.
- **Insurance contingency**: allows buyer to investigate insurance costs.
- **House sale contingency**: allows buyer time to sell an existing property.

While these are the most common contingencies you'll see and use in your contracts, there are literally hundreds of possible contingencies you could create and use as you find necessary.

Tips for Using Contingencies

Now that we've run through a good long list of the contingencies you might use in your offers, it's important to understand how best to use these contingencies in a way that will provide the greatest opportunity to reach an agreement between you and the seller.

Here are three tips that we recommend following when using

contingencies in your contracts:

The fewer contingencies in your offer, the more attractive it will be.

Let's look at contingencies from the perspective of the seller:

She wants to sell her property as quickly and as efficiently as possible, and the contingencies you put in your offer represent opportunities for you to back out of the deal before it closes. As a buyer, you should consider how much leverage you have in the deal before you decide how aggressive you want to be with your contingencies. For example, if you don't have much leverage over the seller, you'll want to limit your contingencies to only those that are absolutely necessary.

We're certainly not saying to never use a contingency—sometimes they're very important—but don't use more than necessary to protect your interests. If you use the fewest possible contingencies in your offer, your offer will be much stronger than competing offers.

Of course, unless you have had the property inspected (or have done it yourself) and are absolutely sure that you want to move forward, you take a risk by not having at least one contingency in your offer.

What we recommend in most situations is:

When possible, limit your offer to a single contingency.

While it may be more reassuring to you to have lots of contingencies in your offer—it means you have more leeway to change your mind, right?—the truth is, that a single contingency often provides all the protection you need. In fact, for 50 percent of the offers we make, the only contingency we use is a well-written due diligence contingency. For the other 50 percent of the offers we make, we use no contingencies at all.

As we discussed above, the due diligence contingency will give you a fixed period of time—generally seven to 14 days, depending on how much you decide you need—to get everything in order to ensure that you want to, and can, buy the property. During that due diligence period, you can get your property inspection completed, ensure that you have your financing lined up, create your rehab plan, have your contractors come out to the property to give you bids, contact your insurance agent to get quotes, and all the other important tasks you should be completing prior to committing to the purchase.

By the time you've used up that due diligence period, you should know if you're ready to move forward on the property. If you come across anything concerning (structural issues, mold, missed repair costs, etc.), you have the option to renegotiate or back out of the deal.

If you need multiple contingencies in your contract, here is what we recommend:

Lump contingencies into a small number of expiration time periods.

The two most common reasons you may need to have more than just one overarching due diligence contingency are:

1. The seller refuses to agree to including an all-encompassing escape clause in the contract; or
2. You have different deadlines for your contingencies.

No. 1 should be pretty self-explanatory. Sometimes sellers just refuse to allow you the option to back out of the contract, except under specific circumstances. This is can be a smart move on their part—they want to protect the sale, and by giving you one overarching contingency, they run a much greater risk of you backing out of the deal.

As for No. 2 this situation arises when you have several different contingencies that you prefer to expire at separate times. For example, what if you're waiting to find out about getting financing, and you don't expect a final answer from your lender for another month?

The seller may be willing to give you a seven-day due diligence contingency, but is unlikely to extend that all-encompassing contingency to 30 days. In that case, you might be able to get the seller to agree to the seven-day due diligence contingency and agree to a separate 30-day financing contingency. Because the seller knows that, after the seventh day, you can back out only on financing issues, she might be more comfortable with the separate contingency.

In general, we like to bundle our contingencies into the smallest number of periods possible. So, let's say we needed the seven-day due diligence period and the 30-day financing period, and we also needed another contingency to get a radon test. While we may only need 15 days for that contingency, we recommend making it 30 days, to coincide with the financing contingency.

By grouping contingencies into a small number of deadlines (in this case, only seven days and 30 days), we make it simpler to negotiate those contingencies together in groups, and we also make easier any renegotiation we may have to do. We'll discuss that more in Chapters 12 and 13.

Other Terms

We talked earlier in the book about how all negotiations consist of *price* and *terms*. We discussed in the previous two chapters how to select the most advantageous price when making an offer on a property. And in this chapter, we've discussed several of the terms that often appear in a contract, and how best to use those terms to maximize your success at getting a great deal.

But while price may be one of the main components of any real estate contract, they are far from the only terms that can be negotiated as part of a deal. And, as we've mentioned several times throughout the book, great negotiators know how to use additional terms to provide value to each side; they even know how to create additional terms that can bridge the gap should the parties not be able to come together on price.

So what are some of the more common terms that can be negotiated as part of a real estate contract? Here are some things to consider:

- **Seller financing.** If the seller wants top dollar for their property, but you can't afford to pay the asking amount, perhaps they'd be willing to finance part of the deal. If you're getting a loan, they may be willing to finance your down payment, so you wouldn't have to bring any cash to the deal. Or, perhaps they'd be willing to finance some or all of the deal themselves.

  We like to ask early on in the discussions if the seller needs all the cash from the sale immediately or if they'd be willing to wait a period of time to receive part or all of the proceeds, in return for getting a higher sale price. Some sellers would actually prefer to have monthly payments coming in over a long period of time—perhaps they prefer an annuity stream or perhaps they're looking for the tax advantages that may come with a prolonged income stream.

  In summary, for you as the buyer, seller financing can be a great option to avoid having to get another loan, reduce your down payment, or provide financing at better terms than you would otherwise be getting. And to the other party, seller financing can often provide more total income and some tax advantages.

- **Personal property.** Are there items in the house or on the property that you, as a buyer, can use or sell? Maybe the seller doesn't want them or doesn't want to move them, and it's easier for them to include these items in the sale.

  Are there construction materials from a rehab that was not

completed or old appliances that can be scrapped for some additional cash? Negotiate these things into the deal. We've negotiated contracts that have included things like furniture, building materials, appliances, and old cars sitting on blocks in the garage.

Not only can the addition of personal property increase the value of the deal for the buyer, but not having to move or dispose of unwanted property can be an added value to the seller as well. Negotiating these things into a sale can often be a win-win for both parties.

- **Quick closing.** The best deals are often obtained in situations where the buyer and/or seller need to get the transaction closed quickly. If you have the ability to provide a quick closing, use that to your advantage. Having the ability to negotiate a quick close (less than ten days, for example) can often get you a better sale price or other important concessions that you might want out of the deal.

- **Closing costs.** For many buyers, cash is extremely limited, especially for investors who look to purchase multiple properties per year. Purchasing a house can require a good bit of cash for down payments, inspections, appraisals, and closing costs. In fact, if you are getting financing on a property, the closing costs alone can easily add up to 3 percent of the loan or more.

  Asking the seller to pay those closing costs can greatly reduce the amount of cash you, as the buyer, needs in order to purchase a property. And because seller-paid closing costs will simply be taken from the sales proceeds, the seller won't need any actual cash to pay these costs, unlike the buyer would.

  In fact, if you otherwise wouldn't mind paying the closing costs, but are getting a loan and are simply looking to reduce your cash outlay, one option is to offer the seller a higher sales price in return for their paying all the closing costs. If structured correctly, a seller can net the same amount of cash on their sale while you ultimately pay less upfront cash.

- **Closing agent.** In most states, the buyer has the right to choose their own closing agent (attorney or title company) when they buy a house. But if you're flexible on a closing agent and the seller has a preferred firm they'd like to use, the seller may agree to pay for title insurance or other closing fees if you agree to use their closing agent.

  On the other hand, if you as the investor use your own closing agent when you're flipping a property, you may be able to use a "hold-open title policy," which will allow you to save some money on the resale if you can use the same title agent when you sell.

- **Possession time frame.** Some sellers have an incentive to sell very quickly (perhaps they are being relocated for work), while others may want a slower sale (perhaps they want extra time to pack and find a new place). Some would even prefer to stay in the house for a long period of time before moving (perhaps they have longer-term plans they aren't ready to act on).

  Regardless, if the seller is interested in staying in the house for a period of time longer than it would take to close the sale, there may be an opportunity for you to negotiate an agreement whereby the seller can stay in the house for a period of time in return for a lower sale price or some other concession.

  In fact, we've had situations where we've allowed the owner to stay in the property as a renter for many months after the sale. We negotiate a separate lease agreement, and provide discounted or even free rent in return for a lower sale price or other concessions at the time of the sale.

  Also, if you're purchasing from a landlord, keep in mind that the tenants will have the legal right to remain in the property through the end of their lease period. This may make it difficult for the landlord to sell to a retail buyer, and could provide you leverage when negotiating the sale.

- **Home warranty.** Offering a home warranty or asking the seller to provide one is another great negotiating tactic. As a seller, offering a home warranty can provide confidence to the buyer that they will not have to make any major repairs. As a buyer, the $400 to $600 the seller might spend on a warranty could save you some cash down the road if there any unexpected maintenance issues that are covered by the warranty.

- **Inspection reports.** When you're selling a home, getting an inspection on the house just prior to sale can provide buyers additional confidence in the purchase, which could translate into a higher purchase price or additional concessions during the negotiation. We will often get a post-renovation inspection and offer it to prospective buyers, giving them the opportunity to save money on their side by not needing to get their own inspection—though we typically will encourage them to do so anyway, for liability reasons.

  As investors, we tend to inspect homes both before and after we make repairs, just for our own benefit. This allows us to make any repairs an inspector might find during the sale process. But as long as we have the results of the inspection, we might as well use them as a concession to the buyer.

Those are just some of the terms and conditions of a real estate contract that can be negotiated; if you're creative, you can probably think of many more. And because every real estate deal is unique, in most deals you'll find additional opportunities for creative deal-making.

Before putting together your initial offer, we recommend making a list of all the terms beyond the price that you'd like to get from the deal and believe the other party would like to get from the deal. This is now your list of concessions that can be used to sweeten the deal for one or both parties throughout the negotiation.

CHAPTER 9
DELIVERING YOUR OFFER

Now that you've decided on the details of your opening bid, it's time to deliver your offer to the seller.

Agents involved in the transaction will obviously have a big impact on how the offer is delivered. If there are agents involved, they will almost certainly be the ones who manage the paperwork and the process. But even with agents, to ensure you have the greatest opportunity at a successful negotiation, there are many details of the process you can and should control.

If there are no agents involved in the transaction, it will be up to you to formally communicate your offer to the seller. How this is done can have a tremendous impact on whether the seller reacts positively or negatively toward the offer, and whether the negotiations proceed smoothly after the offer is made.

In this chapter, we'll discuss the details around formally preparing and communicating your offer to the seller, both with and without agents involved.

Make Most Offers in Writing

For a real estate offer to be legally binding, it must be in writing; but that's not the only reason why we make this suggestion. There are three other—even better—reasons why we suggest always putting real estate offers down on paper:

1. In our society, people ascribe more weight and seriousness to the

written word. While in many areas of contract law, a verbal agreement is considered legally binding, getting an agreement in writing is the best way to ensure that the other party actually follows through on their commitment. When someone sees something in writing, they naturally assume that it's more concrete than something that has simply been discussed; by getting (or offering) a contract in writing, you can be sure that the other party will take the agreement seriously and will be more likely to follow through on the terms. This is especially important given the long period of time it generally takes to get from agreement to closing in a real estate transaction.

2. Putting something in writing creates an emotional commitment. It's easy to throw out an offer without feeling attached to that offer, but when a buyer puts down an offer in writing and signs it, suddenly there is a psychological attachment to what has been written. Adding their signature to the paper has created an emotional extension of themselves in the offer, and once they sign and submit that offer, they're going to be more vested in the outcome. Getting a written offer will psychologically commit the other party to attempt to reach an agreement.

3. It's easy to "forget" all the terms of an offer not made in writing. Assuming you're going into a negotiation with the intent to be ethical, you're going to expect the other party to do the same. When a party makes a verbal offer, it's very easy to later come back and say, "I never agreed to that." When something is captured in writing, it's difficult to argue that it wasn't the true intent at the time of the writing, and it's difficult for either party to later argue that they didn't offer or agree to something. Not to mention, if a contract dispute ends up in court, the first thing a judge is going to ask for is a copy of the agreement.

Now, for these reasons, we could argue that when you're the party making an offer, there are some benefits to *not* putting it in writing—for example, no emotional commitment on your part and the ability to later change your offer. But, in general, we believe that the benefits of always putting your offers in writing outweigh the benefits of trying to get an advantage over the other party by not doing so.

To take this a step further, most smart sellers and almost all agents will refuse to respond to a verbal offer. They will want to see everything in writing so they know exactly what they are getting—and giving—in the transaction. Remember, a real estate sale is typically the most expensive transaction the other party will likely ever make; it's not surprising that even those who have no negotiating experience will want any offer to purchase to be in writing.

All that said, while you should always prepare your offers in writing, whenever possible you should discuss the offer with the seller before handing over the written offer. Later in this chapter, we'll talk about presenting your offer to sellers who aren't represented by an agent; as we'll discuss, you will present your offer verbally, but with the written offer in plain view to reinforce the discussion.

Use State or Attorney Approved Contracts

If you're offering to buy a property represented by an agent, it's almost certain that you will need to use a state approved real estate contract to create your offer. This is because—for liability reasons—most agents and their brokers will only accept offers on state-approved contract templates.

While these contracts can be lengthy and have a lot of legalese, they do a good job of including language that will protect all parties in the transaction. Which means that by using these contracts, you can generally be assured that there are no major loopholes for the seller to take advantage of you.

When you are making an offer to a seller who isn't represented by an agent, you may still be able to use a standard contract for your state, but we generally recommend against it.

The benefit of the state contract is that it may put a seller's mind at ease knowing that you're not roping him into a one-sided legal agreement that doesn't have his best interests at heart. But, there are several significant drawbacks to using a state contract:

- These contracts tend to be long and confusing to those who don't have a legal or real estate background. The sheer length of the contract can overwhelm a seller and force him to think about whether he's qualified to be selling his house without an agent or attorney.
- Many state contracts require *addendums* to make them legal. These are additional legal pages that add information and make disclosures. If you don't completely understand the state contracts, it's

very easy to make a procedural mistake that could deem the entire contract invalid or void.

- Depending on your state, the standard real estate contract may be copyrighted, meaning that it could be illegal to use the contract if you're not a licensed real estate agent or broker.

With that in mind, if you make offers to sellers who don't have agent representation, you should work with a local real estate attorney to draw up a custom contract that will contain many of the same clauses and protections as the standard state contract, but will be much shorter and written with less legalese so that even untrained sellers will understand it.

Keep Offers as Simple as Possible

People will always be more receptive to offers that they fully understand and that are easy for them to be able to "get their head around." In practical terms, this means combining terms or contingencies, rolling together any expenses and credits that you might ask for or offer, and avoiding any confusing or hard-to-explain requests.

We suggest always trying to condense your offer into as few terms and contingencies as possible.

Here's an example of this that I learned early on.

⸝⸝ TALES FROM THE TRENCHES ⸝⸝

In 2009, I got my real estate license. From that point on, I started making offers on houses represented by a listing agent and where I was representing myself as the buyer. As the agent on the buyer side, I was typically entitled to half the commission on the transaction. But I didn't get my license to make extra money—for me, it was the ability to better control my deals. So as an incentive to the seller, I used to add into my contracts that I would waive my side of the commission and allow the seller to keep it as part of the sale price.

Considering that half the commission was generally 3 percent of the sale price, if I were to offer $200,000 for a property, the seller would actually be collecting $206,000 at closing (the extra $6,000 being my 3 percent of the commission). After doing this a few times, one day I found myself in a tough negotiation with a particular seller. I had waived my side of the commission, but we were still about $5,000 apart on price and neither of us was willing to budge. I really wanted this deal, so I decided to increase my purchase price by $5,000 to make the deal happen.

At the closing table, the seller got a copy of the settlement statement (the paper that had all the financials for the transaction) and remarked that they were surprised that they would be walking away with about $7,000 more than they had expected. After listening to their agent discuss it with them, I realized that they didn't understand that my waiving my side of the commission was going to put many thousands of extra dollars in their pocket!

They understood what I was doing, but they never really did the math on how much it added to their bottom line. In other words, I offered a concession worth several thousand dollars and the other party never realized the value of it. *I had basically thrown away $7,000!*

At that point, I realized that my adding this clause to the contract was hurting me more than helping me. I was giving up a bunch of money, but because sellers didn't necessarily "get it," I wasn't getting the full benefit of the concession.

After that deal, I stopped automatically including this clause in my contracts. Instead, if I was willing to pay extra for the property (in our example, if I was willing to pay $206,000 instead of $200,000), I started just adding the extra amount to the offer price and then just collected my commission in the typical way at the closing.

The seller was getting the same amount either way; I was getting the same amount either way; and the listing agent was getting the same amount either way. But by removing the clause from the contract, everything appeared simpler to the seller, there was less explanation that had to go into the offer, and there was no added confusion.

Best Practices When Dealing with the Seller

Agents have a lot of experience presenting offers and receiving offers on behalf of their clients, and the good ones have learned what to say and how to say it when explaining offers to their buyers and sellers. When there are no agents involved in the transaction, the extra responsibility for ensuring that the offer process goes smoothly falls on your shoulders.

And if you want this process to go smoothly—giving you the best opportunity to build momentum in the negotiation—there are a few rules you will want to follow.

Always Deal with the Decision Maker

Let's start with a simple concept that is too often overlooked by novice negotiators:

Never start a negotiation until you're confident that you are dealing with the decision maker. And not just *one* of the decision makers—you want to ensure that *everyone* who is required to make a final decision on the deal is present for all aspects of a negotiation.

When you deal with someone who doesn't have the authority to enter into an agreement, you may then have to repeat the entire negotiation with the person who can make the decision.

In some cases, the reason you're not negotiating with the person who will make the final decision is innocuous—a husband assumes his wife will agree with his decision and doesn't involve her in the talks, or one of the owners of the property doesn't realize that there is someone else on the deed whose signature is needed to complete the deal.

In other cases, the opposing party may be trying to get the upper hand in the deal and is inserting a *gatekeeper* (the initial negotiator who doesn't have the authority to agree to a deal) into the situation. The gatekeeper's job is to negotiate the best deal possible and make you think the deal is imminent, and then hand you off to (or team up with) the ultimate decision maker to grind you down even more.

QUICK TIP *If a person is trying to look tough in front of their spouse or partner, try to get the person alone so they can make concessions without losing face. Often, a person will want to look tough in front of their spouse, and if you risk making them look weak, you can bet the deal is going to go south very quickly.*

Regardless of how you ended up negotiating with someone who doesn't have the authority to make a decision, the outcome for you is going to be worse, as you end up having multiple negotiations over the same deal.

This is going to result in a suboptimal outcome for you because, in the original negotiation, you gave information about what you would accept from the deal. The later negotiator can, and likely will, use that information against you.

So, how do you determine if you're dealing with the decision maker(s) when you start your discussion? One way is to simply ask.

If you've ever walked onto a car lot and talked with a salesman, you know that very early in the discussion, they will ask something along the lines of, "If we can agree on a great price on a great car, are you ready to buy today?"

There are two reasons for asking that question. First, the salesman wants to know if you're a serious buyer or just a tire kicker, so he can determine how much time he wants to spend with you. If you were to say, "I'm just starting my car search and don't really need a new car until the summer, so I'm not actually going to be buying today," you can bet the salesman is going to spend less time and attention on you than if you were to say, "Heck yeah! My car died yesterday and if I don't buy something today, I can't get to work tomorrow."

The second reason for asking this question is to determine if you have the authority to make the purchase. By asking you if you have the intention of buying a car today, he is giving you the opportunity to affirm that you have the ability to make that decision. If you were to answer his question about buying with, "Well, I can't buy anything without my spouse seeing the car and taking a test drive," there's a good chance he'll try to talk you into coming back with your partner before he spends much time with you.

In a real estate transaction, there are several ways you can determine if you're dealing with the decision maker. As we mentioned above, in many cases, it may be easiest to ask flat out, "Are you the one who will make the final decision on this purchase?" This is especially important when dealing with a business entity such as an investor, hedge fund, or institutional buyer or seller where you don't know if the person you're speaking with has the authority to write a check.

To avoid dealing with someone who thinks they're the decision maker but *isn't*, the best question to ask is, "Is yours the only name on the title?" If the answer is "yes," you can safely assume the person(s) you're speaking with has the legal authority to sell the property. But if the response is, "My mom was a co-signer on the purchase, so her name is on the title as well," you now know there will be another decision maker in the mix, at least from a legal perspective.

I have seen several situations where a seller has signed a contract to sell his property, only for the title company to later realize that this person wasn't the only one on the deed. When that happens, the contract is invalid, and negotiations must start again, this time including *all* the people who legally own the property.

If you determine that the person you're dealing with is not the decision maker, you shouldn't necessarily terminate your discussion. This can come off as rude and send the message that you don't care about their input.

Instead, while avoiding giving any indication as to your negotiating position, try to get as much information as you can from the other party. Use your time with the "non-decision maker" to learn new insights that will assist when you do find yourself dealing with the decision maker. Many times the non-decision maker will be a key influencer, so it is crucial you help them feel confident in you and your proposition.

Presenting Your Offer/Priming

When presenting an offer to a seller, there should be a written contract that details all of the terms and conditions of that offer. But, we don't recommend just handing a contract to the seller and waiting for them to read through it.

There are several potential negative consequences that can result from just handing (or emailing) a contract to a seller:

- The seller may not understand what you've handed him. While some aspects of a real estate contract are going to be pretty straightforward, such as the price, there are going to be other terms and contingencies that the seller may not fully understand. If you hand the seller a legal contract and they don't understand something, they may get intimidated and embarrassed. Instead of asking for clarification, they might just shut down and refuse to continue the negotiation.
- The seller may want to argue point by point as he goes through the contract. Without presenting the offer in a structured way, the seller may read the very first term in the contract (which is often the price) and decide not to read any further until there is an agreement on that term. Because an offer is a collection of terms and contingencies, you don't want to start negotiation on one piece of an offer until

the other party fully understands the entire offer.

- The seller may be so anxious to find out what you're offering him that he doesn't read the contract carefully, and misses (or ignores) some of the terms and contingencies. You could find yourself negotiating a completely different offer than the other party thinks they're negotiating, as they skipped (or misread) several of the terms you included in the offer.

For these reasons, it's important that before a seller reads your written offer, you have a discussion to summarize the offer. This way, you control the information that the seller is receiving and you can clarify each aspect of your offer as confusion arises.

There is another important reason to present your offer through a face-to-face discussion, as opposed to just handing it to the seller. This is your opportunity to use *priming* to your advantage.

Priming is the idea that people are susceptible to certain emotional reactions based on the situations, feelings and words presented to them previously. As an example, a study done in 1992 had a wine store alternately play French and German music. What they found was that customers were much more likely to purchase French wine when the French music was playing and were much more likely to purchase German wine when German music was playing.

Without realizing it, customers took sensory clues around them (the music) and translated those cues into desires and actions (which wine they purchased).

We can use the same general principle to help ensure a seller has a positive reaction to our offer. By starting our discussion with information and ideas that the seller finds agreeable, we can create a positive emotional state leading up to the more contentious aspects of our offer.

Specifically, you should try to prime the other party for your offer by starting the discussion with all the aspects of the offer you believe they will be happy with. Elicit as many affirmative responses from the seller ("Yes," "Okay," "That's great," "Sure," etc.) as possible before suggesting anything they might find contentious or might disagree with.

For example, you might place the written offer on the table between you and the seller, and then have a conversation similar to the following:

Investor: *"Thank you for giving me the opportunity to look at your home and to make you an offer to purchase it. I brought a written contract for each of us to sign to formalize an agreement, but first, I just wanted to have a discussion to summarize what's in the contract. Is that okay?"*

Seller: *"Okay."*

Investor: *"Great! As we discussed, you are looking to close as quickly as possible on the sale. I talked to my attorney, and he thinks he can get all the paperwork and title work done in ten days. If we sign the contract today, that means we can close next Thursday, July 14. Does that day work for you?"*

Seller: *"Yeah, that would be great."*

Investor: *"Awesome. Now, just to protect your interests between now and then, my attorney has recommended that I make an earnest money deposit of $500. I'll give this money to the title company to hold, and it basically means that if for some reason I don't follow through on my end of the agreement, you get to keep that $500, no questions asked. Sound good?"*

Seller: *"Sure. I'm good with that."*

Investor: *"Excellent. Now, everything looks great with the property based on what I could see, but I'd like to have my contractor do a walk through as well, since he's the expert. The contract basically says that I have five days to get my contractor to do a walk-through. Assuming he doesn't find any surprises, all is good. If he does find something that I missed, we can sit down again and discuss how to proceed. Are you okay with my contractor doing a walk-through tomorrow or Wednesday?"*

Seller: *"I guess that shouldn't be a problem."*

Investor: *"Great! Now, I know we talked about the fact that you want $110,000 for the house. I already mentioned that I'd be purchasing your* *house as an investment, and unfortunately, I just can't afford to pay that much and still be able to make a profit on the deal. But, here's what I can do. I can either pay you $90,000 in cash for the property or I can pay you $100,000 if you're willing to owner finance the sale. That means we would complete the sale in ten days, but you would wait six months to collect your $100,000. Which of those options would you prefer?"*

At this point, if you've done a good job of selecting your offer prices (e.g., you weren't too generous), there is a good chance the seller isn't going to accept either of those offers without some additional negotiation.

The good news is that we've gotten the seller to implicitly agree to all the other terms and contingencies in the contract. Not only that, but we've now given the seller two options for the sale price, and his response to your final question ("Which of those options would you prefer?") will give insight into which direction the negotiation goes.

If the seller indicates that he might be willing to wait to get his cash, you can start to negotiate seller finance terms. If he indicates that he's not willing to wait, you can start to negotiate the sale price.

QUICK TIP *Be careful about going into too much detail on your offer price—if you give too much information, you may give the seller ammunition to argue. For example, if you say:*

"I can only resell this house for $200,000, so I can't pay more than $100,000."

The seller may be thinking, "He's making $100,000 in profit and HE'S STILL NOT HAPPY!" Sellers likely don't understand the financial aspects of your business (rehab costs, mortgage costs, closing costs, etc.) and now isn't the time to explain to them how your business works.

Be Confident/Don't Justify/Listen

Once you present your offer, you may feel the urge to justify a low price or some term or contingency in the contract that the seller might find unacceptable.

Resist this urge!

By justifying your offer before the seller provides a response, you are subtly communicating that you know the offer isn't going to be satisfactory and you are inviting a debate.

Instead, present the offer confidently, and then *shut up* and give the other party the opportunity to draw his own conclusions. Once you present the offer, sit back and just let them process what you have said.

When they start talking, don't interrupt. Many times, people will attempt to sort out their thoughts by talking through them. As they talk, you should just listen. If they ask a specific question, answer them, and then let them speak again.

By sitting back and listening, you may find that the seller isn't as offended by the offer as you suspected he would be (or even should be). You may find that the seller is okay with the parts of the offer you were concerned about. Or you may find that he has issues with other parts of the offer that you hadn't considered would be a problem.

Ultimately, the seller will accept your offer, reject your offer, or suggest a counteroffer. At this point, the bargaining begins and all of the information the seller provided in their response to your offer will help guide you on how to proceed.

QUICK TIP *Never force "high status" people to lose face in front of "lower status" people. For example, don't demean a real estate agent in front of her broker or a lender in front of his boss.*

Best Practices When Offering through Agents

When you submit an offer on a listed property through an agent, your role of communicator is very much diminished. You'll rarely ever speak with the seller directly, and unless you're a licensed agent representing yourself or you're making an offer without your own agent, it's unlikely you'll be speaking to the listing agent either.

But just because your direct line of contact with the seller and the listing agent is cut off, that doesn't mean you can't communicate to both the seller and the agent through your agent. In fact, this agent-to-agent communication is essential if you want to give yourself the best opportunity at a good deal.

Here are some rules for how you can get the most out of your offers when there is a listing agent as the gateway to the seller.

Communicate in Advance

Good listing agents are busy. They have lots of listings and get lots of offers. Oftentimes, a buyer's agent will call in advance and let the listing agent know that an offer is on the way; but sometimes, a buyer's agent will just email an offer without any notice or warning.

But, just like we did with the seller in our example above, when submitting an offer to a listing agent, it's good practice to review the offer before they start reading the contract. This minimizes any chance of confusion from any terms or contingencies in the offer, and also provides another opportunity to build some rapport with the listing agent, who will have a big influence on the seller.

For example, we often submit offers on behalf of other investors, and prior to submitting the offer we'll call the listing agent. The conversation might go like this:

Buyer's Agent: *"Hi [listing agent's name], this is Mark Ferguson from [brokerage name]. I just wanted to let you know that I'm getting ready to send over an offer for [property address]. Would you prefer I fax that or email it?"*

Listing Agent: *"Email would be great. The email address is in the listing."*

Buyer's Agent: *"Got it, thanks. Just to let you know, my client is an active investor—he buys several properties per year, and is very easy to work with. The offer is an all cash deal with a quick close and just a few small contingencies. Because this would be an investment for my client, and given the condition of the property, we unfortunately can't offer the list price. There is a good bit of work that my client would have to do to get it fixed up and some of the issues are going to be expensive to address. We hope the seller won't be insulted by the offer price—this most certainly isn't our intent. That said, we do have a little bit of wiggle room, so we hope the seller will keep an open mind and will consider our offer."*

Notice that we took the opportunity on the phone to warn the listing agent that the offer would be low, and we also provided some justification for why the offer was low. While we wouldn't have done that right off the bat if we were working directly with the seller, in this case it's important. That's because, if the seller reacts negatively, we won't be there to explain or justify our offer.

We've given the listing agent some ammunition to explain our rationale for the low offer to the seller. Not only did we mention that the buyer was an investor—so the numbers matter above all else—but we also mentioned the rough condition of the property. This subconsciously reminds the agent that the property could be difficult to sell, and gives the agent some incentive to have the seller consider the offer rather than dismissing it outright.

QUICK TIP *If the seller goes with another offer/buyer, ask to have yours be held as a back-up. Deals fall through all the time, and if the seller knows that you'll still be interested, if a problem arises with their other buyer, they may choose to come back to you directly versus putting the house back on the market.*

Summarize Your Offer

When working directly with the seller, we talked about not just handing them the written offer. Instead, we first review the offer with the seller, allowing them to digest the most important points without having to flip through lots of pages of legalese.

When we don't have the luxury of sitting down and explaining our offer to the seller directly, we instead will provide a bullet-point summary that will help the seller digest the offer more easily.

That summary might look like this:

Thank you for considering our offer on your property at 123 Main Street!

Here is a quick summary of our offer:

Purchase Price: $100,000

Earnest Money: $1,000

Closing Date: September 26

Inspection Period: 7 Days

Financing Contingency: 30 Days

Note that the buyer is an investor who purchases several properties per year and has an excellent relationship with his mortgage broker—we have included a pre-approval letter along with the offer, and we expect a smooth transaction.

We like to include this summary not only in the email/fax to the listing agent, but also as the first page of the contract. This gives the best opportunity for the seller to see it without the listing agent removing it from the package.

If there are any other special circumstances or additional reasons why the seller may want to consider your offer over other offers, this is the place to include it.

QUICK TIP *If you know for a fact that the seller will be receiving other offers, do your best to have yours delivered or presented last. Your agent may even be able to get information about offers that were presented before yours. We've even seen situations where a listing agent will tell the buyer's agent what price they need to hit to get their offer accepted.*

Best Practices When You're the Agent

We wanted to talk about one final scenario when offering on listed properties: when you're licensed and you're representing yourself as the buyer's agent. In these situations, you'll get some of the benefits of being able to communicate directly with the other party, and you'll also get some additional leverage.

Extra Commissions

As the buyer agent for your own properties, you will typically be entitled to half of the agent's commission on the deal. While you can keep this cash to offset some of your costs, or use it to offset a higher purchase price, the other option is to offer up some or all of this commission to the listing agent as a bonus.

Since listing agents work purely on commission, this extra cash can provide an incredible incentive for the listing agent to encourage the seller to consider your offer over others.

We'll typically communicate the fact that we're relinquishing our commission to the listing agent during the phone call informing them that the offer is being sent. And, because commission agreements are typically handled separately from the sales contract, the fact that you are handing your commission to the listing agent won't need to be discussed with the seller as part of the offer, reducing the chance of extra confusion on the seller's part.

Let the Listing Agent Sell the Home

If you feel that offering an incentive to the listing agent will help get an agreement with the seller, there's another incentive available. If you will be flipping the property, you can offer to allow the listing agent to resell the property for you after you have renovated it and are ready to put it back on the market.

Listing agents make their money by selling houses. If you can help fill their future deal pipeline, you can be sure they will be rooting for you and may be able to offer you support and assistance in coming to an agreement with their client.

Timing of Offers on Listed Properties

It's typically more difficult to sell a home in the winter than it is in the spring or summer, as there are fewer buyers who are looking to move. As a buyer, if you are looking for houses in the winter, there is a better opportunity to find great deals because sellers are more desperate to sell.

Pretty obvious, huh?

There are plenty of other rules of thumb for when to make offers that are less obvious, but just as effective. This is especially true with listed properties where you are competing with other potential buyers.

In some cases, these rules can also help you when offering on off-market properties.

Here are a few of these rules of thumb to consider:

- **Winter offers.** As we mentioned above, in the winter months (December, January, and even February) sellers tend to be more motivated. There are fewer buyers during this time, curb appeal tends to be at a minimum (it's hard to get good pictures when the house is covered with snow), and the holidays aren't a great time to be scheduling showings and walk-throughs. Especially in northern states where there are tough winters, sellers may be exceptionally motivated to sell, and may be willing to accept an offer much lower than they otherwise would.

- **Beginning/end of month offers.** The very end or the very beginning of the month is often a good time to make offers. Sellers typically make their mortgage payments at the beginning of the month, and it's the week leading up to this payment that sellers may be thinking about how nice it would be to get their house under contract and be able to avoid having to make more payments. Once they've made their payment for the month, the thought of the following month's payment is still weeks away. If you can capture a seller's attention with an offer while they're thinking about that next payment, you may be able to catch them at a weak moment and convince them to accept something lower than they otherwise would.

- **Long holiday offers.** Over Christmas and New Year's break, it's almost always tougher to sell a house than before or after the holiday. If a seller has their house listed during this period of time, they're likely more motivated than average to get their house sold. Likewise, buyers tend to be few and far between during this period, so sellers aren't getting many showings or offers. If you have the ability to look at homes and make offers over long holidays, you may find yourself getting some great deals.

- **Three-day weekend offers.** Buyer traffic tends to be slower on three-day holiday weekends (Memorial Day, Fourth of July, Labor Day, etc.). Sellers typically expect that they won't get an offer the week before or the week after the long weekend, and those sellers who are more motivated will welcome an offer during these ten-day periods. In other words, you may be able to get a lower offer accepted if you make it just before or just after a three-day weekend, as motivated sellers recognize it may be their only opportunity to sell during this period.

- **Tuesday offers.** Tuesdays are a great time to get good deals on listed properties. Most buyer traffic comes through on the weekends when buyers are off of work and agents hold open houses. Some are hoping to get offers on Sunday evening and Monday, and should Tuesday come around without an offer in hand, sellers get dejected. They realize that the buyers who saw the house the previous weekend likely weren't interested in making an offer, and new potential buyers likely won't come around until the following weekend. Sellers may be more willing to consider a lower offer on Tuesday than any other day.

DIG DEEP *In many markets, there are other driving forces around when is the best (and worst) time to be making offers and buying houses. For example, if you live anywhere near Washington, D.C., you'll probably find that the real estate market tends to be frenzied every four years when a new administration takes office.*

CHAPTER 10
NEGOTIATING TACTICS

Now that we've submitted our offer to the seller, it's time for the real action to begin. If your offer was neither too aggressive nor too generous, the seller should respond with a counteroffer. Once you receive that counteroffer, the ball is back in your court, and your next several moves will be crucial to whether you come to an agreement.

In this chapter, we're going to talk about tactics you can use to keep momentum going in the negotiation, and also to ensure that you're keeping control of the process. Many of these tactics aren't specific to real estate transactions; they can be used in nearly any type of negotiation. These are some of the same tactics that expert negotiators use to achieve optimal results when they're closing a deal.

Plan Your Strategy Upfront

By this point, you've likely interacted a good bit with the seller, or—if the seller is represented by an agent—you have a reasonable idea of how cooperative the listing agent and seller are going to be. Before jumping into the back and forth bargaining, it's important to have a plan on how you will approach the bargaining phase. This is especially true if you'll be face-to-face with the seller.

A common mistake many up-and-coming negotiators make is to assume that the stereotypical negotiator persona—tough, stoic, and hard-nosed—will get them what they want. In reality, the exact opposite is often true. Especially when dealing with novice negotiators, any actions that can be interpreted as "bullying" are likely to intimidate the other party and get them to withdraw from the discussion.

While not every negotiation should be approached in the same way, it's typically the case that a friendly and collaborative approach is going to be the most beneficial to reaching an agreement. That said, it's important to gauge the other party's general attitude toward getting things done.

Are they detail oriented? If so, it may be worthwhile to avoid talking only in big picture terms. Are they the "get it done" type? If so, avoid small talk, don't drag out discussions and focus on the big items that each party needs out of the agreement.

By tailoring the discussions to the other party's personality, you keep them engaged and in their comfort zone. Unless you're dealing with an expert negotiator, helping the other party stay in their comfort zone will help keep the momentum going in the discussion.

In addition to the other party's personality, it's also important to assess their attitude toward the negotiation. If they lack basic information to have an informed discussion, spend some time educating them (in a non-condescending fashion).

For example, if the seller thinks her house is worth $200,000 and the data indicates it's worth $80,000, spending some time walking her through the data will do more to get her to consider a lower price than any amount of back-and-forth bargaining. At the same time, you'll be *listening* to her, especially after you gently inquire as to why she believes the property is worth $200,000. She may tell you something revealing about why she's selling the house and what she hopes to accomplish.

DIG DEEP *If the other party is acting unreasonable in their requests, take the opportunity to go back to building better rapport. For example, if the seller starts to get angry about an offer you've proposed, that's typically the result of a lack of trust—the seller doesn't believe you care about her wants and needs. Instead of continuing to discuss the offer, go back to a friendlier discussion, listen to her, and remind her how you are attempting to help her solve whatever problem selling her house will solve.*

Remember, to you the negotiation is over a house. To most sellers, the negotiation is over their *home*. When dealing with something as personal as the sale of a home, many sellers are likely to exhibit a range of emotional responses. It's your job to project empathy toward those feelings, while at the same time guiding the seller toward a mutually beneficial agreement.

QUICK TIP *Don't let negotiations ever become too tense. Try to keep things light by smiling, interjecting with small talk, and making jokes. Negotiations that are too serious often end up failing and creating hard feelings between the parties.*

Focus on Things Both Sides Agree on

When opening a negotiation, you'll find that it's much easier to build momentum and keep the discussion moving forward when you find and focus on things that both sides agree on. Many inexperienced negotiators will get discouraged if an agreement doesn't come quickly—they don't understand that the process can be long and that it often takes many rounds of back and forth before an agreement is reached.

By focusing on the agreeable issues, the other party will get the sense that progress is being made—that an agreement is on the horizon—and they will be more inclined to continue moving forward with the discussions.

For example, you might write down a counteroffer and say to a seller:

Investor: *"Okay, it sounds like we both agree on the major points— we're going to pay for the property in cash, we'll close on your preferred date of February 16, and my partner will need to see the property and sign off on the deal. Now, all we need to do is come together on price. I know you said that you couldn't do $87,500—what if I can increase my offer to $90,000, and we include a five-day inspection period for me to bring in my contractors to take a look at the property? Will that work for you?"*

In this case, even if the parties were far apart in price, we're sending the message to the seller that we're actually pretty close to a deal. In fact, I like to reiterate all the things we agree upon *every* time I make a counteroffer.

This is also a great tactic if negotiations ever stall—revisit the things both parties agree upon and remind the seller of more of those things that may not have been discussed for a while.

For example, if things have come to a standstill in the negotiation, you might say:

Investor: *"I know we haven't yet agreed on price, but I think we're pretty close here. Remember, we're happy to take the house as-is— you don't have to clean out the basement or the garage. And our title company is happy to come here to your house to sign all the paperwork, just to make everything more convenient. My offer of $90,000 really is my top number, but I want you to be confident you are getting a great deal, so I'll give up some of my profit and go to $91,500. Can we close on that?"*

QUICK TIP *If you cannot agree on minor issues, put them aside and complete the main agreement. With the main agreement completed, you'll find minor issues are far easier to settle.*

Keep in mind that if you're working with real estate agents, you can't do as much back and forth, so this tactic will be harder. But you can always include a note with your offer that stresses the most appealing points of the offer terms.

For example, your note might say:

"Our offer is enclosed. We're excited about getting this deal closed quickly and because we don't have any contingencies in our offer, we expect this to be a stress-free transaction for Mr. and Mrs. Smith."

In this case, you've highlighted a point that's likely very important to the sellers—no contingencies in the contract—which hopefully communicates to them that an agreement is right around the corner.

Friction Is Your Friend

At a superficial level, a negotiation that ends quickly and doesn't involve a lot of back and forth may seem quite successful. In reality, the opposite is generally true. It's human nature to place a higher value on things that cost us more, whether that cost is paid in money or in effort.

Think about the last time the other party in a negotiation accepted your offer without too much hemming and hawing. Were you elated? Or was there that little nagging voice in the back of your head telling you that you didn't get as good of a deal as you should have gotten? That the very fact that the other party didn't put up much of a fight meant that they were really happy with the deal, which can only mean that you got the short end of the stick?

Whether you actually did get the short end of the stick or not, people like to feel like they have *earned* something. Like they've worked hard to accomplish a well-deserved goal. And in my experience, parties are more likely to end up backing out of deals that progress too quickly and smoothly, simply because they didn't feel like the other side put up enough resistance.

Good negotiators embrace the friction of negotiation! They'll even manufacture it, if necessary. Especially in real estate transactions, where parties have a long time (days, weeks, or even months) in which they can walk away, it's essential for people to buy into the negotiation through an investment of effort and time. The harder you make them work during the negotiation, the less chance they'll back out when the negotiating comes to a close.

TALES FROM THE TRENCHES

In a community where I had recently purchased a rental property, I decided to make offers on several townhouses. Since I had one property in the neighborhood that was making me money, I figured it was worth trying to get more. There were several townhouses for sale and I decided to submit low offers on all of them, in order to see if any of the sellers were desperate enough to even consider my low offer.

One particular townhouse was listed at $78,000. I decided that I'd probably be willing to pay somewhere around $60,000 for it. Keeping in line with my decision to start by submitting low offers,

I wrote up an offer for $50,150. I had hoped the seller would come back with a counteroffer somewhere closer to the $60,000 I was willing to pay, at which point I'd attempt to close the deal.

To my surprise, the seller accepted my $50,150 without any negotiation. I should have been thrilled—I had just gotten an offer accepted at about $10,000 less than I was willing to pay!

But, I wasn't thrilled. In fact, I was completely deflated. Even though intellectually I knew that I had gotten a great deal, there was a part of me that wondered if I was missing something—was the house worth a lot less than I thought it was? And even if I wasn't missing anything, I still felt as if I could have gotten a better deal— why hadn't I offered $40,000 instead?

Ultimately, I went through with the purchase. But, to this day, the whole deal still doesn't sit well with me. Ironically enough, I would have been happier with the deal had the seller countered my offer and had made me pay more.

A little friction would have gone a long way.

So, how do you introduce friction into a negotiation that seems to be going too smoothly? Simple—ask for more concessions!

In other words, even if the other party is willing to give you everything you want, ask for a little bit more. For example, if you list a property and get ten offers, with one of them being well over list price and no other conditions, you should still counter the offer. Perhaps only ask for $500 more. Or ask for an earlier closing date. Or ask for more earnest money.

It doesn't have to be a big concession you're asking for—just enough that the other party feels like you weren't overly ecstatic with the original offer. That way, the other party can at least think to themselves, "They didn't just accept our original offer... I guess we didn't offer way too much."

QUICK TIP *If the other party makes an offer that is so generous that you'd be uncomfortable asking for any additional concessions, then take a nice, long pause before you accept it. This pause will hopefully introduce enough friction into the transaction that they don't realize they offered too much.*

Use Documentation

In our society, things that are written down tend to carry more weight than the spoken word. This is true, regardless of whether or not the documentation is "official." Heck, even just the *notion* of a written document can create an air of legitimacy.

I recently saw a perfect example of this ...

}} TALES *FROM THE* TRENCHES {{

Just before his inauguration as president of the United States, Donald Trump held a press conference to discuss—among other things—divesting himself of control of his businesses. There was concern among many that he wasn't taking this issue seriously, and this was an opportunity for him to describe his plan. Next to him on a long table were dozens of stacked folders, each folder thick with papers.

Trending on Twitter throughout the news conference was discussion of what, specifically, was in those folders. Unfortunately, we never found out. While Trump's attorney alluded to the fact that the folders contained documents related to transitioning control of his businesses, the folders were never opened or discussed specifically.

But the contents of the folders didn't matter. Whether they were filled with legal documents, blank paper (as some suggested), or even the Sunday comics, the goal of having those folders piled high next to him wasn't to prove anything to anyone. The goal was to psychologically manipulate the media and the general public into more fully accepting the legitimacy of Trump's business plans and to send the message that his business transition was more than just a bunch of talk.

You see, Donald Trump—well known as a strong negotiator—understands the value of the written word when it comes to persuasion. While he could have presented actual documentation (and who knows, it might have been), he recognized just the appearance of having official documents would be enough to create the perception that he was taking his plan seriously, and so should we.

While we don't recommend that you ever create fake documentation or carry around folders of blank paper, the lesson here is that writing things down—or having things written down by others—can send the message that your position is more than just talk. That it is more than just your opinion.

A great example of how I use documentation to support my offers is that I bring a blank worksheet whenever I do a walk-through of a property. As I walk through the house, I make notes, take some measurements, and fill in a bunch of line-item rehab values. At the bottom of the worksheet, I have a line in big print that says:

TOTAL REHAB ESTIMATE: $_____

On that line, I add up the values above, write in the final number in very large print, and circle it.

The truth is, I can do my rehab estimates in my head, and I don't typically need to write things down. I certainly don't need a line-by-line estimate.

But by creating the written estimate, with a big number circled at the bottom, I'm providing legitimacy for my conclusion about the cost to rehab the house. Since I'm going to later use this rehab estimate to convince the seller that I can't pay as much for the property as he might like, it's important to me that he believes that number. The fact that I have something written down—even if it's just my own numbers—will psychologically add credibility to my claim.

Here are some other examples of written documentation that you can bring to your negotiations to support your offers:
- Inspection reports.
- Mortgage pre-qualification/pre-approval letter.
- Comparables printed from the MLS.
- Property appraisals.
- Public data that highlights plans for future growth or possible causes of contraction in your area.
- Reports, articles, and any other information from trustworthy sources that may shed light onto the past and potential future of the local real estate market.
- Graphs and charts that support any claims you are making.

Use Experts

What's even more effective than written documentation? Presenting information that comes directly from an expert source. Individuals who possess expertise in a certain area, industry, or field of knowledge can wield power within negotiations, and utilizing their expertise transfers some of their power to your position.

Do you have any education, professional qualifications, or affiliations that would position you as an expert to the other party? For example, if you have your real estate license, make sure that the other party is aware of it, and make sure to repeat that fact any time you provide information or data where a real estate agent would be considered an expert.

Not a real estate agent? How about an inspector? An appraiser? Previously worked for a lender? Used to be a contractor?

Even if you don't have any expert qualifications, an association with an expert can go a long way toward providing weight to your data. For example, my wife is licensed, so I might say to a seller, "My wife is a licensed agent, and she's sold a lot of houses in this area. She's found that after the summer selling season, values tend to drop by up to 8 percent. For that reason, I really can't offer you the same amount that I could have three months ago."

This information is likely to be much better received than had I said, "In my experience, prices tend to drop a good bit after the summer." My wife's perceived expertise (and the specificity of the data I provided) adds a level of legitimacy that I wouldn't have been able to provide on my own.

When negotiations get tough, great negotiators are often willing to call in experts who can corroborate their assertions. For example, what if the other party doesn't believe that it will cost you $80,000 to renovate the property? Bring in a builder or general contractor who can provide you a detailed bid. Sometimes bringing in an expert can cost a few bucks, but if you've gotten good at negotiating, you should be able to figure out a way to transfer that cost onto the other party.

Again, this is more difficult when working through real estate agents, but it can still be done. Don't hesitate to have your agent walk the listing agent through comps that support your offer, and then follow up with an email that contains copies of those comps. If you have an inspection report on the property, make sure that the listing agent gets a copy of the report. Seeing the inspector's comments first-hand is much more convincing than getting a summary from you or your agent.

Don't Lie

If you ask people if they think lying in a negotiation is acceptable, many will answer, "Isn't that just part of the game?"

Back in the 16th century, ambassador and philosopher Niccolò Machiavelli wrote the book, *The Prince*. Generally considered a political treatise, the book has also been used as a model for how lies and deception can be used to dominate ruthless negotiation. When it comes to getting what you want, Machiavelli believed that deception was not only perfectly acceptable but downright desirable.

Five hundred years ago, he wrote:

> *"A deceitful man will always find plenty who want to be deceived."*

In other words, *caveat emptor,* or buyer beware.

While there's no doubt that Machiavelli was a great strategist, a lot has changed in the past 500 years. Unlike in the past, you have to expect that everyone you deal with these days will have easy access to the ultimate lie detector—Google.

More importantly, if you get caught in a lie even once, there's a good chance the other party will never trust you again.

But we're not saying you need to blab everything all at once! Negotiation is like a good game of poker—you don't cheat, but neither do you show your cards. Especially when you're asked questions like, "What's your bottom line?" a little flexibility in opinion that doesn't cross the line into outright, verifiable deception is an indispensable tool in the negotiator's arsenal.

In other words, always expect the other party to be savvy enough that they'll do their own research, especially if your claims seem far-fetched. And, the real estate industry tends to be pretty tight-knit. If you work in the real estate game for any length of time, you'll get to know the other players and your reputation will precede you in any negotiation. Always maintain a reputation that will work *for* you instead of *against* you.

If you think the other party is concealing information, try asking questions you already know the answer to. "What do you owe on your mortgage?" "Where are you planning to move?" If they lie about those basic things, they are likely also lying about other (bigger) things.

Keep Your Mouth Shut

The most powerful (and often one of the easiest) negotiating tactics can be summed up in a single word:

Silence.

Talking less during a negotiation is almost always a good thing. First, the less we talk, the less information we give that the other party can use against us. Secondly, when we talk less, we tend to listen more, which can provide us information that might be useful later in the negotiation. But, when we say "silence" we don't just mean talking less and listening more. We literally mean *silence*.

After you put out an offer (or counteroffer), shut up. Don't say another word until the other party responds, no matter how uncomfortable you are or how long the silence lasts. The most obvious reason to do this is that the other party might need some time to think about your offer and if you give them enough time to consider it, they may just say, "okay."

This is an important tactic at other points in the negotiation as well. When the other party throws out an offer you can't accept, say nothing. When the other party asks for a concession you don't want to provide, say nothing. Even when the other party offers a concession to you, but you think you can get more, keep your mouth shut.

In our society, most people get very uncomfortable with prolonged silence. Especially when someone else has initiated the discussion and we are now expected to answer. By maintaining your silence, one of two things is likely to happen:

1. The other party will get uncomfortable with the silence, and will break it themselves; or
2. The other party will interpret our silence as anger or disappointment, and will work to rectify the negative reaction.

If the other party is forced to speak again before you do, what might happen? If they've just thrown out an offer, they may decide to sweeten it. If they've just asked for a concession, they may decide to forego it. If they've just offered a concession, they may decide to double down on it. This is especially true if they believe they may have offended you on the initial offer.

In their haste to fill the silent void, the other party is likely to respond with the first thing that comes to mind, which very often will be a concession.

The worst thing you can do when negotiating is to make an offer, and then before receiving a counteroffer, make a better offer! In effect, you'll be negotiating with yourself and offering something better each time you open your mouth.

If you keep silent, you're giving the other party the opportunity to negotiate with themselves and provide you with a better deal without you ever having to respond to them.

And while it may sound crazy, it very often works.

QUICK TIP *Never negotiate with yourself. In other words, once you put out an offer or counteroffer, don't provide any concessions to that offer until the other party responds.*

By the way, this tactic also works when offering and negotiating through real estate agents. When you receive an offer or counteroffer, don't respond too quickly. Make the other party wonder what you're thinking and what your likely response will be. Have your agent let the listing agent know that you weren't very happy with the offer and you need some time to decide how or if you will respond.

The seller may start to get antsy about your position, which may cause them to lower their own standards. I've even seen examples of people submitting a new and better offer when the first one wasn't responded to.

QUICK TIP *Avoid negotiating over text message or email. If the other party wants to ask for a concession, make them ask you face-to-face, or at least over the phone. It's easy to ask for things in writing—don't make it easy for the other party to ask for concessions!*

Don't Interrupt

Letting the other party talk for too long during a negotiation can get very uncomfortable. By not interrupting a long speech, our silence can subtly indicate that we agree with what they're saying—even if we don't. And, oftentimes, the other party will say something that we really want to address or contradict, and we know that if we don't do it right away, we may lose our chance.

Even with those downsides to letting the other party speak too freely and continuously, it's generally wise to let them speak without interrupting them.

First, interrupting is considered rude. We don't want the other party interrupting us when we're speaking, so we should be modeling that behavior ourselves when they are speaking.

But there is a more important reason why it's bad practice to interrupt someone who is speaking during a negotiation: You may be cutting them off right before they are about to offer you a concession!

As we discussed above, when you *listen* more than *speak*, you give yourself an opportunity to collect information from the other party. You also give the other party the opportunity to talk themselves into a corner and potentially offer up more than they should.

Appeal to a Higher Authority

Remember our discussion from the previous chapter about never negotiating with someone who isn't the ultimate decision maker? If so, you can imagine the benefits if you were to negotiate without the other party thinking you were the final decision maker. Of course, you *are* the final decision maker, but the other party doesn't need to know that.

In other words, you can negotiate to the point where you get—or are close to—a deal that you are willing to accept, and then say to the other party, "Okay, I think this will work. I just need to check with [insert "higher authority" here] to make sure they're good with it." The higher authority could be your spouse, your business partner, your boss, or the guy who is lending you money to buy the property. It can be whoever would make sense in the situation. Because she happens to be my business partner and generally doesn't attend my negotiations, I typically will refer to my wife as the person who has the final say.

For ethical reasons, we prefer this person to be real and we prefer them to have a vested interest in the outcome. In fact, I like to use my wife as my "higher authority" because I would rarely finalize a deal without her input and approval. But I do know negotiators who will completely make up a third-party "higher authority," hoping that the other party will never figure it out. This decision is yours, but I would caution about putting yourself in any situation that could cause you to lose the trust of the other party—for example, if they found out you were lying about a nonexistent business partner.

By halting discussions to get the input from another decision maker, you've now done what you worked hard to keep the other party from doing to you. You've put yourself in a situation where they have committed to a deal and all their cards are on the table, but you have not. You now have the ability to consult that higher authority and come back with additional requests or demands from the ultimate decision maker.

As an example, I might negotiate with a buyer to the point where we have a deal that I'm willing to accept, and then tell him:

Me: *"Okay, I think that will work. My wife owns 50 percent of the business that controls the property, so I have to verify that she's good with this, but I don't expect she'll have any issues."*

I'll then step away to call my wife, spend a couple minutes on the phone with her, come back to the buyer, and say:

Me: *"Okay, my wife is good with everything except the closing date— she reminded me that we have a vacation scheduled the week you want to close, so we'd have to close the week prior. Are you okay with an earlier closing?"*

At this point, I'm already off the phone with my wife, so the buyer knows that any further negotiation or a request for more concessions from me would likely result in another phone call and more wasted time. Since I didn't ask for anything too big, there's a reasonable chance he'll just say okay, and we'll get the deal we wanted, plus an earlier closing date.

We don't like to use this tactic too often, but when you want to gain agreement on a relatively small sticking point in the negotiation or need a small concession, appealing to a higher authority can be a quick and easy way to do it.

Bluffing/Take It or Leave It

One final topic I want to touch on is the idea of bluffing in a negotiation. By bluffing, we typically mean telling a lie in the hopes that the other party won't attempt to verify it. A common bluff attempted by many inexperienced investors is threatening to walk away from the negotiations.

This type of situation is often characterized as "take it or leave it," where one party puts out their best and final offer, and suggests to the other party that if they don't accept it, the negotiations are over.

While the use of a strategic bluff can sometimes put a flailing negotiation back on track, there are several reasons why bluffing in general—and "take it or leave it" specifically—is typically not a good strategy during a negotiation.

- Negotiations are much more likely to reach a successful outcome when the parties involved trust one another. Trust is generally earned slowly, throughout the negotiation process, when each party acts in a way that the other respects and appreciates. When one party gets caught bluffing, trust drops—often irreparably—and the likelihood of a successful result is reduced.

- The more likely a bluff is to help your negotiating position, the more likely it is the other party will attempt to check the veracity of your statements. In other words, you might get away with small bluffs that are unlikely to help your negotiating position very much, but you're much less likely to get away with bluffs that will actually help your position. For this reason, you have to ask yourself whether the risk/reward tradeoff for a particular bluff makes the bluff worthwhile.

- With a "take it or leave it" bluff you have the potential of getting the deal you want, but if you're honestly willing to make additional concessions, you run the risk of stalling the negotiations when a deal was still possible. Compounding this, too many novice investors will throw out a "take it or leave it" bluff and then—when the other party decides to "leave it"—will not actually walk away. This sends the message to other party that you are more desperate than you want to admit, giving them additional leverage for the remainder of the negotiation.

If you're going to make a bluff, here are some suggestions on maximizing your chances of success:

- Don't bluff on minor issues that won't give you significant gain should it work. The risk of throwing away a deal over a small gain is typically not worth it.
- If you're implementing a "take it or leave it" bluff, provide a plausible explanation for why you can't budge off your current position. Offer a believable reason, data, or a quantitative analysis.
- Additionally, when making a "take it or leave it" bluff, try to provide an additional concession along with your final offer. This token may be enough to convince the other party that the deal is good enough to move forward.

If you walk away from a negotiation because you really can't concede anything additional to the other party, make a point to keep the door open. Let the other party know that you are still very interested in working together, and should anything change on either side, you'd love to reestablish the discussion and continue working toward an agreement.

QUICK TIP *If you find yourself in a position where you threatened to walk away and the other party let you, but now you really want to come back, the key to is to provide a reasonable excuse for why things have changed for you.*

This "good news" you offer should provide a rationale for why you are now in a position to make additional concessions. You'll still find that your position has weakened, but it may provide a way back to the table without giving up too much leverage.

Dealing with Stalls

Throughout the book, we've touched on the importance of keeping momentum in our negotiations and trying to avoid stalls—situations where the parties are at an impasse and it appears that no further progress can be made because neither party wants to make additional concessions.

Any negotiation that lasts more than a few minutes is likely to eventually lose momentum and, if one or both parties doesn't make a concerted effort to get things back on track, there will be stalls. Once you complete this book, it's safe to say that you will be the more experienced negotiator in many of your negotiations, so the responsibility is often going to fall on you to take control when momentum is waning or when a stall appears inevitable.

Here are some tactics you can use when you feel like your negotiation is losing momentum and is starting to stall:

- **Take a break.** Are either or both of you getting tired? Hungry? Bored? If so, take a break. Walk outside and make a phone call. Offer to come back after lunch. Agree to call it a night and pick up the discussion in the morning. While you don't want to break off negotiations while they have momentum, when that momentum slows, a break might be exactly what each side needs to regain their energy and optimism.

- **Review the progress that has already been made.** By discussing the things you have already agreed upon and ignoring the stuff you still haven't reached consensus on, you can remind the other party that there is reason to be optimistic about reaching an agreement, and that an agreement may be closer than it currently appears.

- **Find more concessions.** You aren't agreeing on how to divide the current set of concessions, so now is a great time to get creative and to try to find some new concessions that you can add to the pot.

- **Remind the other party of the consequences of not reaching a deal.** If other tactics aren't working to get the discussion moving forward again, it may be time to remind the other party of the negative consequences of not reaching a deal. Is the seller facing a foreclosure? Is the buyer's lease about to expire and he needs to find a new place ASAP?

QUICK TIP *To add pressure in a negotiation, and to avoid stalls before they occur, add a time component. For example: "My offer is good until 5 p.m. tomorrow. If we can't come to an agreement by then, I plan to meet with another seller who contacted me this morning about selling his house." Always offer up a brief explanation of why there is a time constraint, so it doesn't like a bluff.*

One final tactic to get a stalled negotiation back on track is to ask the other party a series of questions that you know will result in a "yes" answer. Having the other party hear himself say "yes" over and over will subconsciously lead him to believe that things are progressing forward and that the negotiation has momentum.

The Most Important Tip of All

I want to end this chapter with the most important tip of all—not a negotiating tip *per se*, but a general investing concept that you must consider throughout any real estate negotiation:

No Deal Is Better Than a Bad Deal

When you're deep into a negotiation, it's very easy to get caught up in the idea that reaching an agreement is the only acceptable outcome. After all, you've likely invested a substantial amount of time, research, effort, and energy into making this transaction happen, and you'd prefer to see results of *some* kind.

While this attitude is completely understandable, you need to accept that most real estate negotiations end without an agreement. Oftentimes, real estate negotiations simply reach an impasse that can't be overcome. Real estate deals are the largest transactions most people will ever make, and many people just aren't motivated enough to pursue a deal that big until circumstances require it.

QUICK TIP *To reject an offer or counteroffer, sometimes it's easiest to simply say that you'd lose money by accepting the deal: "I appreciate that counteroffer, but if I were to pay $150,000 for this property, I'd end up losing money—I'm not going to make it long in this business if I do deals that lose me money."*

When a negotiation stalls, many investors—especially those without a lot of deals under their belt—will get desperate and will consider offering concessions just to get to the finish line. They often ignore the fact that the concessions they are offering will turn the deal into a dud.

Remember, it's better to walk away with no deal than to settle for a bad deal that fails to bring you the outcome you need. The effective negotiator knows when and how to say "no" just as they know how to get to "yes."

DIG DEEP *Just because you don't walk away with a deal doesn't mean you shouldn't try to help the seller solve her problem(s) if you have the ability to do so. Perhaps you could refer her to a real estate agent who can help her? Your goodwill may come back to you in the form of a deal further down the road.*

CHAPTER 11
CONCESSIONS STRATEGIES

We talked earlier about how concessions are the currency of a negotiation. Thinking about concessions as a currency is a great analogy. If you were literally bargaining with dollar bills, it's unlikely you'd be throwing them around and handing them out without regard for what you were getting in return.

Likewise, concessions represent the monetary value you're getting or giving in the deal. And, if you don't manage them wisely, you'll find yourself receiving less value from the deal than you're giving.

In this chapter, we'll talk about how concessions can be used, how you can use them to gain leverage in the negotiations, and how you can avoid giving more than you get.

Rules of Concessions

Before we jump into the more complex aspects of using concessions, let's start with the basics. Below, we list some of the common rules for how concessions should and should not be used, and how you can ensure that concessions are being used to create a win-win deal for both sides.

- **Avoid giving concessions—instead, trade them.** When you offer a concession to the other party, you nearly always want to ask them for a concession in return. For example, let's say you're negotiating with a mortgage broker to get a loan financed. You might say:

Investor: *"I have another broker who is offering to only charge me three-quarters of a point for the origination fee, and you want a full point. I'd love to work with you, but your fee is pretty steep. If I would be willing to pay the one point origination, will you prioritize this loan, pull in the schedule and get it completed in the next 15 days?"*

- **Suggest conditional concessions versus giving them.** Phrasing your concessions as hypotheticals can often avoid locking you into a concession. For example, you want to avoid the following happening if you were to negotiate with a smart seller:

Investor: *"Okay, I guess I can go up to $90,000. Would you be willing to seller finance 30 percent of that amount for the next 12 months?"*

Seller: *"Great, so it sounds like we agree on the $90,000. But, there's just no way I can seller finance any of the deal. Oh, by the way, my wife is adamant that we use our title company to close this deal. Can we agree to that?"*

What just happened? This smart seller just took your offer of a concession (going up to $90,000) without giving anything in return. And, at the same time, asked for another concession from you!

To avoid this type of situation, we prefer to always phrase our concessions as an "if-then" expression: "I might be willing to give A if you were to give B."

With that in mind, your offer in the example above might have instead been phrased as:

Investor: *"I'm not sure I can make $90,000 work. If you'd be willing to seller finance 30 percent of that amount for the next 12 months, then I can run the numbers and see what I can do. Will you seller finance under those terms—you'll get most of your money right now and the rest no later than January?"*

In this case, you haven't committed to anything with your offer. And, you've even left the door open to getting more than what you've proposed:

Seller: *"I don't need all the money now, so I guess I can do that."*

Investor: *"Okay, let me play with the numbers a bit..."*

[Spend the next couple minutes doing some calculations on your notepad.]

Then you say:

Investor: *"Even with that seller financing, $90,000 is a bit too high for me. But, I can do $88,000. So, that would be $88,000 with 30 percent seller financing for 12 months? Do we have a deal?"*

- **Typically start with the highest priority concessions.** The order in which you offer and ask for concessions should generally be aligned with the importance of those concessions. You want the other party to gauge how important various parts of the deal are to you, and introducing terms early indicates that you care about those points. Likewise, you should generally assume that the issues the other party mentions early on are the most important to them.
- **Make sure you get equal value when you give.** Never accept a concession that's worth less than the concession you are offering. If the other party starts to realize that you're willing to give up concessions of greater value than they have to give up, they'll start looking to trade lots of non-equal concessions.
- **Concessions lose value as soon as you make them.** If you don't ask for a reciprocal concession right away, you'll likely never get it. The reason being that the value of a concession goes to zero shortly after you give it. Getting something makes people happy, but once they have it, they quickly take it for granted.
- **Use "giveaway concessions" to your advantage.** During any negotiation, there are going to be some aspects of the deal that you may consider completely unimportant but that the other side may see as valuable.

  For example, as the investor/buyer, when dealing with a seller, it's natural that you would take care of getting the contract to the title company and arranging all the closing details. But, the seller may not be aware of this. During the discussion, you might use this "giveaway concession" to your advantage in the following way:

Investor: *"If I'm hearing you correctly, it sounds like I'm willing to put up $500 in earnest money and you'd prefer $1,000. How about this—we agree to the $500, but I'll also handle all of the paperwork and closing details. I'll coordinate with the title company, get the title search completed, and handle the settlement statement. All you'll have to do is show up to the closing! Agreed?"*

By making all the paperwork and closing coordination seem like a concession—and positioning it as a lot of work—we can get value for something that we had planned to do all along. And while the seller never even thought about doing any of this work, he now feels there's a weight lifted from his shoulders.

- **Point out and remind them of the value of concessions you gave.** We just mentioned that once they're made, concessions quickly lose value. You can somewhat counteract this by reminding the other party of the concessions you've previously made and the value of those concessions, especially when asking for new concessions.

For example, when you get down to the last point of disagreement, you might say something along the lines of:

Investor: *"Okay, I've already agreed to allow you to stay in the house for a week after closing, which my lawyer is going to kill me for doing. I've agreed to pay all closing costs, which is going to put about $5,000 more in your pocket. All I'm asking for in return is that you leave the big screen TV mounted over the fireplace so I don't have to repair the holes it will leave in the wall if you remove it. That seems like a good deal for you...do you agree?"*

In most negotiation scenarios, sticking with those basic concepts around offering and negotiating concessions will give you a big advantage. But, there are some additional, more advanced tactics we can use to maintain control over our negotiations.

QUICK TIP Always express gratitude for the other party's concessions. Even a simple, "Thank you, I appreciate that," can encourage them to continue the beneficial behavior.

Always Ask for a Final Concession

Great negotiators learn how to *train* the other party into doing what they want, without them even realizing it. This is especially important when it's not just a one-time negotiation and you expect to be negotiating with that person over and over again in the future (like a contractor, mortgage broker, or inspector).

One way of doing this is to always make sure you ask for—and get—the last concession in any negotiation. By always asking for the final concession, the other party will, over time, learn to stop asking for things once he essentially has what he wants or needs from the negotiation.

If the other party realizes that every time he asks for something, he will need to give something up, he will naturally shy away from asking for more than what he needs, in fear that he will be asked to give up something important in return for additional non-essential demands on his part.

For example, when negotiating with a contractor, let's say he throws out a final price that you would be happy to accept. But instead of just saying:

Investor: *"I agree with that price, we have a deal."*

We might instead say:

Investor: *"I can agree with that price if you can start first thing tomorrow morning."*

If he comes back with:

Contractor: *"I can't start tomorrow, how about the following day?"*

Your response might be:

Investor: *"That works, but then I'll really need you to finish in three days instead of four."*

If his response to that is:

Contractor: *"Half of my crew is on another job I need to finish by Saturday, so there's no way I can finish in three days. Is four still okay?"*

Your response could be:

Investor: *"Okay, so you can't start tomorrow and you can't finish in three days. That would put us at next week, which makes my schedule pretty tight. I'll make you a deal—cut $100 off your price and I'll figure out a way to make that work."*

For as long as he continues to counter your requests, continue to ask for additional concessions. Eventually, you will train him that by "resisting" he's encouraging you to continue asking for more. He'll also learn that by simply giving in, he'll end up sacrificing less in the end.

And if he never happens to learn this lesson, at the very least you'll continue to get more and more concessions from him.

Again, this tip is especially valuable when you expect to be negotiating repeatedly with the same party. We have had contractors who we've worked with on dozens of projects, and negotiations with them were always easy. They knew to just get an agreement as quickly as possible to avoid my continuing to ask for concessions; in fact, they would typically just agree to any reasonable price I suggested right off the bat.

QUICK TIP *While you should always ask for the final concession, good negotiators will also "hold back" a concession that can be given to the other party at the end of negotiations to reinforce good faith and to encourage the other party to walk away feeling as if they got the better end of the deal.*

Typically, a hold back concession is non-financial and has more value to the other party than it has to you. For example, when selling a house, you might choose to throw in the washer/dryer that you were hoping not to have to move anyway.

Implement a Penalty for Concessions

Have you ever been on the phone with a customer service representative haggling over something small (for example, you're on the phone with your cable company trying to get your monthly fee reduced by $10), and you find that every time you ask for something, the rep puts you on hold for ten minutes while they "check to see if they can do that."

You can bet that it doesn't really take them ten minutes to determine whether they can give you $10 off your bill. But, they realize that when you ask for $10 off, then wait for ten minutes, and then they come back and counteroffer you $5 off your bill, you're going to be less likely to go another negotiating round (like saying, "How about $8 off?") if it means you'll have to wait another ten minutes to get the response.

What they've done is implemented a *penalty* for each time you ask for a concession. While you're sitting on hold, you're powerless. You have the option to wait for some unknown amount of time, or hang up and get nothing.

If you want to discourage others from asking for concessions in your negotiations, do the same thing—implement a penalty each time they ask for something additional (though, of course, don't let them know you're doing it on purpose). And keep in mind that the penalty doesn't need to be same for each "offense."

Making them wait (like the example above) is a great example of a penalty. Perhaps you say to the other party:

Investor: *"I'll have to think about that, I'll give you a call tomorrow and we can discuss further."*

Or perhaps the penalty is that they have to fill out a bunch of forms to get their desired concession:

Investor: *"My attorney says that would put me at risk of liability, but I'm willing to do it if you're okay signing an indemnification agreement?"*

Or perhaps they'll have to drive somewhere to pick up that extra thing that they want:

Investor: *"Sure, I'm willing to pay for the materials upfront, but my light fixture vendor is in the next town over, so it's going to be an extra drive for you if you want to do it that way."*

If you make the penalty for asking more cumbersome than what they asked for, it's quite possible they'll decide it's not worth the effort—like having to wait ten minutes to find out if you can save $10 extra.

QUICK TIP Whenever the other party suggests that they might be able to make a specific concession, take the opportunity to turn that "suggestion" into an "agreement." For example:

Homeowner: *"We might be able to throw the refrigerator into the deal..."*

Investor: *"Okay great, so you'll throw the refrigerator into the purchase. That will really help. Now, let's talk about the closing costs..."*

Taking Concessions off the Table

You've probably heard the phrase, "Everything is negotiable." In fact, if you like haggling, you've probably used that phrase once or twice yourself. But what if you're entering a negotiation and there is a particular concession or set of concessions that are non-negotiable on your side?

For example, I know many real estate wholesalers (people who get a property under contract and then sell the contract to another investor) who don't have a lot of cash and therefore don't have the ability to offer a seller a large earnest money deposit as part of the contract.

For someone in those shoes, offering a large deposit is out of the question, and a negotiation can get difficult if they constantly have to offer up other concessions to avoid having to give in on that one. If the party on the other side of the table is astute, they'll probably realize that the wholesaler is trying to avoid putting down a big deposit, and will use that as leverage to get a much better deal.

In these situations, it can be advantageous to take these non-negotiable concessions off the table as soon as they come up in the negotiation. Or even before.

TALES FROM THE TRENCHES

An investor friend and I had decided to work together on a deal that I had a lead on. We visited the seller at his property, did our walk-through and sat down to start our negotiations for the property.

After exchanging pleasantries and asking the seller a bunch of questions to determine their motivations for selling, we got down to business. A few minutes into the discussion, the seller asked for a big concession—he mentioned that he was likely going to be moving in with his girlfriend in a few months, and he wanted to be able to stay in the house until he was ready to make the move.

In general, I'm not a fan of letting sellers stay in the house after the closing takes place. There are far too many things that can happen that will have a negative impact on the deal. For example, the seller may damage the property; or he may not leave as promised. Then we would have to go through an eviction process.

This particular situation seemed especially risky, as it hinged on a major relationship decision between the seller and his significant other, and we all know how quickly a relationship can go badly. I didn't want to risk the seller deciding not to go through with his move while living in a house we owned. And, without even discussing it, I was fairly certain my partner was thinking the exact same thing.

I knew allowing the seller to stay in the house after closing was going to be non-negotiable on our end, and I was ready to address it with him. But, before I could say anything, my partner jumped in:

Investor: *"You'd be surprised how often sellers ask if they can stay in the house for a couple of months after closing, and I completely understand how important that is to you. Unfortunately, on the advice of our attorney, there are just some things that we aren't allowed to agree to, as it puts us at too much liability risk."*

As he was saying this, he reached into his folder and pulled out an official looking piece of paper on attorney letterhead. It was titled "Calhoun Properties—Corporate Policies," and contained what appeared to be a list of "policies" that my partner and I were required to adhere to.

About halfway down the list was a line item:

Possession of property must transfer to buyer at time of closing.

The seller said, "okay," and never even asked to see the full list, and that was the last time this request was discussed during the negotiation.

My partner had found the perfect way to take a whole list of potential concessions off the table. And the best part was that we could act just as exasperated as the seller about it, agreeing that it was a ridiculous policy, but unfortunately, it was "out of our hands."

The "corporate policies" document leveraged two aspects of the tip we offered in the last chapter—it put the list in writing, providing it more weight than if my partner had just talked about it; and it came from a recognized authority—our attorney—which provided an air of legitimacy that we likely couldn't have provided ourselves. To this day, I carry my "corporate policies" list to every real estate negotiation. It contains all the concessions that I prefer not to give, including not allowing the seller to stay in the property after closing.

On rare occasions—for example, when I know a seller must have one of the concessions and I'm prepared to provide it—I can still use the policy list in my favor. I will point out that while I'm not allowed to agree to the point, I'm willing to talk to my attorney to get his input and see if there is a way we can work around it.

Of course, I come back with good news: "My attorney says it can be done!" But, I also point out that it provides some liability risk on my company, so I'm going to need a big concession in return...

It Never Hurts to Ask

Have you ever asked someone for something and were surprised that they said "yes" without any hesitation? Sometimes, people will hand you a lot more than you might expect—and all you have to do is ask.

We typically assume that other people are going to react to situations and requests the same way we would. We assume that because we wouldn't say yes to a supposedly crazy request, nobody else would either. But not everyone has the same desires, needs, or dreams as everybody else. You might not hand a dollar to every person on a street corner asking for money, but that doesn't mean other people won't. If nobody did, they wouldn't still be asking, would they?

So why don't more people simply ask for what they want? At the negotiating table, many see asking for concessions as a sign of weakness. They want the other party to *offer* concessions instead. Unfortunately, if you wait for the other party to offer you everything you want or need, you could be waiting for a long time. It's your responsibility to get what you want or need—to do that you must be willing to ask.

The best part is, even if the answer isn't "yes," it may not be "no." Here's a great story to illustrate that point:

} TALES *FROM THE* **TRENCHES** {

At a Real Estate Investors Association (REIA) meeting in Atlanta, I was talking to a local investor. I asked him what he was doing to find investment properties. He mentioned that he was finding most of his houses on Craigslist.

In the past, I had looked at a few houses listed on Craigslist, but since most of the listings didn't contain many pictures or a detailed description, I found it difficult to separate the motivated sellers from the unmotivated sellers. I asked him how he decided on which houses to make offers.

His answer surprised me. He said that he offered on *every* property he saw listed on the site. Because each property listing included a link to initiate an email, he could quickly fire off emails to each person who listed a house for sale. Each of the emails was a short, three-sentence cut-and-paste that read, "Hello. I saw your property listing on Craigslist and I might be interested in making an offer. Would you be willing to accept $XXX for the house?"

The $XXX that he filled in for each email was exactly half of the list price for the house. So, if a house were listed for $200,000, his email would ask if they were willing to accept $100,000.

Obviously, he didn't expect anyone to actually agree to his half-price offer, but what he found was that a small number of sellers would respond with something along the lines of, "I can't sell for that little, but I would take $YYY," where $YYY was a significant reduction from the list price!

By spending about five seconds to send a form email, he was able to not only determine which sellers were highly motivated, but was also able to use the $YYY price as the new starting point for negotiations!

By the way, this idea that everyone sees the world differently is an especially important lesson to learn as a real estate investor. Not just from a negotiation standpoint, but in many aspects of investing. For example, many investors assume that their buyers are going to require the same level of amenities in their properties that they would require for themselves. I often hear investors say, "I can't invest in a property that I wouldn't live in myself!"

That's ridiculous! I may not know where those investors live, but it's safe to say that there are plenty of people who live in homes not nearly as nice as those investors live in, and plenty who live in homes that are much nicer. Again, everyone has different desires, needs, and dreams.

Never assume that the other party thinks the way you do or wants the same thing you might want. And because of that, never be afraid to ask for something "crazy." The worst they can do is say "no." And sometimes, you just might get it!

QUICK TIP *When making a large price concession, don't concede in round numbers. For example, if you up your offer by exactly $10,000, the other party is likely to think you just made a ridiculously low offer in the first place.*

Instead, perhaps you might concede $8,192, with the explanation, "I just got a big refund on some unused materials that I returned, so I guess I can afford to make a little bit less on this deal." This will sound more like you really are working off meaningful numbers and not just padding all of your offers to generate large profits.

Negotiate Concessions in Chunks

The human brain is excellent at storing large amounts of information for long periods of time. Unfortunately, the part of the brain responsible for storing short-term memory (also called "working memory") is not nearly as efficient. In general, the average adult can remember between five and nine pieces of new information at a given time; and that's assuming the information is relatively simple, such as a word or number.

In fact, one of the most highly cited papers in psychology ("The Magical Number Seven, Plus or Minus Two: Some Limits on Our Capacity for Processing Information") deals with this specific topic. Published in 1956 by cognitive psychologist George A. Miller of Harvard University's Department of Psychology in *Psychological Review*, the idea that the number of objects an average human can hold in working memory is seven plus or minus two is frequently referred to as Miller's Magic Number.

Despite this, many inexperienced negotiators will attempt to put together a complex deal by trying to negotiate many important terms all at once. It's not uncommon to hear an offer along the lines of, "I'll give you A, B, and C if you give me X, Y, and Z and we can keep discussing P, Q, and R while we await the outcome of T, U, and V."

If you have trouble remembering a ten-digit number, how are you going to keep all these terms—and all the concessions that go along with them—straight? While these types of complex deals might be okay when you're playing Monopoly with your kids, when you're buying and selling *real* houses and hotels, it's important to focus on breaking down the negotiation into smaller pieces.

The biggest risk of negotiating too many terms at once is that one or both parties is likely to get confused about what has been agreed to. This can be especially risky to the deal when one of the parties doesn't act in good faith and purposefully attempts to confuse the discussion by pretending not to remember earlier agreements or tries to convince the other party that they agreed to something they didn't.

There are two important rules to keep in mind when negotiating deals with more than a few terms:

1. **Negotiate terms in small chunks.** For example, if price is the most important concern to both parties, discuss that first, without bringing any additional terms into the mix. While you may not come to an agreement on price without pulling in additional considerations, the goal here is to define a range to where both parties might be

willing to compromise. Once the most important aspects of the negotiations have been discussed, and both parties have a general idea of where each side stands, introduce additional terms one by one (or in small groups).

2. **Write everything down.** As I mentioned above, our working memory is limited in how efficiently it can remember information. By writing down each offer, the parties can be certain they—and the other party—are perfectly clear on the details of the offer being discussed. There is no risk of anything being forgotten or lost in the discussion.

QUICK TIP *Be skeptical. Take nothing at face value. While the other party may be acting in good faith, there's always the chance they may be trying to "get one over on you."*

Bundle Concessions to Reduce Complexity

We've discussed negotiating concessions in small chunks to keep from causing confusion. While that's always good advice, it doesn't mean that each and every concession should be discussed in a vacuum. There are times when bundling concessions together can be done in a way that's not confusing and that can also substantially reduce time and complexity in a negotiation.

This is important because, while you might be happy to negotiate for hours on end or go back and forth with 20 counteroffers if you're working through an agent, your typical buyers and sellers probably won't want to do this. And, if you're working with a "get it done" type of seller, you may find that you're able to avoid frustrating them, and may get a much better deal, by grouping concessions into batches.

When bundling concessions, focus on those things that:
1. Naturally go together as part of the deal.
2. Are likely to be uncontroversial.

For example, you might bundle several related contingencies together when you don't believe the seller will have a big objection:

Investor: *"Let's talk about the closing. How about if we use my title company? I'll have them come here to sign the paperwork so you don't have to travel, and we'll split the closing costs right down the middle. Does that work for you?"*

Because all three of those concessions being discussed were related to the closing, and because they were well balanced in terms of giving and getting value, it's likely that we could get the seller to agree to all of these terms much more quickly than if we were to have discussed them one by one.

You'll Have to Do Better Than That

When one party makes an offer or counteroffer, the appropriate response is typically for the other party to make a counteroffer where, in a show of good faith, he makes a concession that brings the parties closer to an agreement. In fact, this is the basis for most successful negotiations—the parties go back and forth, each giving an appropriate amount until a successful outcome is reached.

But, there are going to be situations where the proper response to an offer is not a counteroffer—a more appropriate response is a resounding "No!"

For example, times when the other party—often innocently—throws out an offer that is so far from acceptable that a counteroffer wouldn't make sense. Or, when you offer a concession and the other party reciprocates with a much less valuable concession.

There will also be times when the other party isn't acting innocently. For example, you might be up against a good negotiator and he may decide to test your emotional strength by purposefully making a ridiculous offer, asking for a completely unreasonable demand or not properly reciprocating a concession you've made to him. Good negotiators know that when someone receives an offer—even one that doesn't meet their satisfaction—the natural tendency is to want to give in, at least a little bit, to show appreciation for the offer that was made.

An aggressive negotiator may test you to see if you are unable or unwilling to shoot down a farfetched request; and if they find that you don't shoot them down, they will start to bombard you with more and more unreasonable demands in hopes that you won't defend your own best interests.

In other words, he wants to know early on if you have the ability to say "No!" and stick to it.

Regardless of whether the crazy offer is made in good faith by a naïve buyer or seller, or whether it's made by a strong negotiator to test your intestinal fortitude, saying "no" is not only appropriate, but absolutely necessary in order to ensure that the balance of power isn't tipped too far in favor of that other party.

That said, there are risks when you flat-out reject an offer, the biggest being that you risk closing the door on the negotiation. Essentially, you're saying that you don't accept the offer and you're not proposing an alternative. While it's okay that you're not proposing an alternative (again, you don't *want* to counteroffer), you also don't want to completely shut down the discussion.

For this reason, just saying "No!" is probably not the best response.

So how can you reject an offer without countering and without shutting down the discussion?

My favorite response in this situation is:

Investor: *"You'll have to do better than that."*

That simple phrase serves a dual purpose. It sends the message that you don't believe the other party's proposal merits a counteroffer, but also gives the other party the opportunity to try again. In other words, it leaves the door open to continuing to try to reach an agreement.

Keep in mind that the natural tendency after saying "no" to someone is to want to justify your rejection and make a concession to "soften the blow." Don't do this. After saying, "You'll have to do better than that" (or whatever other form of "no" you choose), keep silent. Don't explain why you are rejecting the offer (they'll already know why) and don't offer a concession. It's important to send the message that you are inflexible in your ability to consider their current offer.

CHAPTER 12
DEFENSE & COUNTER TACTICS

We've spent much of the past few chapters discussing the tactics and strategies you should be using to ensure that you come out on top in your real estate negotiations. We haven't yet discussed what to do when you encounter a buyer, a seller, or another investor who is also skilled at negotiation and who attempts to use the techniques we've presented here against you. Or worse yet, someone who is willing to use unethical tactics against you.

In this chapter, we're going to discuss how to defend against those negotiating techniques that will most commonly be used against you.

First Things First

The more you negotiate, the more likely you are to run into a seasoned negotiator who attempts to use many of the tactics we've presented here against you. There will be times during a negotiation when you know the other party is trying to get one over on you, even if you don't know exactly what they are doing or how to defend against it.

In those situations, the very first thing we recommend is slow down the process so you can try to determine what's going on and how you should react. Slowing down the process could mean talking less and listening more; it could mean taking a break to gather your thoughts; it could even mean stopping negotiations for the day so you can regroup and start fresh after thinking things through.

A good negotiator will try to use those situations where you are uncomfortable and "off your game" to get more concessions or even to try to close the deal. The moment you start feeling uncomfortable during a negotiation, stop talking. As long you're not saying anything, you won't find yourself giving anything away or making any foolish concessions. Take time to regroup and come back when you're ready.

Defending against Lowball Offers

The longer you're in this business, the more times you'll experience a buyer throwing out an extremely low offer on one of your properties. This could be a retail buyer, but will more likely be another investor trying to score a great deal on a property they can wholesale, rent out, or flip themselves.

While you can't necessarily blame him for trying, you need to handle this situation properly to avoid letting it lead to a bad deal. While many negotiating books will tell you never to reject an offer outright—in other words, always respond with a counteroffer, even if that counteroffer is near full price—when the other party's offer is ridiculously low, we actually prefer the outright rejection.

By rejecting their offer, you are sending the message that you are refusing to even engage in a negotiation until they are willing to be reasonable and act in good faith. By countering an unreasonable offer, you can send the message that you are desperate or that you can be taken advantage of, and we believe those are two messages you should never send during a negotiation.

QUICK TIP *When rejecting an unreasonable offer, don't mince words. For example, don't say: "That's a little bit out of my range," when what you really mean is, "That's ridiculous. I won't even consider that."*

Defending against the Nibble

A common strategy for some buyers and sellers is to use a technique known as "the nibble" in order to slowly drain a seller of concessions. Nibbling involves making the other party feel cheap and shaming her into giving up lots of little concessions. You may also hear the phrase "nickel and diming" to refer to this tactic as well.

For example, you may be close to an agreement when the buyer says:

Buyer: *"I'm purchasing this $600,000 house from you…the least you can do is spend $2,500 to replace the windows for me."*

If the buyer does this once and it's a reasonable negotiation request, you might consider it. But, if the buyer repeatedly uses shaming or intimidation techniques to try to get you to make lots of little concessions, it's important that you push back and make it clear that you won't allow him to nibble away at you.

Buyers will sometimes act as if they are entitled to a concession. For example:

Buyer: *"I assume you're going to leave all the appliances, right?"*

In this case, we'd recommend responding in a way that not only shuts down this request, but shuts down all the buyer's future attempts at nibbling as well. For example, you might respond with:

Investor: *"You shouldn't assume that I'm going to give anything away for free."*

Defending against a Trial Balloon

Smart negotiators will attempt to get information about your negotiating position, or even get concessions, by throwing out informal offers or ideas that are often referred to as "trial balloons." Trial balloons are questions that one party will ask in order to gain clues about the other party's position without giving up any information about his own position.

For example, a buyer might be walking through your property that's listed for $200,000 and throw out:

Buyer: *"So, would you take $160,000 for this place if I paid all cash?"*

Notice that the buyer didn't offer $160,000, and he certainly didn't say that he'd be willing to pay cash. More likely than not, this was an attempt to gain information that he'll likely use later when he makes a formal offer. Many investors might get excited and respond to this type of query with:

> **Investor:** *"I don't know if I'd take $160,000, but if you can pay cash, I'm certainly willing to come down off my asking price."*

By saying this, you've essentially just made it clear that your list price is highly negotiable, and you can be sure that any offer this buyer might make will be well below full asking price, and probably won't be for cash.

The only reasonable response to this type of question is:

> **Investor:** *"I'll be happy to look at any offer that you present to me in writing."*

Defending against Higher Authority

We discussed earlier how using a "higher authority" to gain a quick concession can be a powerful tool. Indicating that someone else needs to make the final decision and that the other person needs a change to the agreement can provide you benefit without much risk.

But what happens when the *other person* claims that they don't have the authority to make the final decision, and they attempt to use the strategy of appealing to a higher authority to gain leverage and concessions?

First, if you took our advice to never negotiate with anyone who is not the decision maker, this generally shouldn't be a problem. But, there will be occasions when someone represents themselves as the decision maker, and then backtracks, either because they weren't really the decision maker or because they are trying to take advantage of you.

In these situations, the best defense is to simply say:

> **Investor:** *"When can the person who has the authority to make the decision meet with us?"*

If the other party was bluffing about having a higher authority, he's likely to give in at this point and decide that he *can* make the decision himself. If there really is a higher authority (or if he continues to insist there is one), it's in your best interest to continue to push to make that person part of the negotiations before giving any further concessions.

Defending against Take It or Leave It

When a novice negotiator feels backed into a corner, he will often use the "take it or leave it" tactic to attempt to regain some control. But, just because the other party says, "This is the best I can do," doesn't mean that it's true.

Sometimes, people will employ "take it or leave it" simply because they are frustrated. Sometimes they are just looking to exert power. Sometimes they just don't know a better way to say, "I'm not sure what to do next," and are looking for you to lead the way.

Regardless, when the other party gives a "take it or leave it" ultimatum, your job is to determine whether it's really their final offer or it's just an idle threat masking some other emotion or issue.

The best way to handle the other party's "take it or leave it" offer is to just keep talking. Don't acknowledge the threat of walking away, and either keep negotiating or change the subject. If the other party doesn't actually start to walk away, you know they were bluffing and are still willing to negotiate.

QUICK TIP *Always ensure that your words and your actions are in agreement. For example, if you say that you are displeased with an offer, make sure your face and body language replicate that displeasure. When words and actions are out of sync, this will subconsciously register as a red flag with the other party.*

Defending against Silence

We talked earlier about how powerful silence can be when negotiating. When the other party throws out an offer or counteroffer, simply not responding can often elicit a concession or a completely new offer from them.

But, what about when you put out an offer or counteroffer and the other party tries to use this tactic against you? Instead of responding to the offer or making a counteroffer, they simply sit in silence waiting for you to say something more.

When this happens, the best tactic is to repeat the offer you just made. Then sit back and wait.

Defending against Lies

We recommend always being honest in your negotiations, especially when discussing factual information that can be verified. But, there are times when your counterpart won't adhere to the same high standards and will be happy to lie to you during the negotiation process.

Unfortunately, studies have shown that despite their confidence that they are good at it, most people are very bad at detecting lies; so expecting that you will be able to spot a lie isn't the best way to handle a dishonest negotiator. Instead, the best tactic is prevention—encouraging the other party not to lie in the first place.

There are a couple ways of doing this:

- Early in the negotiation, casually mention that you take your ethics seriously, and that you would never engage in lying or deceit just for business or personal gains. Simply reminding the other party that ethics is important (and that you're thinking about it) will diminish the likelihood that they attempt to deceive you.
- Divulging private information will encourage the other party to do the same. For example, I've had several conversations with sellers that go something like this:

Investor: *"You know, just to be transparent, I wanted to let you know that if I buy your house, I'll likely try to get zoning approval to turn it into a multifamily property, then tear it down to build a duplex."*

Homeowner: *"Well, just so you know, we had another investor approach us last year to do the same thing, but the zoning department said they wouldn't allow it, so the deal fell apart."*

Not only did you get the homeowner to give you information that could save you time and money but you got her to admit that the highest and best value of the property was lower than you thought.

Finally, if the other party makes a statement that you suspect may be untrue, but that can be easily verified, make it part of the terms of the contract. For example:

Homeowner: *"We wouldn't sell for anything less than $500,000. We talked to the zoning department last year, and they said it could be subdivided into three lots, so you could build three houses. Even at $500,000, you're getting a great deal!"*

Investor: *"I didn't realize that. Okay, in that case, I'm willing to pay $500,000, but we'll have to make the contract contingent on my getting this same verification from the zoning department."*

If it turns out that the homeowner was lying and that the zoning department wouldn't approve the subdivision, you can reopen negotiations with more leverage.

QUICK TIP *When the other party makes a suspicious statement, make a point to write yourself a note about it in front of them. If they believe you're writing down the things they're being dishonest about (in other words, they realize they've been caught), they are less likely to continue the behavior.*

Defending against Interruptions

As we discussed early, we recommend never interrupting the other party when they are speaking or making an offer or counteroffer. You could be interrupting a concession they are about to make!

But, what about when the other party is constantly interrupting you? Some seasoned negotiators will do this as a way to throw you off your game, but it's more likely you're dealing with an inexperienced negotiator who feels the need to interject his opinion as often as possible.

While this can be frustrating, it's also an opportunity to gain information and leverage. If you were simply in the middle of a discussion, letting the other person interrupt and start talking may provide you with new information. On the other hand, if you were in the middle of making an offer or counteroffer, the interruption probably just stopped you from making a concession—use this interruption to get a concession from the other party instead!

For example:

Investor: *"Okay, it sounds like my $126,600 offer won't work for you because it won't provide enough money for you to pay off the loan on the property. What if I was willing to..."*

Homeowner: *"Wait. Not only will it not allow me to pay off my property, but I also need money to cover my moving expenses as well."*

Investor: *"Oh, I understand. Well, do you think that if we could come to a deal that would give you the money you needed, you'd be willing to leave the hot tub instead of taking it with you?"*

Homeowner: *"Yeah, sure...I'd be willing to do that..."*

While you were about to increase your offer price, the homeowner's interruption gave you an opportunity to ask for another concession, without having to give up anything in return.

Defending against "Tactical Criticism"

If you're selling renovated properties, you're much less likely to run into this buyer tactic, but we've seen it used on several occasions. It essentially involves the buyer, and sometimes their agent, telling you all the negative points of your property in preparation for delivering you a lowball offer.

We learned this lesson early on in our investing career.

TALES FROM THE TRENCHES

Back when we were new to flipping, we had an agent call to ask us to meet at one of our fully renovated houses to do a walk-through. He was an investor and he was looking to purchase a rental property in the area. We were skeptical about our property working well as a rental, but we were always looking to build relationships with investors and agents, so we agreed to meet him.

As we walked through the house, the guy started nitpicking every detail—even going so far as to make things up. His very first comment was that the siding on the house was a composite siding that had been recalled and was prone to cracking. (Not true—we were very well-versed in that type of siding and always replaced it when it was on one of our houses.) Next, he complained that the roof appeared to be old and in need of replacing. (The roof was less than five years old and looked to be in perfect shape.)

He complained about the electrical panel (it was brand new and up to code); he complained about the plumbing (the supply lines were new and everything was working great); he complained about the materials we used for the wood flooring (it was solid oak); he complained about the "cheap countertops" (they were granite). For 15 minutes, as we walked the house, the guy literally complained about every little detail.

After the walk-through, we listened to him chastise us for another ten minutes about the lack of attention to detail our contractors must have had, the poor choice of finishes we used, and anything else he could think to insult us about. We told him we had to leave for another appointment, and he said he'd be in touch if he decided to make an offer. We were completely dejected from all the negative feedback we had just received, and were quite certain we'd never hear from him again.

But, we did! The next morning, there was an offer in our email from that very guy. It was a very low offer, and it was accompanied by a note reiterating all the negative feedback he had given us in person the previous day. We quickly realized that he didn't hate the house. The truth was just the opposite: he wanted the house, but thought that if he could make us feel like we'd never be able to get a reasonable offer for it, we just might accept his low offer.

We rejected his offer. A few days later we got a full price contract on that house, which reaffirmed our suspicions that the agent/investor was using all the criticism in order to get a better deal.

Whenever you meet a buyer who tries to use this strategy to wear you down and make you question the value of your property, we suggest a simple reply:

Investor: *"Thank you for looking, but it sounds like this just isn't the right house for you."*

QUICK TIP *Always communicate respect, even if the other party doesn't earn it or deserve it. Remember, the goal is to get what you want and communicating respect is the best way to do that.*

Defending against Threats of Competition

One of the more common tactics we see when dealing with off-market sellers (properties that aren't listed on the MLS or any other place publicly) is being told by the seller that she is talking to other investors as well. She may even say that she has other offers on the table that we'd be competing with.

Because the property is not listed publicly, the chance of this being true is less than if the property were listed on the MLS or was actively being marketed. But, you can't rule out the possibility that the seller is telling you the truth and that there really are other interested parties or other offers.

The best strategy in these situations is to try to determine:

1. Is the other party telling you the truth?
2. If so, what are the other offers you are competing against?
3. What is their level of motivation to work with you?

Typically, the answer to the first question can be gleaned by asking the seller for some details:

"Who are the other investors you're speaking with? Perhaps I know them."

"How long have you been negotiating with them? Is there a reason you haven't been able to come to an agreement in that time?"

"Did you contact them or did they contact you?"

"Have you met with them face-to-face? Are you planning to talk to them again soon?"

While asking these questions isn't likely to get the seller to admit she's lying, her answers—and specifically the details she chooses to either reveal or conceal in her answers—are likely to give you an idea of whether she's telling the truth.

QUICK TIP Always verify claims that the other party is making about their hands being tied. For example, if a buyer says:

Buyer: "While I'd love to pay the full $300,000 asking price, I'm only qualified for a loan up to $270,000."

Ask if he's willing to talk to your mortgage broker to see if your broker can help him increase his qualification amount. If the buyer is lying about $270,000 being his qualification amount, you'll soon find out.

If you determine that the seller may be telling the truth about other interested parties or other offers, it's now time to get as much information as possible about those people and offers, as they are going to be your competition.

We suggest asking questions such as:

"Is there an offer on the table? What is that offer?"

"Have you accepted their offer? Is there a contract or commitment?"

"Are they willing to pay cash? What other terms are they offering?"

Finally, ask some probing questions to determine their level of motivation to work with you or the other party. This can give you some indication of how aggressively you should be approaching your offer:

"Are you planning to sign a contract with the other investor in the near future?"

"Would you rather hold off discussions until you finish talking to the other investor?"

If the seller isn't confident that she is close to a deal with another party, or if she's bluffing about having other interested parties, the answers to these questions may serve to encourage her to stick around and keep negotiating.

Defending against a Rejected Offer

In the previous chapter, we discussed how important it is to say "No!" when you receive an unacceptable offer or counteroffer from the other party. And we mentioned that a great way to say "no" during a negotiation is to instead say, "You'll have to do better than that."

So, what happens when the person on the other side of the table refuses to counter your offer and tries to force you to make additional concessions? Remember, a good negotiator may try to use this tactic against you to induce you to respond with a better offer or more concessions, even when your offer is perfectly reasonable.

Don't do it! Instead, if you get, "You'll have to do better than that," the appropriate response is:

Investor: *"How much better do I have to do?"*

Or, if the other party just says, "No!" you should respond with:

Investor: *"Why don't you tell me what you're looking for?"*

By asking those questions, you're subtly (or not so subtly) putting it back on the other party to make a counteroffer, which restores the natural pattern of the negotiation.

QUICK TIP *When you reach a final agreement, try to ensure that you (or your agent) prepares the final contract. This will allow you to avoid any tricks or mistakes by the other party and will also allow you to write stipulations and contingencies in the most favorable way.*

CHAPTER 13
RENEGOTIATION PRINCIPLES

You've done your due diligence, research, and planning; and you've met with the seller of the property, built rapport, and ultimately negotiated a deal that satisfies both sides. For most types of negotiations outside of real estate, this would mark the end of the transaction, and you could now walk away happy with what you achieved and prepare for your next negotiation.

But, in a real estate transaction, things may not be quite that simple. If you had any contingencies in your contract—inspection contingency, financing contingency, appraisal contingency, or any other contingency—now is the time the two parties are trying to complete those contingencies and get to the closing table.

What happens when one of your contingencies doesn't work out as hoped? For example, when your inspection results indicate an issue with the property? Or when your lender hits a snag and says he can't get the loan done as promised? Or when the appraiser determines that the property you want to purchase isn't worth what you're offering to pay and the lender refuses to finance the deal?

These are all common scenarios in real estate, and the more contingencies you have in the contract, the more likely an issue will come up that will jeopardize the transaction. In this chapter, we're going to talk about the basic principles of negotiating back to an agreement when your transaction hits a snag due to failed contingencies.

What Is Renegotiation?

Some contract contingencies are written in such a way that, if the contingency fails (e.g., an inspection turns up an issue or a loan falls through), there is a clear path to resolution. For example, an inspection contingency may give a seller the option to fix any inspection issue that arises and, assuming the seller makes the fix, the transaction will continue forward toward closing.

But in other cases, contingencies are written in a more open-ended fashion. If a problem arises with a contingency, one or both parties may either try to work out a solution through renegotiation or they'll back out of the contract.

While this seems pretty straight-forward, there are some nuances here worth noting:

- Renegotiation often gives one or both parties the option of backing out of the contract completely. This is one of the reasons why it's so important that both sides be happy with and feel like they got what they wanted and needed from the original agreement. If either side was having second thoughts after the initial contract was signed, a failed contingency could be an easy opportunity for either party to bail on the deal.

- Renegotiation often provides one party with leverage over the other party. For example, if a buyer has a property appraisal that indicates the property is worth $10,000 less than the contract price, the seller is going to find herself in a much worse position than the buyer. Ultimately, in order to keep the deal moving forward it will be up to the seller to make the bulk of the concessions in this situation, and likely lower the sale price. This can create a fragile renegotiation that is more likely to fail.

- Renegotiation often shifts the balance of power to one of the parties. For example, if a buyer has a generic "due diligence" contingency that gives him the right to back out of the deal for any reason, the buyer can use this contingency to ask for new terms without necessarily providing a good reason for those new terms. This shifts the balance of power toward the buyer, but also reduces trust and goodwill between the parties. These types of situations are likely to result in failed renegotiations unless the party without the power is significantly motivated. And in some cases, even a motivated party will happily spite himself to keep from letting the other party take advantage of the situation.

- Renegotiation situations often arise from one party running into a problem that can't easily be solved by renegotiating the contract. For example, if a buyer determines that he doesn't qualify for a loan to purchase the property, there may not be any concessions that either side can make that would allow a new agreement to be reached. In these situations, both sides might be motivated and willing to act in good faith, but it still may be impossible to revive the deal if the issue is unresolvable.

For all these reasons, renegotiation is often more difficult than the original contract negotiations, and without both sides having a strong desire to get the deal done, renegotiation runs a high risk of failure.

DIG DEEP *The potential for renegotiation is one reason why it's so important to build a strong relationship early and to continue working on that relationship throughout the transaction. A deal that requires renegotiation is much more likely to be successful if the parties respect and trust one another.*

Risk of Over-Using Contingencies

Before we go any further, we think it's important to point out a pitfall that many new investors make when it comes to contingencies and renegotiation.

A story will best illustrate our point:

⟩ TALES FROM THE TRENCHES ⟨

We have an investing friend named Dan (not his real name). Dan makes offers on lots of properties, sight unseen. His methodology is that he'll write up an offer based on pictures he sees on the MLS or pictures that sellers send him of the property.

He'll often write offers that are attractive to the seller based on his best-case analysis of the property. Dan will also include a standard due diligence contingency in his contracts that allows him to do his inspections and other due diligence after the seller accepts his offer, and gives him the right to renegotiate or back out of the deal if he isn't satisfied with his due diligence results.

In most situations, Dan's due diligence will turn up issues that he's not happy with—a roof that needs to be replaced or a house situated on a busy street, for example. These will invariably be issues that Dan would have noticed *before* making the offer had he actually visited the property beforehand, but because he didn't, he then will go back to the seller and try to negotiate a better price.

I was having lunch with a real estate agent friend of ours one day (her office specializes in REO and foreclosure deals), and since she knew that we are pretty well connected in the investor world, she asked if we knew Dan.

I said yes, and asked her why she was asking. She said:

"He's been quite the topic of discussion around our brokerage recently. Apparently, he's made offers on three of our agent's REO properties in the past couple of weeks, and all three times he's come back and tried to renegotiate a much lower price based on his inspection results. Since they were all issues that he should have known about before making his offer, our sellers refused to renegotiate and all the deals fell through.

We've heard similar stories from another agent at a different brokerage and one of our brokers has told us that we should recommend to our sellers not to seriously consider his offers anymore."

In other words, Dan had pretty much ruined his reputation among a set of very popular local real estate agents. And once you gain a bad reputation in this industry, it's often difficult—if not impossible—to fix it.

In a market that was heating up and already getting difficult to find great deals, Dan was making it near impossible to get any deals where a local real estate agent was involved.

We're not saying you shouldn't use contingencies in your contracts, and we're not saying that you shouldn't rely on those contingencies when something goes wrong. But, if you use contingencies simply as a way to renegotiate every one of your contracts after the seller has committed to a sale, you're likely to find yourself with a bad reputation; and we can promise you that agents, sellers, wholesalers, and other investors *will* find out.

Remember, sellers—whether retail sellers, institutional sellers, or investors/wholesalers—are interested in getting rid of their property as quickly and efficiently as possible, and if they think you're just going to waste their time by backing out of the deal, they won't even bother to accept your offers.

Common Renegotiation Resolutions

In some cases, the resolution of a failed contingency is very straightforward. For example, a buyer who needs to sell their property before purchasing another may have a contingency that basically says, "If we don't sell our property by March 1, we aren't obligated to buy the new property."

One of two things will happen: The buyer sells his property, in which case he's obligated to move forward with the purchase or he doesn't sell, in which case he can (and likely will) back out of the deal.

But many other types of contingencies can open up the entire contract to renegotiation. For example, a generic inspection contingency may essentially say, "If the buyer isn't happy with the inspection results, the buyer can renegotiate or back out of the deal." In this case, a buyer could come back and say, "I wasn't happy with the inspection results, let's renegotiate everything!" That would be his right if the contingency were generic enough, and in many cases, they are.

While a failed contingency could open up a contract to a big renegotiation, in reality most failed contingencies result in the buyer pursuing one of the following resolutions:

- **Ask for nothing.** Is the buyer already getting a good deal? And are the contingency issues that came up relatively minor and easy for the buyer to deal with? For example, perhaps an inspection turns up a couple minor repair issues that the buyer is happy to fix himself once the purchase is completed. If so, the best tactic may be for the buyer not to ask for anything from the seller and to move forward with the contract as agreed.
- **Ask for lender-required changes.** Is the lender requiring repairs based on the inspection report? Is the lender asking for concessions from the seller, or perhaps additional information from the seller? Banks can be very demanding prior to approving a loan, and if a

lender needs something in order to provide financing, it's common for the buyer to pass this requirement on to the seller. If the seller is unwilling to fulfill these requests, it's possible that neither this buyer, nor any other buyer getting financing, will be able to purchase the house.

- **Ask for other repairs to be made**. If there are costly or risky repairs required over and above what was known at the time of the original contract agreement, the buyer may ask the seller to make these repairs prior to the closing.
- **Ask for a price reduction**. In the case of surprise inspection issues or a low appraisal where the lender is unwilling to lend against the full purchase amount, the buyer may ask the seller for a price reduction to compensate for the loss.
- **Cancel the contract**. In some cases, a failed contingency may be so disastrous that the only acceptable resolution is to cancel the contract. For example, if the buyer can't get financing under any conditions, if an inspection turns up a catastrophic issue or if the title work indicates that there is a legal issue with the seller's ownership, the best option may be to simply cancel the contract.

While the buyer can ask for any of these things, unless the contract requires the seller to agree, the seller is free to reject the buyer requests and either attempt to reach a compromise on the renegotiation requests or to cancel the contract herself.

Next we'll discuss how we approach renegotiation scenarios as the buyer, and how we determine what to ask in a renegotiation scenario.

Renegotiate to Make the Parties "Whole"

Let's be clear—running into contingency issues and having to renegotiate *can* threaten the success of a deal. If renegotiations aren't treated carefully, it's easy to destroy the trust that has been built up throughout the transaction and you may find the other party using a renegotiation process as an opportunity to reconsider the entire deal if they were having doubts or getting "cold feet."

With that in mind, the best way to ensure that a renegotiation goes smoothly is to approach it with the following principle in mind:

The goal of renegotiation should be to make each party whole—no more, no less.

Let's talk about what this means. Prior to the renegotiation, both parties agreed to a deal that they found satisfactory. Each side felt they were receiving adequate value for what they were providing and each side was walking away with a very clear result. At the end of a renegotiation, the goal should be that each side is still walking away with the same amount of value, minus the specific liability that they incurred due to the contingency issue.

For example, if an inspection issue comes up that would cost $1,000 to fix, and the issue is the seller's "fault" (e.g., the seller didn't disclose a known issue), then the buyer shouldn't suffer any loss on his side of the agreement and the seller shouldn't suffer any loss greater than the $1,000. This ensures that the buyer stays "whole" (gets what he agreed to) and that the seller gets the same value from the deal as promised, minus the cost of the extra issue for which she was responsible.

Now, you might be thinking:

Wouldn't it be a better tactic to ask for more than we expect to receive during a renegotiation (or to offer less than we expect to pay during a renegotiation), both because that will give us room to negotiate and because that way we might get even more than we wanted?

That's a very reasonable assumption, but in the case of renegotiation, we typically recommend not doing that for two very important reasons:

1. **We don't want to violate the other party's trust.** In many cases, there is a well-defined cost associated with the renegotiation issue. For example, perhaps the buyer's inspector found a termite infestation that would cost $800 to remediate. Or perhaps the buyer can't close on schedule, and it's going to cost the seller an extra $1,500 in mortgage payments to extend the closing an extra month.

   By asking a seller to pay more than the actual cost of the renegotiation issue, or by offering to pay less than the actual cost if we're the seller, the other party may interpret this as us trying to take advantage of the situation. Doing this late in the process can erase any trust we've accrued with the other party, and should another issue come up later in the process, the other party is going to be much less apt to be reasonable about working with us in good faith.

2. **We don't want to reopen the entire negotiation.** If we ask for more than the actual value of the renegotiation issue (or, if selling, offer less), the other party is going to interpret this as an opening bid

in a new negotiation. This sends the message that we're willing to negotiate this item, when in fact, we'd prefer to send the message that making ourselves (and them) whole is non-negotiable, which will be much more likely to result in a successful outcome.

If we send the message that we want to reopen negotiations, we're essentially starting from scratch, and the likelihood of a successful outcome drops. Plus, we'll be giving the seller the psychological approval to back out of the agreement or to renegotiate other parts of the contract as well, which could result in a worse deal for us.

Instead, we'd prefer the other not to recognize this as an opportunity to renegotiate, as that runs the risk of us losing value in our agreement, or losing the entire agreement altogether.

QUICK TIP *If the renegotiation was the result of something the seller purposefully omitted telling you or lied to you about—for example, you find evidence of a roof leak the seller didn't disclose—don't call the seller out on a lie.*

Saying, or even implying, that the seller lied to you will risk embarrassing the seller and hurting the relationship. Instead, express surprise that the seller didn't know about the issue (she'll get the message), and make it clear that you expect her to handle the issue.

Determining Who Should Pay

While it's clear to us that the goal of making each party whole should be a guiding principle of any renegotiation, it's not always going to be clear which party should be responsible for covering the cost of a specific renegotiation issue.

Sometimes it's fairly obvious. For example, if a buyer is unable to close on schedule and that results in a seller having to spend an extra $250 on his mortgage payoff the day of closing, it probably won't be too controversial for the seller to ask the buyer to pay the extra $250 in additional cost.

But in other situations, the buyer and seller may not agree who is responsible for the additional costs. In these situations, it may be necessary to enter in a limited renegotiation. By "limited" we mean that you should try to limit the negotiation specifically to the additional cost related to the issue at hand, as opposed to opening up the entire deal to renegotiation.

For example, let's say that a buyer's inspection indicates that the roof of the house is 17 years old, and has about three to five years of life left. In this situation, the buyer faces the cost of replacing the roof in the next three years, and it's not unreasonable for him to expect the seller to cover at least part of that cost. On the other hand, there are no immediate issues with the roof (no leaks, etc.) and it does have some life left in it, so it's not unreasonable that the seller expects the buyer to replace the roof when it's time to do so, at the buyer's own expense.

While the buyer might ask the seller to replace the roof, and while the seller might refuse, a reasonable strategy in this case would be for the buyer and the seller to split the cost. Whether the parties split the cost 50/50 or whether one side pays more, we'll generally make it clear to the other party that the goal of the negotiation is to determine the cost split for this specific item, and not open the negotiation back up further than that.

When to Ask for More

In this chapter, we've talked about how the goal of a renegotiation is simply to make both parties *whole* in the transaction. And that's true. But, there will be some situations where, as a buyer or seller, it's necessary to ask for more than the actual cost of the renegotiation issue, simply because the issue will cause us to incur additional time and/or increase the risk of unforeseen expenses.

Here's an example:

⟩ TALES FROM THE TRENCHES ⟨

After we had negotiated a deal on a property in Milwaukee, we did the inspection ourselves and didn't see anything that appeared to be very serious. But given that most of the houses we saw in that area had foundation and water intrusion issues, during our inspection period we had our foundation company take a closer look.

It turns out that the house had some major foundation issues that I had missed because they were in a part of the basement that wasn't easily accessible. Luckily, our foundation contractor found the issue before we completed the purchase. Our contractor felt like there was a reasonable chance that they could remediate the problem by reinforcing the foundation walls with steel beams, at a total cost of $4,000.

But there was a chance that they would get into the work and determine that instead of just steel beams, there would need to be some excavation on the exterior of the house as well, to reset the walls and place a water-proof barrier between the soil and the foundation. If it turned out that this was necessary, the cost would be closer to $12,000 for the additional work.

We decided to go back to the homeowner and ask for a reduction in the sale price of $8,000. The owner asked to see the contractor bid, and when he saw that the cost of the work was only $4,000, he got justifiably annoyed. We explained that the cost could be significantly higher, and that the extra $4,000 was to compensate us for the risk of having to spend an extra $8,000 should excavation be necessary, not to mention the additional risks of potentially having to excavate. In a worst-case situation, a foundation wall could even collapse.

Ultimately, we negotiated a reduction of $6,500 on the sale price. It turns out that excavation wasn't needed, but it was nice to know that if we had hit any additional snags, we had some extra money to cover the overages. It was also decent compensation for the extra few days it took us to complete the foundation repairs.

In short, when an inspection issue is going to introduce a major time delay or increased risk to the project, any renegotiation should aim to reimburse you not just for the repair, but also for the delay and the risk of additional unforseen expenses.

CHAPTER 14
RENEGOTIATION SCENARIOS

In the previous chapter, we discussed some general principles around renegotiation based on issues that come up while working through contract contingencies.

There are literally hundreds of potential situations that can put a deal at risk if there isn't a successful renegotiation. In most cases, it will be the buyer who runs into a contingency issue—such as inspection, financing, or appraisal issues—and needs to renegotiate the contract. But these situations affect the seller as well, and there are sometimes situations where the seller is the one who runs into a roadblock and needs to renegotiate for their own benefit.

While it's impossible to discuss every potential renegotiation situation, below we will discuss, in detail, two of the most common scenarios you'll face: renegotiation related to inspection issues and renegotiation related to financing issues. Once you have a basic understanding of how to renegotiate in these two common situations, you will likely be able to handle the other situations just as effectively.

Inspection Contingency Renegotiations

By far the most common renegotiation scenario arises from a bad inspection report. Most contracts contain either generic due diligence clauses or inspection clauses, and they are often written in a way that allows for renegotiation should there be a major inspection issue, or in some cases, any issue whatsoever.

As we discussed above, when these situations come up, we typically assume that both parties were happy with the deal as it was originally agreed upon, and our goal with this renegotiation is simply to ensure that both sides remain as whole as possible through the renegotiation.

Inspection Issues When We're the Buyer

For the first part of this discussion, let's assume we're the buyer in the transaction. Perhaps after we come to an agreement to purchase a property for $110,000, our inspector finds that the back deck was not built properly and needs some major repair to be made safe and to be brought up to code. The cost of repairing the deck would be $3,000.

Generally speaking, in this situation, we'd be looking for one of the following four concessions from the seller:

1. Drop the sale price by $3,000;
2. Place $3,000 into escrow to be used to repair the deck after closing;
3. Repair the deck using one of our preferred contractors; or
4. Provide some other concession that we felt was worth $3,000.

In general, we will always try to get the seller to reduce the sale price over any of the other scenarios. The reason for this is that the $3,000 reduction is now in the form of cash to us, and we can use it however we like. We don't necessarily have to use it to repair the deck, and if we did decide to repair the deck, we don't have to use the full amount toward that work.

DIG DEEP ⟩ *One of the benefits to both parties of reducing the sale price (versus other concessions) is that it will reduce the amount paid to any agents in the form of commission, and it will also reduce the title insurance, transfer taxes, and potentially other closing-related costs that are tied to the sale price. The total cost to both the buyer and seller is reduced.*

Ultimately, if the seller didn't want to reduce the sale price for some reason, the other three options would be acceptable to us as well. But, what happens if the seller refuses to provide the full value of the repair at all—in other words, they refuse to reduce the price or to provide some other concession?

We now have two options:

1. We could accept a lesser concession if it still provides an acceptable deal above our MAO; or
2. We will consider the renegotiation of the entire contract to be on the table and we will consider any terms and conditions of the contract to be renegotiable at this point.

As we discussed above, we typically don't like reopening all negotiations in situations where we were happy with the original contract, as the chances of coming to a new agreement that is suitable for both sides is lower than it was originally (and remember, we now need a better deal to accommodate for the repairs). But, in some situations, we may not have any other choice, and we'll often have to accept the fact that a second agreement may never be reached.

Inspection Issues When We're the Seller

Despite your best efforts to renovate and ensure that your properties are of the highest possible quality, there will invariably be times when your buyer finds inspection issues with the property. Sometimes, it will be small stuff—poorly wired electrical outlets or a toilet that doesn't stop running. But sometimes your buyer is going to run into larger, unexpected issues.

For example, we were selling a property and the buyer's inspector found a large amount of water under the crawl space. When we had purchased the property, it was in the middle of a drought, so our inspector never saw an indication of any water problems. When an inspection issue like this arises, expect that the buyer will request repair of the problem.

When we receive a request like that, the very first thing we'll do is to ask for a copy of the inspection report from the buyer's inspector, and verify that the issue really is an issue. We'll also verify the cost of the remediation with our contractors.

From there, we will do one of three things:

1. If this issue was something that we had disclosed to the buyer prior to them making an offer (for example, if it was listed in a disclosure statement we had given them) or if the issue was obvious during the buyer's initial walk-through of the property (for example, a stain on the hardwood floor), we might refuse to make the repair.

   Additionally, if we believe that the buyer is already getting a great deal on the property and that we could easily get another contract at the current price or higher, we might refuse to make the repair. Ultimately, any refusal to do repairs will be because the buyer should have known about the issue before making an offer or because we would be okay losing the contract.

2. If we determine that the issue is real and that it should have been addressed prior to our listing the house for sale (for example, termite damaged joists that should have been replaced but hadn't been), we will offer a reduction in sales price up to the actual cost of repair.

   Depending on whether we believe it's reasonable for the buyer to contribute to the cost of the repair (again, we can use the example of a roof that is older but has a few years of life left), we may offer a reduction of less than the full amount of the repair, and explain to the buyer that we expect to share the cost.

3. If a lender is requiring repairs be performed in order to allow the buyer to close on the property, or if the buyer insists on having the repairs completed prior to closing, we will have our contractors do the repairs. If we determine that the buyers should contribute to the repair cost, we may even negotiate the purchase price up to cover their portion of the cost, or we may ask the buyer to provide us an additional credit at closing for this purpose.

Note that when we have the option of either doing a repair for the buyer or just providing a price reduction in the same amount as the repair, we generally recommend the price reduction. By giving a cash credit and not having to do the repair, we reduce the risk of causing or finding other unknown renovation problems during the repair process.

There is also another benefit to offering a cash credit that is illustrated by this story:

⟩ TALES FROM THE TRENCHES ⟨

We were helping some good friends sell their personal residence. We got the house under contract, the buyers had a quick inspection, and everything seemed great. Unfortunately, the inspector found evidence of a buried old oil tank that was used to heat the house many, many years ago.

The buyers got a bid to have the tank removed—all said, it was going to come to just over $14,000, which included some potential clean-up costs should it be discovered that the old tank had corroded and leaked. The buyers submitted a contract addendum (a change to the contract) that basically said:

"Seller will reduce the sale price by $14,000."

We thought it was a little strange that the buyers asked for a reduction in sale price as opposed to just having the tank removed—if they were actually worried about a hazardous old oil tank, they likely would have preferred it be remediated before the sale completed and before they moved in.

On a hunch, we suggested that our friends submit the following counteroffer to the buyer's addendum (this is a simplified version of the actual legalese we used):

"Buyers may choose from either of the following options:
• Seller will, at seller's expense, remove the buried oil tank from the property prior to closing; or
• Seller will reduce the sale price by $7,000."

The reason for this counteroffer was that we had the feeling that the buyers weren't planning to have the tank removed, and were just looking to save $14,000 on the sale price. If it were true that they didn't care much about the oil tank, then a $7,000 price reduction was likely more important to them than having the tank removed.

If that were the case, the sellers could save $7,000 by not having the tank removed, the buyers could save $7,000 on the price of the house and both sides would walk away satisfied.

Ultimately, we negotiated a $9,000 reduction in the sale price. This saved the sellers $5,000. They were happy with this, as most other buyers would have required the removal of the tank at a cost of $14,000, which the sellers would have had to pay.

Occasionally, you'll have a buyer who is unreasonable and who requests a larger concession than the cost of the repair. Except in very specific circumstances—for example, the market has turned and we don't think we could easily get another buyer should this contract fall through—we will refuse to provide more of a concession than the cost of the repair itself.

Conceding too much tips the balance of power in favor of the buyer, sending the message that we're willing to give more than we get in order to keep the deal alive. This isn't a message we generally want to be sending to our buyers.

Financing Contingency Renegotiations

The second most common renegotiation issue you'll face during your real estate transactions concerns financing and appraisal contingencies. Since most contracts won't have an appraisal contingency unless the buyer is getting financing (in which case, the lender will require the appraisal), the financing and appraisal contingencies often go hand in hand.

When a buyer runs into an issue with his ability to get his loan, this often necessitates renegotiation of the terms—or, worst case, canceling the contract. The two most common financing issues that come up during a transaction are:

1. The buyer needs more time to get their loan closed.
2. The appraisal comes in below the purchase price.

Let's discuss each of these situations in more detail.

When the Issue Is Time

With buyer financing there are lots of potential issues, but by far the most common is the loan officer or lender dragging their feet on getting the loan completed. Oftentimes, there is nothing holding up the loan other than the lender being busy and not getting around to submitting paperwork in a timely manner, not getting an appraisal ordered, or not pushing the buyer to get documents signed.

In fact, in our experience, about 75 percent of all financing issues are simply the lender or loan officer being lazy and not delivering on their commitment to their customer, the buyer. When this happens, it can slow down a transaction, and in some cases even put the transaction in jeopardy. Below, we will discuss how you should handle situations in which a loan is not completed prior to the expiration of a financing contingency.

Timing Issues When You're the Buyer

As an investor, it's part of your job to ensure that your financial situation is in order before you start making offers on properties. If you make cash offers, you should ensure that you have the cash available to buy; if you make financed offers, you should ensure that your lender is capable of getting the loan closed in the time and fashion to which you agree in the contract.

In addition, it's your job to ensure that your lender is getting things done quickly and efficiently. Did they get you the paperwork ASAP? Did they immediately order an appraisal? Did they schedule any necessary inspections? If not, you need to take the initiative and make sure your lender stays on top of your loan every step of the way.

With that being said, there are going to be times when you make an offer with a financing contingency, and for some reason, your lender won't be able to get the loan closed in the time frame promised. If this is strictly a timing issue—say, the lender just needs more time to finalize the loan—and there are no other major risks to getting the financing you need, then your best option is just to be upfront with the seller.

Let her know that your loan has been delayed, but that you're confident that with a bit more time, you will be able to close. Be specific when you present this information. If the seller is hesitant to give you an extension on the financing contingency or the closing date, we'll sometimes offer to increase our earnest money deposit, especially if we'll need to bring cash to the closing anyway.

If you're very confident in your loan getting closed in the time frame you indicate, you can even offer to allow your earnest money to become non-refundable; this gives the seller some comfort in knowing that if you don't close as promised, they'll at least get some cash out of the deal. But we only like to do this as a last resort, as we don't like to take any risks that aren't absolutely necessary.

Timing Issues When You're the Seller

When you're the seller in the transaction and your buyer tells you that due to financing issues he needs to extend the financing contingency or the closing date, the first thing we recommend is asking the buyer's agent and mortgage broker how confident they are that the extension they've requested will be long enough to get the deal closed.

Nine out of ten times, they'll tell you that they are certain or near-certain the extension will be enough time to conclude the deal. But in our experience, if a mortgage broker believes he *won't* be able to get a loan approved, he'll ask for more time, hoping he can perform a miracle. As the seller, you don't want to hang your sale on the hope of a miracle, so we recommend saying to the buyer's agent something along the lines of the following:

> **Seller:** *"If you're certain the extension will be sufficient to get this deal closed, I'll grant the extension if the buyer puts up additional non-refundable earnest money. Since they'll need the money for the down payment at closing anyway, and since you are certain the deal will close, there's no reason the buyer can't put the money in escrow today, right?"*

By telling the buyer, his agent, and his mortgage broker that you'll only grant the extension if they are willing to put up additional non-refundable money, you'll quickly learn how confident they are about getting the loan closed. If the broker isn't confident he can get the loan done, he's not going to let his client throw away more money.

How much extra earnest money to ask for is up to you, but anything up to the entire down payment is reasonable, especially if the agent or broker tells you they are "certain" it will close. In addition, for the first extension try not to give more than seven days.

If the buyer requests a second closing extension, we recommend only doing it under the following two conditions:

- If they haven't already, the buyer puts up the entire down payment as non-refundable earnest money.
- You get a "kick-out clause" added to the contract.

A kick-out clause is a term you can add to the contract that will allow the buyer to keep the house under contract, but will, at the same time, allow the seller to look for another buyer. Should the seller find another buyer, the original buyer will have a fixed amount of time (generally 24-48 hours) to remove any remaining contingencies in the contract and prove that he can get the deal closed. Otherwise, the seller will have the option of moving forward with the new buyer.

Here is an example of what a kick-out clause might look like:

"Seller shall have the right to continue to offer the property for sale. In the event that Seller receives an acceptable offer to purchase the property, Seller shall give Buyer written notice of the same. Buyer shall then have 24 hours after receipt of the notice to deliver to Seller an Amendment to this agreement, signed by Buyer, in which Buyer agrees to remove all contingencies in favor of Buyer, along with ability of proof to retain financing.

In the event Buyer does not deliver, within 24 hours, the signed amendment and proof of ability to obtain financing, the agreement shall terminate and earnest money shall be refunded to Buyer. In the event Buyer does deliver, within 24 hours, the signed amendment and proof of ability to obtain financing, Seller shall execute amendment and deliver a copy of same to Buyer."

The nice thing about a kick-out clause is that you, as the seller, can both move forward with the current buyer in hopes he can get his financing approved, and can also continue to look for another buyer—perhaps one willing to pay even more!

If the buyer still can't get his financing in order and requests a third contingency or contract extension, you now have two choices:

- If you already have a kick-out clause in place from the second extension, you can pretty much extend it as long as you want, as you always have the option to go with another buyer if one comes along. The only drawback is that you don't get the earnest money until you ultimately terminate the contract, though that shouldn't be your goal; or
- The other option is to terminate the contract and tell the buyer that if they figure out their financing issue and can get things resolved, you're happy to sign a new contract and apply the earnest money from the original contract, but you'll have a right to renegotiate terms and perhaps ask for additional earnest money for the new contract.

Typically, we'll stick with the first option (the kick-out clause) and continue to market the property to other buyers. In our experience, if a buyer asks for three extensions to get their financing in order, there's a very good chance they will never get approved for their loan, so finding another buyer should be your top priority.

When the Issue Is the Appraisal

When a lender gets involved in a transaction, it's nearly certain that there will be an appraisal involved. If the lender is a bank or federal institution, the appraisal will be formal and likely completed through a third-party organization hired by the bank. If the lender is a hard money or private lender, it's likely they will—at the very least—do an informal analysis of the value of the property.

If the lender doesn't believe the value of the property is at least as much as the purchase price, it's nearly certain they will refuse to lend the full amount. More likely, they will only agree to lend an amount based on the value indicated by the appraisal. So if a buyer has a contract to purchase a property at $100,000 and the appraisal indicates that the value of the property is only $90,000, there's an excellent chance the lender will only lend based on a $90,000 purchase price.

This means that either the buyer will be expected to provide the difference (in the example above, $10,000), the seller will be expected to drop the purchase price (in the example above, down to $90,000), or a combination of both of these things (in the example above, perhaps the seller drops the price to $95,000 and the buyer brings an extra $5,000 to the closing table). Below, we will discuss how we typically approach situations where an appraisal comes in low, both as the buyer and the seller.

DIG DEEP *For FHA loans, any appraisals completed on the property will get recorded and stay with the property for up to six months. So, a bad appraisal on an FHA loan will affect any buyer attempting to get an FHA loan on that property for up to 180 days. On the other hand, if the loan is not FHA, the appraisals do not typically "attach" to the property.*

Appraisal Issues When You're the Buyer

A low appraisal when purchasing a property can be a great renegotiation tool. Because an independent third party has indicated that the value of the property is less than the agreed upon purchase price, it's often not difficult to convince the seller that she would be unlikely to get the originally agreed upon price from *any* buyer, and therefore should be willing to lower the price for this transaction.

The first thing we will do when an appraisal comes in low is to simply request that the seller drop the purchase price to the appraised value. We will indicate that our lender refuses to lend at the agreed upon price, and we'll remind the seller that, if they refuse, this will likely be an issue for any buyer they might work with in the future.

In many cases, especially with agents involved, the seller will be willing to drop the price to the appraised value or close to it. They won't want to lose the sale, and their agent will recognize that terminating the contract and trying to find a new buyer will waste the time and effort of both the agent and seller.

That said, on occasion, you may deal with a seller who is either not motivated enough to reduce the price, can't reduce the price because of how much they owe to a lender, or simply don't want to reduce the price because they believe the price is fair and that you should pay the difference. In these situations, we will ask ourselves a few questions:

- How badly do we want the property? The agreed upon price was good enough that we were willing to make the deal in the first place. Has anything other than the appraised value changed since we made the deal?
- Will the low appraisal impact our ability to make a profit on the deal? For example, if we are planning to rehab and resell, does the low appraisal indicate that our expected resale was off or that the market is softening?
- How motivated do we believe the seller is? Would she really walk away from the deal? What are her alternatives if she doesn't sell?

Based on our answers to those questions, we can decide how tough we want to be with our renegotiation. Perhaps it's still a great deal, we have the cash available to make up the difference, and it's worth agreeing to pay the original price for the property. Or perhaps the appraisal has made us realize that the original price wasn't as good as we thought, we don't have much cash on hand, and we're willing to walk away if the seller won't agree to drop the price.

When you're the buyer, in many instances a low appraisal plus a seller who is unwilling to reduce the sale price is a recipe for a failed transaction. This is a situation where either the deal will be successfully renegotiated or both parties will have to walk away without an agreement.

Appraisal Issues When You're the Seller
As a seller, the best way to handle a low appraisal on the property you're

selling is to keep it from happening in the first place. Remember, appraisals are just as much an art as a science, and much of the value of an appraisal will be based on the appraiser's opinion of value. By using the same techniques we've already discussed in this book, it's possible to help an appraiser recognize the value of the property.

Remember, while it's tremendously important to ensure that your rehab is top-quality in all respects (visually, functionally, price-to-value), the key to ensuring consistently successful appraisals is to focus on your interaction with the appraiser himself. Because the appraiser does have leeway in making decisions on comps and adjustments, while he's preparing the appraisal his attitude toward you and the property can impact the result.

Specifically, when dealing with the appraiser, we strive to do three things:

1. Provide information
2. Build rapport
3. Build trust

Based on earlier discussions in this book, those things shouldn't be too surprising. When we're negotiating—and our interaction with an appraiser is very much a negotiation—providing information and building rapport and trust will go a long way toward getting the other party (the appraiser, in this case) to err on the side of trying to help you rather than hurt you.

With that in mind, here are some rules we have when dealing with appraisers:

- Always ensure that you know when the appraiser is coming to your property. We make sure that our properties are on an agent lockbox and are alarmed. We then tell the lender or broker that to get access to the property, the appraiser needs to call us or our agent.
- Always make sure you or your agent are present when the appraiser is doing his walk-through. This is your opportunity to build rapport, provide information about what work you did, brag about the fact that you pulled all required permits and only used licensed contractors and to generally take credit for the great rehab your team has done.
- At the end of the walk-through, you have an opportunity to provide information to the appraiser that he can take back to the office and

review. This is the information that will help him do his appraisal and help him justify the number he comes up with. We typically provide a full list of renovations we completed, a breakdown of the rehab costs, before and after pictures of the rehab, and a list of comparable properties that support the value of the property.

It's rare that an appraiser will be bothered by the fact that you stick around during the walk-through; anything that makes their job easier is typically welcome and I've never had an appraiser who didn't want the extra information I had to provide. But you should ask the appraiser upfront if it's okay for you to be present, and if he seems uncomfortable with it, just leave the information for him and go.

If despite your best efforts an appraisal comes in low for your buyer, it's time to make some tough decisions. You will typically have three options:

1. You can encourage the buyer to appeal the appraisal. With most lenders, the buyer can submit evidence to support a value higher than what the appraiser determined; while this is a long shot, we've seen it work on occasion when the appraiser has made an obvious mistake in his analysis or the comps he chose.
2. You can terminate the contract and find another buyer. Keep in mind that some types of appraisals (FHA, specifically) will stay on file for up to six months and will be available to future appraisers, so the tactic of finding another buyer and getting a new appraisal often won't work.
3. You can negotiate with the buyer some combination of a price drop and the buyer contributing more cash to the purchase.

Realistically, No. 3 is often our only reasonable option, and this is where it's important to be able to gauge both your buyer's motivation to purchase the property and his ability to come up with additional cash. The more motivated you believe the buyer to be and the more you believe he has the cash available to pay the difference in value, the tougher you should push not to drop the price to the appraised value.

QUICK TIP *Always include a term in the contract that requires the buyer's lender to order the appraisal immediately after the contract is signed; we normally stipulate three days. This way, if an appraisal comes in low, you'll know as soon as possible, and lose the minimum amount of time should you have to find a new buyer.*

Appealing an Appraisal

If an appraisal comes in below the sale price, there is a chance that the buyer can work with their mortgage broker, lender, and appraiser to get the appraisal revised. This generally requires the appraiser to recognize that he made one or more errors when determining value and having the appraiser correct those errors to generate a new value.

In other words, don't expect to get an appraisal changed just because you're not happy with it—you will need to have some factual basis for any challenge you make to an appraisal.

That said, when we get a low appraisal on a property, the first things we will look at are:

- Was all the information for the subject property entered correctly? For example, did the appraiser mistakenly claim our property had two bathrooms when it really has three?
- Were the comparable properties in the same neighborhood or market? Were there other comparable properties that were closer and could have been used?
- Were the comparable properties within the same age range? Typically, appraisers should be using properties that are within ten years of the subject property.
- Were the comparable properties within the same size range? Typically, appraisers should be using properties that are within 20 percent (higher or lower) of the square footage of the subject property.
- Were the comparable properties sold within the previous six months? A property sold more than six months previous might not reflect the current market conditions.
- Were the adjustments the appraiser made realistic?
- Were the comparables in the same condition as the subject?
- Were there any REO properties or short sales used to value a fair

market sale? If you're purchasing a house through a retail sale, there shouldn't be any "distressed" sales used as comparables.

To challenge an appraisal, you'll need to work through the mortgage broker, who will often be your biggest ally in the process. The broker has an incentive to get the loan done, and if a bad appraisal is going to risk that (and risk his getting paid), he'll be happy to help you try to get the appraisal fixed.

Keep in mind though, even with glaring errors and a horrible appraisal, there is no guarantee the appraiser will agree to change it or the lender will agree to a higher value.

One last thing: If an appraisal comes in lower than is justified and the appraiser refuses to fix his errors, the buyer may be able to find a new mortgage broker or lender, start the loan process over, and (assuming it's not an FHA loan, which "attaches" to the property) get a new appraisal along with the new loan process.

CHAPTER 15
NEGOTIATING THE SALE

We've spent the bulk of this book discussing how to negotiate real estate deals as the buyer in the transaction. And while most of the negotiating tactics we've discussed will be the same whether we're the buyer or the seller, there are some situations that are unique from the selling side.

In this chapter, we're going to talk about some of those negotiation strategies and tactics that are specific to when we're on the selling side of the transaction and learn how to take control of a real estate sale to ensure that we get the deal we want.

Agent versus FSBO

Assuming you're not a licensed agent yourself, the first decision you're going to need to make prior to listing your property is whether you'll list it "for sale by owner" (FSBO) or whether you'll list it with an agent. We won't go into detail here, but suffice it to say, there's convincing evidence that using a professional listing agent will net you a greater amount of cash from your sale than trying to do it yourself.

The biggest reason for this is buyer traffic. Most retail buyers work with real estate agents, and therefore will be getting their lists of available houses from their agents. Because buyer's agents choose the houses they will show their buyers from MLS, as a seller you'll want to be listed on the MLS in order to get exposure to the largest number of qualified buyers.

Flat-Fee Listing Services

Now, you might be thinking that even with an FSBO listing, you can still get your property on the MLS using a flat-fee listing service or broker. Flat fee listing brokers are real estate brokerages that specialize in allowing sellers to list their properties on the MLS. Some of them don't do anything other than list the property, while others will do additional services such as provide a lockbox, provide a sign, and help with paperwork, each for a separate fee.

In general, we're not very big fans of flat-fee listing services, for the following reasons:

- Many flat-fee listing brokerages are known for poor service, and many buyer's agents don't like to deal with them or their clients. This means that if you are listed under a well-known flat-fee brokerage name, some buyer's agents will avoid your properties.
- Sellers who use flat-fee listing services are often less responsive than a listing agent, and for that reason, many buyer's agents don't like to deal with sellers who use flat-fee services.
- Buyer's agents realize that if the flat-fee lister doesn't provide any back-end support, they may have to do a lot of hand-holding of the seller through the process. This means that the buyer's agent will do twice the work for the same amount of commission on these deals.
- Finally, because many of the larger flat-fee listing brokerages offer lots of á la carte services, the cost of a flat-fee listing can often be more expensive than just using a full-service real estate agent.

Long story short, to list and sell your properties we highly recommend using a professional listing agent who is very familiar with your area.

Setting Your List Price

Potentially the most important decision you will make as a seller is the list price of your property. While you or your real estate agent can review the local comps and get an idea of what the property is worth, ultimately it will be your decision to determine what your initial list price will be.

If you price the property too high, you risk not getting many buyers or offers and the listing eventually getting "stale." If you price it too low, you risk putting yourself in a situation where you leave money on the table and don't get top dollar for all your hard work and time. Just like determining your initial offer when you're the buyer, the importance of choosing your list price as the seller can't be overstated.

To achieve maximum value on your sale, we recommend listing your property for a price somewhere between the fair market value (based on comps) and 5 percent above fair market value. The stronger the market is for sellers, the closer your list price should be to that top number.

Some sellers will attempt to list their properties well above fair market value in the hopes of getting a high offer. Unfortunately, this approach has several drawbacks:

- Most buyer's agents will recommend against their clients looking at or making offers on properties that are overpriced. By listing your property more than 5 percent above fair market value, you are likely to limit the amount of traffic you get through the property and are unlikely to get any serious offers.
- The bulk of the traffic you will get through your property will come in the first two weeks of the listing. If an overpriced listing doesn't attract much attention in the first two weeks, you run the risk of severely limiting your buyer pool.
- If you're lucky enough to get an offer well above fair market value, there's an excellent chance that you'll run into appraisal issues, and the buyer will find it difficult to get financing at the inflated price.
- If you find that you have to lower the price after not getting much traction on your listing, you will be inviting buyers to submit low-ball offers, as they will think you are getting desperate to sell.

For these reasons, we recommend you stick with the general rule of thumb of listing your property for somewhere between fair market value and 5 percent above it.

Price and Terms

As the seller, it's important to remember that not all offers are created equal, and a higher purchase price doesn't always make for a better deal. When we're selling a property, there are three aspects to the offer that we look at when determining how attractive that offer might be:

1. How much money will the offer net us?
2. How likely is the deal to close? Is it a high-risk transaction?
3. How much frustration is this offer/buyer likely to cause?

When selecting an offer to negotiate and a buyer to work with, while No. 1 is certainly important, there will be transactions where the other two considerations are just as important.

Here's an example of where this has come into play for us.

On one of our first flips, in the first few days the property was listed we received several offers. Most of the offers were below list price—between 3 to 8 percent—while just one of the offers was at the full asking amount, and with a relatively short closing period. The only red flag on the offer by "Mr. Jones" was that the buyer included a laundry list of terms and conditions.

Things like:

"Seller agrees to hold the closing at the buyer's place of choosing."

"Seller agrees to provide receipts for all work completed."

"Seller agrees to replace the kitchen faucet with [specific brand of faucet]."

There were about a dozen of these little requests, and while our guts were telling us that Mr. Jones was going to be a pain in the butt to work with, each of the requests was relatively small and easy for us to accomplish. So, we decided to negotiate and ultimately accept that offer.

Big mistake! We should have trusted our guts. Over the next 30 days, between the buyer's inspection and financing contingencies, we received about 20 more of these little requests. Not only did they take up an inordinate amount of our time, but the cost of completing each little item added up.

We could have, and should have, pushed back; but we were new to this business and were so excited at the prospect of getting the sale closed at our full price that we just said "yes" to every request in order to keep the deal alive.

In the end, we probably spent more money, and certainly more time and frustration, than we would have lost had we just gone with one of the lower offers. We decided then and there that we never prioritize a little bit more in price over having smooth and low-frustration transactions.

When evaluating any offer, determine what's important to you and look for the offer most likely to provide that. For many investors who are looking to scale their businesses and do lots of deals, price is often not the most important consideration. Only you can decide where your priorities lie, but it's an important question that you should consider.

Important Terms for Your Sales Contracts

The buyer will obviously be looking to negotiate the most favorable terms and contingencies in the contract. While you want to give him a reasonable opportunity to perform his due diligence, the best time to protect yourself and ensure that greatest likelihood for a successful deal is before the contract is signed.

With that in mind, here are our best tips for managing the terms and contingencies that go into the contract to ensure that your negotiated agreements close more often, faster, and with less hassle:

- Always encourage the buyer to use a mortgage broker that you know and trust. Most mortgage brokers are average at their jobs at best. When a buyer uses an experienced broker, there is a much higher likelihood the deal will close, and will close on schedule. At the very least, we recommend that you require your buyers to get pre-qualified with a broker you trust. If the buyer will use your recommended broker, all the better. But if not, make sure to call the buyer's mortgage broker to chat with them to make sure they are familiar with any flip rules that might be applicable, ask about the buyer's qualifications and discuss the broker's biggest concerns about getting the loan done. If it's not the broker you recommended, they probably won't tell you anything worthwhile, but you may be able to pick up something from asking the questions.
- Get the most amount of earnest money as you possibly can. While on the day the contract is signed everyone likes to be optimistic, we can't count the number of times we've looked back a few weeks later and wished we had gotten a lot more earnest money to protect

ourselves should the deal go south and the buyer not be able to close.

- Limit the buyer's financing contingency to 21 days. Regardless if it's FHA, VA, or conventional, there is no reason it should take longer than that to get a loan commitment letter for the buyer. If the broker balks at the 21 days for financing contingency, this is a red flag that there is either an issue with the buyer's finances or the broker isn't very good. Encourage the buyer to use another broker.

- Keep the closing date to 30 days or less. Unless you live in a state where a 30-day closing is really tough (like New York), there's no reason it should take longer than that to get a loan funded and a deal closed. Good mortgage brokers can get FHA, conventional, and VA loans done in three or four weeks, and that's even when two appraisals are needed. At the *very most*, and only if there's a good reason for the long wait, give five weeks to close the contract. Remember, it's easier to push the date out if there are problems than to get everyone to work harder to pull a closing date in.

- Have a stipulation in the contract that the mortgage broker will order all necessary appraisals within 72 hours of a signed contract. Holding off on ordering an appraisal is one of the most common reasons for closings to get delayed, and having a contractual obligation to get this done sooner rather than later will help all your deals close faster and more reliably.

- Any financing contingency in the contract should stipulate that the broker submit a "loan commitment letter" no later than the day the financing contingency is up. If you don't get a loan commitment letter, you need to be willing to kill the deal, unless the buyer is willing to put up more earnest money.

- Include a stipulation in the contract that allows you to call the seller's mortgage broker once a week to get a status on the loan. When you call, ask what has been done, what the next steps are, if there are any issues that have come up, and when the broker thinks the loan will go to underwriting. In addition, once the loan is in underwriting, have the broker tell you every time the underwriter comes back with conditions and what—specifically—those conditions are. This will keep you updated on exactly how close you are to the closing and what is holding it up.

Disclose, disclose, disclose! The biggest reason for sellers to end up in lawsuits with buyers is that they didn't disclose known issues with the property. We recommend providing the buyer a detailed written disclosure statement (these templates are standard with state contracts), along with any inspection reports you may have received since the renovation was complete.

You'd rather give the buyer too much information about any property issues than not enough. It's better to lose the deal over an existing issue than to complete a deal and then get sued because you weren't completely forthcoming about something.

Multiple Offers Situations

Especially in hot markets, there will be times when you'll find yourself in situations where you receive multiple offers on a property you're selling. This is obviously a great opportunity, but knowing the right strategies for maximizing those offers is key to ensuring that you capitalize on the opportunity and walk away with the best deal.

In this section, we're going to look at three different strategies for how to navigate the situation where you receive multiple offers on a property.

Negotiate One Offer at a Time

While we don't generally recommend it, as a seller you always have the option to negotiate a single offer at a time in the hopes that each negotiation will get you closer to the best deal. That said, there are several issues with this approach:

- It is time consuming. Negotiating one offer can take multiple days. Multiply this by several offers and you could end up negotiating for a week or more, during which time you run the risk of one or more buyers getting frustrated and walking away.
- You don't have the ability to easily leverage each offer against one another. While the leverage you gain over the buyers is the biggest advantage you have with multiple offer situations, it's difficult to capitalize on that leverage when you negotiate each offer individually.
- You may leave money on the table. By negotiating each offer individ-

ually, you're likely to find yourself in a situation where you propose an offer or counteroffer that is accepted by one buyer before you determine what the other buyers would have been willing to offer. That accepted offer or counteroffer could be well below what another one of the buyers had been willing to offer, but you won't have the opportunity to find out.

For these reasons, we typically don't recommend trying to negotiate multiple offers individually. That said, there is one situation where this might make sense:

If you have multiple offers, but one offer stands out far-and-away better than the rest, it may be worthwhile to just focus on that offer and ignore the others. This is especially true if the one offer has better financing terms than the other and is more likely to actually close.

By focusing on one offer—as opposed to using one of the other tactics we discuss below—you will send the message to that buyer that you are interested in negotiating with him specifically, which will build trust and an emotional commitment on both sides and will likely garner a smoother transaction overall.

Highest & Best

We mentioned earlier in the book the use of the "highest & best" selling tactic when a seller has a multiple offer situation. Our previous discussion focused around our being the buyer and how to navigate highest & best situations to help us lock up a deal. On the flip side, when we're the seller, using a highest & best tactic can help us to quickly negotiate the best offer.

When you receive multiple potentially acceptable offers and want to leverage each of the potential buyers against one another, setting a deadline for all buyers to submit their best offer is often a great strategy. Because buyers realize they may only have one opportunity to get the deal, they will often submit an offer at their MAO, giving them the best chance of "winning."

We will typically have our agent call for highest & best offers under the following conditions:

- We have at least three potentially acceptable offers.
- None of the offers stands far-and-away above the others.
- We believe at least three of the buyers are motivated to buy our property.

While the upside to using a highest & best scenario is that you'll often get the highest value from the transaction, the downside is that this technique can intimidate—and therefore scare away—some buyers. Further, some buyers and agents view highest & best scenarios as the seller simply taking advantage of buyer competition (they're not wrong!), which will potentially impact trust throughout the rest of the deal.

Additionally, some buyers and agents are skeptical when a seller says they have multiple offers, and we've seen plenty of buyers try to "call the seller's bluff" by threatening to walk away from a situation, or actually doing so.

When you call for highest & best offers as a seller, you should be prepared for one or more of the buyers to walk away at this point and not submit a highest & best offer. While you can still use their original offer as their highest & best (with their permission), this may negate some of the advantages of using the tactic in the first place.

DIG DEEP *Some sellers will use highest & best when they only have a single offer. They will tell the potential buyer that they have multiple offers and ask for the highest & best in the hope that they can get the most value out of the deal for the least amount of negotiating effort.*

While this will sometimes work, the risk of the buyer not wanting to participate in a highest & best situation, or the buyer not believing the seller and walking away, is relatively high. While we never recommend lying during a negotiation, the risk here is more than just ethical—you are also likely to lose that one buyer.

For these reasons, we never recommend telling a buyer you have multiple offers when it isn't the truth.

Mixing Both Techniques

In many cases, we like the idea of combining both tactics above to get the most value from our sale. If we are confident that calling for highest & best offers will garner a better offer than what we currently have on the table, we will ask for highest & best.

Once we have the highest & best offers in hand, we'll evaluate them from all aspects of the deal. Which offer has the highest likelihood of closing? Which offer nets us the highest amount of cash? Which offer will provide the smoothest transaction and closing?

Once we determine which offer is most preferable to us, we'll go back to that buyer and negotiate the aspects of the deal that we're still unsatisfied with. For example, we might reply to a buyer's highest & best offer with the following (this could be in person or in writing, depending on the logistics of the negotiation):

> **Investor:** *"Thank you for your offer! While your offer wasn't the highest, overall it was more attractive than any of the other offers we received and we'd really love to work with you. But, for your offer to make sense over the others we received, we'd need to change two of the terms in the contract: 1. We'd need to pull the closing in by one week; and 2. We'd need to increase the earnest money from $1,000 to $2,500. Are you willing to accept these two changes? If so, we have a deal!"*

Assuming we are not attempting to make any major changes to the contract, this will allow us to work with the contract that is most appealing to us overall, and will also allow us to improve any aspects of the deal that we may not have considered good enough.

Keep in mind that some buyers will take offense at your trying to continue to negotiate a highest & best offer, so tread lightly when using this technique and be prepared to address a buyer who gets a little irritated at your attempts to get more than their highest & best.

QUICK TIP *In a seller's market, it often makes sense to take your time with the offer review process, and to hold off making counteroffers for as long as possible. This will give you an opportunity to receive more offers, and will increase the pressure on the buyers who submitted offers, in hopes they will raise their offer prior to your response.*

Escalation Clauses

There is one other offer strategy that we should probably mention: "escalation clauses." An escalation clause is a stipulation in your contract that says the buyer is willing to pay $X (where the buyer defines X) above the highest offer the seller might receive, up to some maximum amount.

A typical escalation clause might read:

> *"In the event that Seller receives one or more bona fide offers acceptable to the Seller, then the Sales Price stated in this offer will be $500.00 higher than the highest bona fide offer, net of concessions, not to exceed a sales price of $195,000. Further, Seller will provide Buyer with a copy of the next highest bona fide purchase agreement offer."*

In this example, the buyer is offering $500 more than any other offer, including the value of other stipulations and concessions in the contract, but only up to $195,000. So if the highest offer received by the seller were $191,000, this offer would automatically escalate to $191,500.

Typically, we don't recommend using these clauses as a buyer, as you are basically telling the seller what you are willing to pay for the property, and the seller will have the opportunity to negotiate you up to that price, even without a competing offer. When we do use them as a buyer, we do so *very* sparingly.

But as a seller, there will certainly be times when you receive an escalation clause from one of your potential buyers. Receiving an offer with an escalation clause is a great indication that the potential buyer is highly motivated. In addition, the escalation clause generally gives us a lot of information that we can use as leverage in the negotiation.

As a seller, when we receive an offer that contains an escalation clause and we are happy with the highest price the buyer has indicated they'll pay, we will typically counter the offer at that highest price. For example, if we receive an offer containing an escalation clause that starts at $110,000 but will go up to $130,000, we will typically counter at $130,000.

Many investors feel this is unethical, but remember, just because a buyer submits an offer with an escalation clause, you are under no obligation to be bound by the terms of the clause. There is nothing unethical about countering at any price you'd like to counter at, including the highest price the escalation clause indicates the buyer is willing to go.

Additionally, because our counteroffer removes all of the terms of the escalation clause—and simply counters at a higher price—we are under no obligation to provide the buyer proof that there were any other offers at any amount. The buyer may not like the fact that we are using the information they provided us against them, but remember, they already indicated that this was a price that was acceptable to them, so hopefully they should be satisfied with the deal as well.

A good agent will likely have warned their buyer that an escalation clause can backfire, causing the buyer to pay their top offer amount.

DIG DEEP *If you counter a buyer at the highest price of their escalation clause, you may want to throw in a nominal concession in the process, just to mitigate the risk of them feeling as if you took advantage of them. For example, perhaps offer to pay for their inspection or offer to help with closing costs.*

CHAPTER 16
BUYING FROM INSTITUTIONS

We've discussed many of the buying scenarios you'll encounter when buying from private sellers, but we haven't discussed the scenario of buying properties from institutions, which for some buyers is very common. These include banks (both large and small), as well as government agencies like the United States Department of Housing and Urban Development (HUD).

While buying from these institutions can be very competitive, there are some specific negotiating tactics that can give you a leg up on the competition and help you secure some fantastic deals. In this chapter, we're going to discuss the two most common types of institutional deals—REO purchases from banks and HUD purchases from the government.

REO Properties

REO stands for "real estate owned." This is the term most banks use to describe properties they seize after the home goes through foreclosure. In most cases, when a bank forecloses on a home, the bank will then sell that property on the open market using a listing agent who specializes in selling bank-owned properties.

Working with the real estate agent, a representative from the bank called an "asset manager" will be making all the final contract decisions. The asset manager is responsible for setting the price, determining if repairs will be made, negotiating, and other tasks. The listing agent will have some input on the price; she will likely provide a broker price opinion (BPO), which is basically a watered-down appraisal that tells the asset manager what the listing agent thinks the home will sell for.

The asset manager will usually get BPOs from other agents as well; and, in many cases, also get a formal appraisal. So, when you see an REO that seems priced way too high or way too low, it is not generally the listing agent's fault, and in many situations, the listing agent may agree that the price is too high, yet not have any control over the pricing decision.

When you submit an offer on a REO property, there are some important things to consider:

- The REO listing agent and asset manager are usually very busy people. Making their job easier by not wasting their time will go a long way in getting them to want to work with you.
- Most REO listings have detailed instructions for exactly how to submit offers. Make sure you or your agent follow those instructions carefully.
- Many offers on REO properties do not go directly to the listing agent. They are submitted online by the buyer's agent directly to the asset manager through a third-party system. The listing agent may or may not see the offers before the asset manager sees them.
- Do not include a list of repairs to justify your offer (at least not with your initial offer). The asset manager does not care at this point and it will make the listing agent look bad, as it's the listing agent's job to communicate to the asset manager what repairs are needed and how they affect the value of the home. You don't want to insinuate that the listing agent or asset manager don't know what they are doing.
- To make an offer on a bank-owned listing, you must have a pre-qualification letter from a reputable lender or proof of funds such as a bank statement indicating you have the cash available.
- Asset managers typically oversee the sale of dozens or hundreds of houses, so any attempt to contact the asset manager directly—or to influence the asset manager by writing a letter or sending any other type of private communication—is unlikely to be successful.

Despite what some people think, banks are typically not desperate to get rid of their REO properties; they want to get the most money for them, just like any seller would. Having said that, it is still possible to get a great deal on a bank-owned property.

Specifically, some REOs need substantial amounts of work, some won't qualify for financing, and in some cases the asset managers and listing agents risk losing the property if they don't sell it in a certain period of time. There is a lot of competition for REO properties in many markets, but you can get a great deal if you know how to make the seller happy.

QUICK TIP *The one place where you might be able to buy REO properties before they're listed is a local bank. Local banks will some- times sell their REOs to investors before they list them for sale. If you can build a good relationship with a local bank, you may be able to get their deals.*

Not only that, but many smaller, local banks will provide financing for their REOs—often at much better terms than if you were to work with a traditional lender or a large bank.

Focus on Price and Terms

Because there won't be any face-to-face discussion with an asset manag- er, and because there is absolutely no emotion involved in the sale of REO property, your chance of getting an REO offer accepted often depends on the terms of your offer. Banks and asset managers care about their bottom line, so that's what they will be looking at first.

But, that's not the only thing they care about, and there are other con- tract terms that can sway an asset manager to consider your offer, even when it's lower than they'd like and even when your offer is competing against other offers.

Here are a few ways to make your offer appealing to a bank asset manager:

- **Large earnest money deposit.** Banks don't like to play games. They want to know that you are serious about purchasing the property and that if a contract is in place, you'll follow through. Increasing your earnest money is a great way to communicate that you are serious and intend to make good on the purchase.
- **Short closing period.** The sooner a property closes, the sooner the asset manager gets the property off the books. Asset managers are usually paid a salary, but they also get bonuses for how many houses they sell. Most banks cannot close faster than 15 days, because it takes time to get the title policy and other documents prepared.

But, when they see a short closing period (seven to 15 days), they know you're serious. They will probably tell you that they need a month, but your ability and willingness to close sooner will make your offer attractive.

- **No (or very short) inspection period.** Most banks expect the buyers to perform inspections in ten days or less. If you can shorten the inspection period or remove it, it will show the seller you are serious. If you combine a large earnest money deposit with no inspection contingency, your offer can be very attractive, as it reduces the risk of you backing out to almost zero.

- **All cash offers, when possible.** On properties that need a lot of work, or even properties that do not, banks prefer cash offers. There is a better chance of a cash offer getting to the closing table, and that's the goal of every asset manager with their REOs.

QUICK TIP *In our experience, when offering on an REO property, the seller's first counteroffer will typically be near or at full price, while the second counteroffer will generally represent their biggest price reduction.*

Avoid End-of-Month Closings

When making offers on REOs, avoid asking for a closing date at the end of the month. There are two reasons for this:

1. Closing agents are exceptionally busy at the end of the month, and end-of-month closings are more likely to get pushed out, delayed, or rescheduled.

2. Asset managers get bonuses based on the number of closings they have each month. If a closing on the last day of the month gets pushed out, it will cause the asset manager to miss out on a bonus they were expecting that month.

Scheduling a closing at the beginning of a month removes pressure on the closing agent and reduces the chance of any hard feelings with the asset manager if there is a delay. Likewise, if you can close earlier than you planned in the previous month, it will likely make the asset manager and REO agent very happy. This could even help you get future deals.

Time Your Offers and Closings Around Financial Events

REO sellers such as big banks are often public entities required to report their financial well-being to investors and to the public on a regular basis. For that reason, they often want and need to get houses sold quickly and by certain financial deadlines.

The most common deadlines are quarterly and annually. For example, a simple Google search will indicate that Wells Fargo has a financial year that ends on December 31, with their financial quarters ending on March 31, June 30, September 30, and December 31. These are the dates in which the bank closes its financial books for that quarter (or year) and reports how much money they made or lost during that period to Wall Street and their shareholders.

While selling a property on December 31 versus selling that same property on January 1 may seem like a difference of only one day, to a bank like Wells Fargo that ends its fiscal year on December 31, it's a huge deal! By selling on December 31, Wells Fargo can get credit for the sale (both in terms of number of houses sold, lower existing inventory, and money made) in the earlier year. If they don't sell until January 1, they have to wait an entire year to get credit for that sale.

There are few things more important to public companies than reporting financials to their shareholders, so if you want to make your offers really attractive, do your best to close right before the end of the bank's fiscal quarter or fiscal year. Banks are often willing to accept less money if it means that they'll get credit for that sale in an earlier financial period, so even a low offer may be attractive if you can get the closing in just under the quarter or annual deadline.

Some of our very best REO deals have been negotiated in early- to mid-December, with a promise of closing before the New Year.

Track Price Drops

Banks typically drop the prices of their REOs in regular intervals. It may be 45 days, 90 days, or some seemingly random amount of time, but in many cases, there is a pattern to the reduction in prices. If you submit an offer just before a price drop, the bank may be more willing to consider the offer, as they are already prepared to drop the price.

For example, if you see an REO property that has had price drops every 40-50 days for the past six months, and it's been about 40-45 days since the last price drop, there is a reasonable chance the bank may be ready to drop their price again, and may be more open to considering a low offer. The advantage to offering before the price drop is that, if you were to wait until after the price drop, you would likely have to compete with other investors who find the new price attractive.

Look for Properties Just Back on the Market

Banks hate when the REO properties fall out of contract. The asset manager risks losing his bonus and the listing agent risks losing the listing. If you can submit an offer shortly after an REO comes back on the market, the bank is likely to be much more willing to negotiate a favorable offer. And this is the perfect time to offer a large earnest money deposit and/or a short inspection period, as this will reduce the risk of a second contract falling through.

QUICK TIP *Instead of waiting for an REO contract with another buyer to fall through, many REO listing agents will accept backup offers when another buyer is currently under contract. By submitting a backup offer to the listing agent or asset manager—or even just notifying the listing agent that you are interested in making an offer should the contract fall through—there is a reasonable chance that instead of relisting the property should the contract fall through, the asset manager or agent will come back to you directly.*

TALES FROM THE TRENCHES

In 2016, the Colorado REO market was hot—it was difficult to get any REO deals for a reasonable price. I had my eye on a Freddie Mac REO that was listed for $175,000 and I knew I needed to buy it for $130,000 to make my profit—a hefty discount!

I didn't bother to offer on it at first—I knew there was no way they'd accept $130,000 on a house listed at $175,000 in this market. The property went under contract with another buyer, but about a month later, the sale apparently fell through and the property came back on the market at $160,000. The property then went under contract two more times at the $160,000 price, but both buyers ended up backing out based on inspection issues with the foundation and roof.

The property was relisted at $150,000 and I felt this was a good opportunity to swoop in and attempt to solve the bank's problem of getting this property sold. My first offer was $110,000, as I knew it would take some negotiations to get the price down. The bank countered at $142,000. I countered at $117,000. The bank countered at $135,000. I countered at $124,000. The bank countered at $130,000 and said that was the lowest they would go. This was my price! I accepted the offer.

The only thing that had changed between the time the property was listed at $175,000 and now was that it had fallen out of contract three times. I knew there was no way the bank would have accepted my $130,000 offer earlier, but after several issues with other buyers, they got motivated and suddenly my offer wasn't so ridiculous.

Get Offers in During First Look Period

Many government REO sellers like Fannie Mae and Freddie Mac have a period of time (generally about two weeks) after an REO listing is first posted when they will only consider offers from owner occupants (often called the "first look" period). Investor offers are not considered during this time period, but you can typically submit offers during this period that will be considered if the bank doesn't get a contract with an owner occupant in that first look period. Ask the listing agent or have your real estate agent ask the listing agent for the best time to submit your offer.

By submitting your offer before the end of the first look period, you give the seller the opportunity to work with you immediately after the first look period has ended, while other investors—who were waiting for the first look period to end—haven't yet submitted an offer.

DIG DEEP *If a property is not in move-in-ready condition, there is an excellent chance that a homeowner will not be able to get financing to purchase the property. This means that there is a much lower chance of the property getting sold during the first look period. Seasoned investors are good at determining which properties will get sold during first look and which won't and can tailor their offer strategy to those properties likely to still be available when investor offers are considered.*

Work Directly with the Listing Agent

In the past, the listing agent on REO properties had a lot of influence over which offers might get accepted and which offers would not. Asset managers would often listen to the listing agent when she said, "I've worked with this buyer before and he's easy to work with and will always close on schedule." In addition, we knew of many listing agents who would help a favorite buyer get their offer accepted by purposefully not submitting other offers. While this is against the law, it did happen.

To prevent unequal treatment, the banks have since changed many of their practices to make sure all offers get submitted (for example, by using online submission systems that go directly to the asset manager), and some banks have even prohibited listing agents from representing the buyer on their own listings.

But while listing agents don't have as much influence as they used to with asset managers, working directly with the listing agent on REO properties (e.g., letting them be your buyer's agent) may still be a great way to get a deal that you may not otherwise get. For example, one advantage to working with the listing agent directly is that they will know the ins and outs of their listings and the bank's policies. They will know exactly when to submit offers to get their client the best chance of getting the deal. They can also explain to you how likely that particular bank is to accept low offers, if the bank is willing to make repairs, or other pertinent "inside" information.

And remember, if you use the listing agent to represent you, she is able to get both sides of the commission (the seller and buyer side), so even if she doesn't have much influence with the asset manager, she will at least be motivated to do what she can.

Highest & Best with REO Properties

When banks receive multiple offers on a property, they will often come back to all the potential buyers and ask for their highest & best offer. In fact, if you're going to be making offers on REO properties in a hot market, you should expect that the majority of offers will result in a highest & best situation.

When we're faced with a highest & best on an REO, we will simply make the highest offer that makes sense for us. We don't try to guess how many offers there are, how many other offers are cash or what the other buyers are doing. Too many investors will overthink a highest & best situation, which can lead to bad outcomes.

Here's an example:

The first time we made an offer on an REO property, it had been listed on the MLS for nearly six months. There wasn't a lot of investor activity in the area, and we were fairly certain we could pick up this property well below list price, as there apparently wasn't much interest by any other investors.

We submitted an offer of $63,000, about 25 percent below the list price of $80,000. Our target price was $68,000 and our MAO was $75,000. Our offer was below our target price and far below our MAO, so even if we had to negotiate up, it was still a great deal.

The bank then asked for highest & best.

This made me angry. I was nearly certain there were no other interested buyers and I felt like the bank was just trying to play hardball to get us to raise our offer. We chose not to raise our offer at all—part of that decision was that we didn't think there were any other bidders, and part of it was just plain spite (we didn't want the bank to "get the best of us").

We ended up losing the property. It turned out there was one other bidder and he had offered $66,500, with similar terms. In other words, even if we had only raised our offer to our target price (still a great deal for us!), we would have gotten the deal. In retrospect, we could have raised our offer to somewhere near our MAO, and we still would have been thrilled with the deal.

The moral of the story here is that we shouldn't have let emotion get in the way of our decisions and we shouldn't have tried to overthink or outsmart a highest & best situation.

HUD Foreclosures

A HUD home is a property that was purchased with an FHA loan (a loan made by the Federal Housing Administration), but the borrower defaulted and got foreclosed upon. HUD homes are owned by the government. The HUD listing and sale process isn't simple, but once you figure it out, HUD can be a great source of deals for investors.

When HUD forecloses on a property, they will quickly turn around and assign those properties to a HUD listing broker (a real estate broker who partners with HUD). Offers on HUD properties must be placed online at HUDHomeStore.com by a registered HUD real estate agent. Only HUD registered agents can place bids, though most real estate agents can gain access to the system.

Unlike REO properties, where the seller often cares about terms other than price (closing date, earnest money amount, etc.), HUD properties are typically evaluated specifically on the net amount of money that HUD will generate on a sale. If one offer will net HUD $10 more than another offer, HUD will typically accept that offer, regardless of any of the other terms of the contract.

HUD Offer Process

The HUD offer process is broken up into several "periods," during which only certain buyers will have access to the property. For example, during the first period after a property has been listed ("exclusive listing period"), only owner occupants, nonprofit organizations, and government agencies will have the ability to place an offer.

The length of the exclusive listing period depends on the condition of the property; if the property is in reasonably good condition ("insurable") than the exclusive listing period will be longer than if the property is in bad condition ("uninsurable").

Here is a breakdown of the listing period times:

	INSURABLE PROPERTIES	UNINSURABLE PROPERTIES
EXCLUSIVE LISTING PERIOD	15 DAYS	5 DAYS
EXTENDED LISTING PERIOD	180 DAYS FROM LISTING	180 DAYS FROM LISTING

If there are no acceptable offers during the exclusive listing period, HUD will open up the bidding to all buyers, including investors. This period is called the "extended listing period." This period lasts for 180 days from the date of the original listing.

Once in the extended listing period—either on the sixth or 16th day after the exclusive listing period has started—HUD will review property offers every business day (from the day prior).

When to Bid

Good investor deals on HUD properties will invite a lot of competition, and will often go under contract the first day of the extended listing period. An investor cannot bid before the exclusive listing period expires, so getting your offers in as soon as possible once the period opens up is very important.

- On 15-day exclusive listing periods (insurable properties), you can and should bid on the 16th day. Waiting even one day can, and often will, cost you the deal.
- On five-day exclusive listing periods (uninsurable properties), you can and should bid early on the sixth day. HUD accepts bids during the day and a home may be available for investors to bid on early, though owner occupants may still get priority. If HUD accepts an owner occupant bid on day six, an investor who bids early could have their offer held as a backup, and, if the owner occupant backs out for some reason, the investor may get their bid accepted without the home going back on the market. To have the best opportunity at the deal, we recommend submitting your bid before 10 a.m. on the sixth day.

How Low Will HUD Go?

While a buyer can submit any bid amount they want on a HUD home, HUD has certain pre-defined guidelines that determine what net offer amount they will accept. Typically, HUD will accept a net offer amount of between 10 and 12 percent below the list price. This net amount is what HUD will receive after commissions and closing costs are paid.

HUD always pays the listing broker 3 percent commission and the selling broker can also get up to a 3 percent commission. Keep in mind that if HUD is paying a 6 percent total commission, the net amount they will receive is already 6 percent less than list price, even on a full priced offer. If the buyer wants closing costs, that amount drops even further. Note that HUD will accept different amounts in different areas of the country, but the 10 to 12 percent below list price is relatively standard.

QUICK TIP *Play around with submitting low offers on HUD properties until you have a feel for what percentage below list price they will accept in your area. Once you have an idea of the discount they will accept, this should allow you to quickly determine which HUD deals make sense to offer, and how much.*

Submitting Low Offers on HUD Properties

Even if you don't believe your offer falls into the acceptable price range to HUD, it still might be worthwhile to submit the bid. If HUD accepts a higher bid, you will have the option to have your bid held as a backup. This means if an accepted offer cancels their bid, HUD will automatically accept the next highest bid as long as it is an acceptable amount, which can change if and when HUD lowers their list price.

Specifically, if HUD lowers the price on a property, they will review bids they have already received to see if they are now an acceptable amount after the price change. If you had submitted your offer prior to the price drop, your low bid could be accepted before anyone else gets a chance to submit a new bid after the price change.

There are also occasions when a low bid that does not meet HUD guidelines is accepted. This usually happens on "aged" assets that have been on the market over 90 days. The asset management company can ask for special approval from HUD to accept these low bids. In some cases, your bid could be rejected in the morning, and then, later in the day, HUD could notify your agent that they have "changed their mind," and have accepted your bid.

Basically, the bid was initially rejected because it didn't meet the price guidelines, but the asset management company sent it to HUD for special approval and HUD granted it later in the day. The longer a HUD home is on the market, the better chance you have of a low bid being accepted.

QUICK TIP *To verify how long a HUD home has been on the market, have your real estate agent look up the history on the MLS. This is because the dates on the HUD website are often not accurate; they are skewed by price changes and relisting of properties when they fall out of contract.*

HUD Counteroffers

Unlike banks and REO properties, HUD will not go through a back-and-forth offer and counteroffer process. Once you submit your offer, HUD will either accept it or reject it. If they reject your offer, they may "suggest" a counteroffer to you. But, this is not a legally binding counteroffer; it is simply an indication of what HUD might accept if you were to submit a new offer.

You can submit a new offer at this counteroffer price (or higher), but because offers are only opened once per day by HUD, if any higher offers come in that same day, your new offer may not be accepted. We recommend that if your offer is rejected by HUD and you find the suggested counteroffer to be acceptable, immediately submit a new offer at the suggested price in order to have your new offer reviewed the next day.

HUD Property Inspections

If you get a HUD offer accepted, expect the inspection process to be considerably different than if you were purchasing a retail property, or even an REO property.

First, HUD will not turn on any of the utilities. When HUD signs your purchase contract, they will email your agent a "utility turn-on" request form. You will have 15 days to request that all utilities be turned on and then complete your inspections. It can easily take a week or more to get the utilities turned on once the form is submitted, so you'll want to ensure your agent submits the request as soon as possible.

HUD will not pay any fees to have the utilities turned on and they will not de-winterize the property. If you live in an area that requires winterization, you will have to pay $150 with your turn on request form if you want to turn on the water during the winter season (typically October 1 through April 30). This fee is for the property preservation company to re-winterize the property after you complete your inspections.

Remember this important fact: HUD homes are sold in "as-is" condition, and HUD will make no repairs, even if your lender requires them. If you find issues during your inspection, you have two choices:

1. Cancel the contract and lose your earnest money; or
2. Proceed to closing without any repairs.

Unless your inspection finds substantial issues that were not originally disclosed by HUD, expect that you will not receive your earnest money back under any condition.

DIG DEEP HUD does an inspection before listing each property, and the basic results are listed on HUDHomeStore.com. To find the inspection, look under addendum on HUDHOMESTORE and you will see a document called PCR. This will list the general condition of the plumbing, electric, HVAC, and roof.

Do not depend on these inspections to be perfect, as many times the HUD inspectors are only able to do a visual check since the utilities are not on. But, the PCR should be able to give you a reasonable idea of the condition of the property.

Appraisals on HUD Properties

Another risk you should be familiar with on HUD properties is the appraisal. If you plan to get financing for the purchase of the property, and the lender orders an appraisal that comes in low, it's almost certain that HUD will not drop the agreed upon price. Your options will be to purchase the property at the originally agreed upon price or to back out of the deal.

For this reason, we highly recommend that if you make offers on HUD properties where you will need an appraisal, that you either:

- Do a good amount of due diligence to ensure that you are comfortable that the appraisal will come in at least at the agreed upon price; or
- Expect and plan to bring additional cash to the deal if and when the appraisal comes in low.

FINAL THOUGHTS

We've covered a lot of ground in this book. From basic concepts to advanced techniques and tactics, there's a lot to know about being an expert negotiator. But, you can always learn more negotiating tips on the BiggerPockets Podcast or within the forums on the site: www.BiggerPockets.com.

Negotiating skill is like a muscle—the more you use it, the stronger it gets. In your first negotiation, you don't need to use every concept and tactic we've discussed. Just pick one or two strategies that you found appealing, and work those into your everyday negotiating situations.

As those start to become natural, and you find that you're more comfortable using the concepts, add a few more. With practice, the strategies we've presented here will become part of your everyday negotiation skill set.

With that in mind, we leave you with two final tips:

QUICK TIP *When you win a negotiation, don't gloat. Make the other party feel like they're the winners by acting like you're still a little bit disappointed by everything they managed to get in the deal.*

QUICK TIP *After an agreement is reached, compliment the other party on their negotiating skill. Don't pile on false praise, but find something they did well and offer them a sincere compliment. They will walk away feeling they negotiated a great deal.*

Before you know it, you'll find that you're a negotiator that others look toward to solve problems and control the room.

About the Authors

J and Carol Scott

J and Carol are full-time entrepreneurs and investors. Now living in the suburbs of Washington, D.C., they both spent much of their early careers in Silicon Valley, California, where they held management positions at several Fortune 500 companies.

In 2008, J and Carol decided to leave behind the 80-hour work weeks and the constant business travel. They quit their corporate jobs, moved back East, got married, started a family, and decided to try something new. That "something new" ended up being real estate, and since their move they have bought, built, rehabbed, sold, and held over $30 million in property.

J and Carol have detailed their real estate adventures on their blog: 123flip.com.

J can be reached at j@123flip.com.

Carol can be reached at carol@123flip.com.

Mark Ferguson

Mark became a real estate investor and agent after graduating from the University of Colorado in 2001. Mark has flipped over 120 houses in his career and owns over a dozen rental properties. Mark currently runs a real estate team with six licensed agents who have sold over 200 homes a year.

Mark also created InvestFourMore.com, a real estate blog with up to 300,000 views a month. Mark's focus in the current market is flipping, and he shows all the numbers on his active flips (up to 19 at a time) on his blog. Mark has a weekly podcast with over 100 episodes, has written multiple books, and his blog has over 450 articles.

Mark has been married to his wife since 2008 and their twins were born in 2001. Mark is an avid fan of golf and cars.

More from
BiggerPockets Publishing

Real Estate Note Investing

Are you a wholesaler, a rehabber, a landlord, or even a turnkey investor? *Real Estate Note Investing* will help you turn your focus to the "other side" of real estate investing, allowing you to make money without tenants, toilets, and termites! Investing in notes is the easiest strategy to make passive income. Learn the ins-and-outs of notes as investor Dave Van Horn shows you how to get started—and find huge success—in the powerful world of real estate notes!

If you enjoyed this book, we hope you'll take a moment to check out some of the other great material BiggerPockets offers. BiggerPockets is the real estate investing social network, marketplace, and information hub, designed to help make you a smarter real estate investor through podcasts, books, blog posts, videos, forums, and more. Sign up today—it's free! **Visit www.BiggerPockets.com.**

The Book on Rental Property Investing

The Book on Rental Property Investing, written by Brandon Turner, a real estate investor and cohost of the *BiggerPockets Podcast*, contains nearly 400 pages of in-depth advice and strategies for building wealth through rental properties. You'll learn how to build an achievable plan, find incredible deals, pay for your rentals, and much more! If you've ever thought of using rental properties to build wealth or obtain financial freedom, this book is for you.

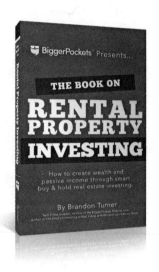

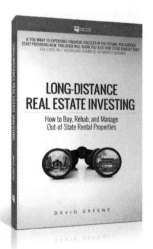

Long-Distance Real Estate Investing

Don't let your location dictate your financial freedom: Live where you want, and invest anywhere it makes sense! The rules, technology, and markets have changed: No longer are you forced to invest only in your backyard. In *Long-Distance Real Estate Investing*, learn an in-depth strategy to build profitable rental portfolios through buying, managing, and flipping out-of-state properties from real estate investor and agent David Greene.

More from
BiggerPockets Publishing

The Book on Investing in Real Estate with No (and Low) Money Down
Lack of money holding you back from real estate success? It doesn't have to! In this groundbreaking book from Brandon Turner, author of *The Book on Rental Property Investing*, you'll discover numerous strategies investors can use to buy real estate using other people's money. You'll learn the top strategies that savvy investors are using to buy, rent, flip, or wholesale properties at scale!

The Book on Tax Strategies for the Savvy Real Estate Investor
Taxes! Boring and irritating, right? Perhaps. But if you want to succeed in real estate, your tax strategy will play a huge role in how fast you grow. A great tax strategy can save you thousands of dollars a year. A bad strategy could land you in legal trouble. That's why BiggerPockets is excited to offer *The Book on Tax Strategies for the Savvy Real Estate Investor*! You'll find ways to deduct more, invest smarter, and pay far less to the IRS!

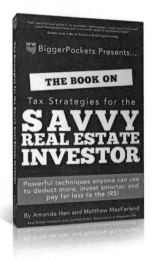

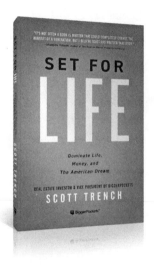

Set for Life: Dominate Life, Money, and the American Dream

Looking for a plan to achieve financial freedom in just five to ten years? Scott Trench's *Set for Life* is a detailed fiscal plan targeted at the median-income earner starting with few or no assets. It will walk you through three stages of finance, guiding you to your first $25,000 in tangible net worth, then to your first $100,000, and then to financial freedom. *Set for Life* will teach you how to build a lifestyle, career, and investment portfolio capable of supporting financial freedom to let you live the life of your dreams.

Raising Private Capital

Are you ready to help other investors build their wealth while you build your real estate empire? The road map outlined in *Raising Private Capital* helps investors looking to inject more private capital into their business—the most effective strategy for growth! Author and investor Matt Faircloth helps you learn how to develop long-term wealth from his valuable lessons and experiences in real estate: Get the truth behind the wins and losses from someone who has experienced it all.

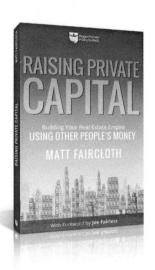

CONNECT WITH BIGGERPOCKETS

and Become Successful in Your Real Estate Business Today!

Facebook
/BiggerPockets

Instagram
@BiggerPockets

Twitter
@BiggerPockets

LinkedIn
/company/Bigger
Pockets

Website
BiggerPockets.com